Implementing Data-Driven Strategies in Smart Cities

Implementing Data-Driven Strategies in Smart Cities

A Roadmap for Urban Transformation

Didier Grimaldi
Associate Professor, La Salle-Ramon Llull University, Barcelona, Spain

Carlos Carrasco-Farré
Researcher, Ramon Llull University—ESADE Business School, Barcelona, Spain

Elsevier
Radarweg 29, PO Box 211, 1000 AE Amsterdam, Netherlands
The Boulevard, Langford Lane, Kidlington, Oxford OX5 1GB, United Kingdom
50 Hampshire Street, 5th Floor, Cambridge, MA 02139, United States

Copyright © 2022 Elsevier Inc. All rights reserved.

No part of this publication may be reproduced or transmitted in any form or by any means, electronic or mechanical, including photocopying, recording, or any information storage and retrieval system, without permission in writing from the publisher. Details on how to seek permission, further information about the Publisher's permissions policies and our arrangements with organizations such as the Copyright Clearance Center and the Copyright Licensing Agency, can be found at our website: www.elsevier.com/permissions.

This book and the individual contributions contained in it are protected under copyright by the Publisher (other than as may be noted herein).

Notices
Knowledge and best practice in this field are constantly changing. As new research and experience broaden our understanding, changes in research methods, professional practices, or medical treatment may become necessary.

Practitioners and researchers must always rely on their own experience and knowledge in evaluating and using any information, methods, compounds, or experiments described herein. In using such information or methods they should be mindful of their own safety and the safety of others, including parties for whom they have a professional responsibility.

To the fullest extent of the law, neither the Publisher nor the authors, contributors, or editors, assume any liability for any injury and/or damage to persons or property as a matter of products liability, negligence or otherwise, or from any use or operation of any methods, products, instructions, or ideas contained in the material herein.

Library of Congress Cataloging-in-Publication Data
A catalog record for this book is available from the Library of Congress

British Library Cataloguing-in-Publication Data
A catalogue record for this book is available from the British Library

ISBN: 978-0-12-821122-9

For information on all Elsevier publications
visit our website at https://www.elsevier.com/books-and-journals

Publisher: Brian Romer
Acquisitions Editor: Graham Nisbet
Editorial Project Manager: Andrea Dulberger
Production Project Manager: Swapna Srinivasan
Cover Designer: Christian J. Bilbow

Typeset by STRAIVE, India

Contents

Contributors	xi
About the editors	xiii
Foreword	xv
Preface	xix
Acknowledgments	xxi
Memoriam	xxiii

1. From smart city to data-driven city
Didier Grimaldi, Kristi Shalla, Ignasi Fontanals, and Carlos Carrasco-Farré

1.	Urban challenges	1
	1.1 Environment issue	1
	1.2 Economic competitiveness	2
	1.3 Quality of life	3
	1.4 Sustainability	3
	1.5 Resilience	4
2.	Definition of a smart city	4
	2.1 Taxonomy of smart city	4
	2.2 Technology-oriented approach or top-down	5
	2.3 People-oriented approach or social smart cities	5
3.	Smart city as an opportunity for innovation and entrepreneurship	6
	3.1 Social entrepreneur	6
	3.2 Urban entrepreneur	7
4.	Resilient city	18
5.	Sustainable city	20
	5.1 The risks of ICT to environmental and social sustainability	21
	5.2 The contribution of ICT to environmental and social sustainability	23
6.	Augmented city	24
	6.1 From small data to big data	24
	6.2 Big data applications for cities	26
	6.3 Smart mobility	26
	6.4 Smart school	27
	6.5 Smart energy	28

v

	6.6 Smart facility management	29
	6.7 Smart hospital	29
	6.8 Smart security	30
	6.9 Smart public governance	30
	6.10 Smart economy	31
7.	Is a data-driven approach progress?	32
	7.1 False promises of big data	32
	7.2 Potential benefits of big data	32
8.	Data-driven smart city architecture	33
	8.1 Evolution of the smart city models	33
	8.2 The architecture of the solution	33
	8.3 Real-time urban platform	36
	References	40

2. Governance, decision-making, and strategy for urban development

Didier Grimaldi, Eula Bianca Villar, Laurent Dupont, Jose M. Salian, and Carlos Carrasco-Farré

1.	Data-driven approaches for smart city	47
	1.1 A systematic literature review	47
	1.2 Evolutionary path to data-driven resilience in a private sector network	56
2.	Smart urban governance	57
	2.1 Definition of a big data citizen-centered approach	69
3.	Big data citizen-centered organization change	70
4.	Architecture of a big data citizen-centered urban governance	72
	4.1 Data life cycle management	75
	4.2 Real-time urban platform	77
	4.3 Master Data Model	80
	4.4 Data quality management	82
	4.5 Data security and privacy	82
	References	83

3. Data Science technologies

Carlos Carrasco-Farré, Manu Carricano, and Didier Grimaldi

1.	What is data science?	89
2.	Organizing for data science	93
	2.1 Managing data science teams	94
	2.2 Managing data science departments and organizations	96
3.	Managing data science projects to solve urban issues	96
	3.1 Problem statement	97
	3.2 Developing the solution	97
4.	Interview with Miami's CIO	100
	4.1 The backbone of data-driven cities	100

		4.2	The shinning projects of data-driven cities	101
		4.3	The team	101
		4.4	Linking data teams with the whole organization	101
		4.5	DTFT: Do the fucking thing	101
		4.6	Do something useful	102
	5.	Indicators for urban retail		103
		5.1	The importance of indicators	103
		5.2	How to select indicators	104
		5.3	Retail streets and the principle of agglomeration	104
		5.4	Retail location	105
		5.5	How to revitalize empty premises?	106
		5.6	Indicators to measure the health of urban retail	108
	References			109

4. Roadmap to develop a data-driven city

*Didier Grimaldi, Jose M. Sallan,
Josep Miquel Piqué Huerta, Jesús Soler Puebla,
Kristi Shalla, and Carlos Carrasco-Farré*

	1.	The data-driven strategy decision		111
		1.1	The smart city approach	111
		1.2	The transformation to a data-driven city	112
	2.	Roadmap for developing data-driven smart cities		113
		2.1	Smart cities need to include urban, economic, and social development	113
		2.2	The lifecycle of a smart city from inception to maturity	114
		2.3	Quadruple helix agents develop different functions in the development of smart cities	116
		2.4	Effective roadmap	118
		2.5	Smart index	120
	3.	Legal, security, and ethical considerations for a data-driven smart city		123
		3.1	Legitimation for the use of big data	123
		3.2	Legitimation basis	125
		3.3	Information principle	127
		3.4	Main problems	129
		3.5	Solutions	129
	4.	Value model in a data-driven smart city		130
	5.	Case study of Nice (France)		132
		5.1	The Nice City Pass app	132
		5.2	Benefits of the *Nice City Pass* app	133
		5.3	Value model	136
		5.4	Nice in the third stage in the roadmap	137
	6.	Case study of Seoul		138
		6.1	Data strategy: Smart public transport planning system	139
		6.2	Data capture: Automated fare collection system	140
		6.3	Data cleaning: Assessing available data	141
		6.4	Data analysis: The evolution of the TRIPS tool	142

		6.5	Data modeling: A proactive city government tool	143
		6.6	Other cases: Integrate with other big data	144
	A.	Appendix I: Questionnaire		147
		A.1	Organization	148
		A.2	Technology	148
		A.3	Data management	149
		A.4	Involvement of stakeholders in the data-driven city (quadruple helix)	149
		References		150

5. **Enabling technologies for data-driven cities**
   Carlos Carrasco-Farré, Ramon Martín de Pozuelo, and Didier Grimaldi

	1.	Data-driven cities and smart cities: Technology is the tool, not the goal		153
	2.	Which technologies are needed in a data-driven city? From IoT to big data		155
		2.1	Data collection	158
		2.2	Data transportation	159
		2.3	Data storage	161
		2.4	Data preparation	164
		2.5	Data analysis	164
		2.6	Data visualization	165
		References		172

6. **Data analysis, modeling, and visualization in smart cities**
   Carlos Carrasco-Farré, Ignasi Alcalde, and Didier Grimaldi

	1.	Introduction		173
	2.	What is data visualization?		174
	3.	Data essentials		175
	4.	Data types		176
	5.	Methodology		177
	6.	Charts and data relations		177
	7.	Data design principles		178
		7.1	Color	179
		7.2	Form	179
		7.3	Movement	180
		7.4	Spatial positioning	180
	8.	Dashboard basics		180
		8.1	How to lie with maps	181
	9.	A data-driven approach to predict the COVID-19 effect on urban retail		184
		9.1	Measuring the effect of COVID-19	184

		9.2	How EIXOS identified the retail categories most affected by the COVID-19 lockdown?	186
		References		195

7. Data-driven policy evaluation
Marçal Farré, Federico Todeschini, Didier Grimaldi, and Carlos Carrasco-Farré

1.	Introduction		197
2.	Types of policy evaluations and evaluation questions		197
	2.1	The role of evaluation in the decision-making process	198
	2.2	Needs assessment	199
	2.3	Implementation or process evaluation	200
	2.4	Impact evaluation	201
	2.5	How to (correctly) identify the counterfactual situation?	202
3.	Experimental and quasiexperimental methodologies		204
4.	The role of data in urban policy evaluation		206
	4.1	Typologies of data in public policy evaluation	206
5.	Challenges and opportunities of big data		210
6.	Examples of policy evaluation		213
	6.1	Big data contribution to impact evaluation	214
7.	Case study: Fudging the nudge: Information disclosure and restaurant grading in New York		214
8.	Case study: Consumer response to the COVID-19 crisis		215
9.	Case study: The impact of public health interventions during the COVID pandemic		217
10.	Case study: Effect of smart technology on consumer's behavior		218
11.	Big data contribution to needs assessment		219
12.	Case study: Mapping poverty using mobile phone and satellite data		220
13.	Conclusions		221
	References		223

Index 227

Contributors

Numbers in parentheses indicate the pages on which the authors' contributions begin.

Ignasi Alcalde (173), Ramon Llull University, La Salle Faculty, Barcelona, Spain

Carlos Carrasco-Farré (1, 47, 89, 111, 153, 173, 197), Ramon Llull University—ESADE Business School, Barcelona, Spain

Manu Carricano (89), Department of Operations, Innovation and Data Sciences, Universitat Ramon Llull—ESADE Business School, Barcelona, Spain

Ramon Martín de Pozuelo (153), Research Group on Internet Technologies & Storage, Department of Engineering—La Salle University, Manila, Philippines

Laurent Dupont (47), Université de Lorraine, ERPI Laboratory/Lorraine Fab Living Lab, Nancy, France

Marçal Farré (197), Catalan Institute of Public Policy Evaluation (Ivalua), Barcelona, Spain

Ignasi Fontanals (1), Expert in Organizational and Urban Resilience and Director Europe at Rezilio Technologie, Beloeil, Canada

Didier Grimaldi (1, 47, 89, 111, 153, 173, 197), Ramon Llull University, La Salle Faculty, Barcelona, Spain

Josep Miquel Piqué Huerta (111), Technova, Ramon Llull University, La Salle Faculty, Barcelona, Spain

Jesús Soler Puebla (111), Virtual Abogados, Barcelona, Spain

Jose M. Sallan (47, 111), Universitat Politècnica de Catalunya, BarcelonaTech, Barcelona, Spain

Kristi Shalla (1, 111), Smart City Consultant, Washington, DC, United States

Federico Todeschini (197), Catalan Institute of Public Policy Evaluation (Ivalua), Barcelona, Spain

Eula Bianca Villar (47), Asian Institute of Management, Manila, Philippines

About the editors

Didier Grimaldi is Doctor in Smart City and Innovation. He is Associate Professor at Ramon Llull University—La Salle Faculty (Spain). He is the Coordinator of Executive Education of Big Data for Executives. His research looks at supporting public policies to resolve traffic, mobility, education, and resilience issues. As a data scientist, he has managed different projects to reveal, analyze, and predict urban trends. With 20+ years' experience in consulting, he has developed solutions from diagnostic to development and implementation, providing him with large international experience in this domain. He is co-editor of the *Smart Cities Journal* from MDPI Publisher. His publications are accessible at https://www.researchgate.net/profile/Didier-Grimaldi.

Carlos Carrasco-Farré is a doctoral researcher at ESADE Business School, in the Department of Operations, Innovation, and Data Science. His research focuses on the impact of AI and Data Science in management and decision making. Previously, he spent 7 years doing research at IESE Business School, where he participated in the creation of the Cities in Motion Index and conducted research on Smart Cities. He is also partner and Chief Data Scientist at EIXOS Economic Observatory. He has published in leading journals like *California Management Review*, *Social Science Computer Review*, and *Strategy Science or Technological Forecasting and Social Change*.

Foreword

By Carlos Grau, CEO of Mobile World Capital, Barcelona

We live immersed in the digital age, which is marked by a technological revolution whose vehicle is digital information and communication technologies. The digitization that characterizes the global economy today is spreading much faster than we estimated and is already affecting all areas of our lives. One of the biggest changes we are witnessing is our city lifestyle and habits; 21st-century cities are considered smart cities because they are smart and digital, two complementary aspects that, as of today, make the future of all cities dependent on the connection aspect.

In fact, the European Commission defines a smart city as the place where traditional networks and services are more efficient thanks to the use of digital and telecommunications technologies that benefit both its habitants and businesses. We must not ignore that the concept of connected cities is an emerging reality that is growing to fulfil our needs and address the urgencies of our times.

At a time where data is the main tool for cities to develop as a new functionality and provide uses for public use, we must consider it as an inevitable process of evolution of our technology. It is undeniable that technology is a protagonist in the social, cultural, and economic evolution of our society, where our commitment to technological evolution, such as 5G technology, is very high. It incorporates tools that may improve the quality of life of people through efficiency in management, from the most traditional such as energy supply, water cycle or waste cycle, to mobility, health, culture, and leisure, or current existing new technologies based on 5G enabling technology, that can enable a qualitative leap in the services that citizens receive in the coming years.

In this scenario, digital transformation plays a key role for citizens to take advantage of the large improvement technology can provide, a scenario where the city adapts to the public's new ways of living and working, not vice versa. Precisely at times like the present, where the COVID pandemic has deeply changed our lives, we are facing a historical moment that opens the door for us to take advantage of all these opportunities generated by the digital age itself. We must be capable of incorporating the tools that the digital revolution offers and place the people at the center of technological development to empower citizens.

This book seeks to serve as a manual and guide to how cities can make public services more efficient and better serve the needs of the population through data management. Each chapter gives a clear explanation of the theory and case studies of cities and regions that have successfully implemented data-driven policies. The first chapter looks at how to move from a smart city to data-driven city and provides the example of NYC's Office of Data Analytics. In the second chapter, we look at issues of governance and strategy for urban development and examine our home city of Barcelona. Next, we delve into data science theory in Chapter 3, and in Chapter 4 we create a road map for the development of data-driven cities, examining how Nice and Seoul have been doing with parking and public transportation data. In Chapter 5, we look at the technology being developed to make use of the data and improve processes, and we look at the beginning of the 5G era in South Korea. After that, we move on to the analysis and visualization phase of data management and end the book with a chapter on data-driven policy evaluation.

Indeed, the opportunities offered by technology and big data in the field of smart cities are very wide and diverse. We tried to cover everything in this book. However, it is necessary to add the current context of digital emergency that happened after we started work on this book. We have all heard, are aware, and have acquired a commitment to the climate emergency. In addition, for a year now, with the impact of the global coronavirus pandemic, we are dealing with a health emergency through drastic measures that we have had to adopt to try to solve as soon as possible. We are very clear about these emergencies in our order of priorities, but perhaps what we are still not so aware of is the digital emergency we are living in.

To face this emergency, the different agents present in this global ecosystem must be equipped with the necessary tools. Cooperation and collaboration between all actors and interest groups is the most effective response to face the complexity of these challenges. This must involve the public sector, i.e., administrations, governments, and legislators; to the private sector, i.e., corporations, companies, and platforms; and, of course, to civil society, made up of organizations and individual citizens.

In any case, it seems clear that a large part of the future of smart cities depends on the optimization and correct use of big data. A clear opportunity to create truly personalized services that help improve city management and, what is more relevant, people's lives. Without a doubt, a path with infinite possibilities opens up for us.

If the pandemic of 2020 taught us anything, it is that we are all in this together and we are going to have to find solutions for the future of mankind together. Knowledge sharing and brainstorming must be engaged in at a global level, and this is the main reason why we at Mobile World Capital decided to launch the Digital Futures Society and why I am so excited about this book.

The publication of this book involved the hard work of many talented people and I am deeply grateful for their efforts to create a tool with the potential to take advantage of the opportunity to implement real change and benefit so many people around the globe.

Preface

By Pilar Conesa, Anteverti CEO
   Smart City Expo World Congress Curator
   Cities have dramatically increased their political and social roles worldwide. According to the UN, 68% of the world's population is projected to live in urban areas by 2050. Today, cities are where society faces the greatest challenges of the 21st century such as the climate emergency, inequity, and resilience to disasters and pandemics.
   The combination of accelerated growth of urban areas with the disruption of digital transformation has expanded the concept of smart cities worldwide as a paradigm of innovation and transformation to improve people's quality of life. However, technology is a disruptive means to accelerate change and not an end in itself.
   As William Shakespeare said, "What is the city but the people?" The city is made up of its infrastructures, its public space, and its surroundings, but what defines a city is its people and its culture. The massive use of technology through mobile and social networks encourages citizen involvement and the development of communities.
   Smart cities are people-centric. The goal is to develop more livable, sustainable, healthy, equitable, and participatory cities. But this was not the first approach to smart cities. In 10 years since the Smart City Expo World Congress, the evolution of the concept of smart cities has been clearly seen, from a tech-centric vision to a people-centric vision.

That is why it is so important to continue the global debate about the challenges and different approaches of smart cities—a debate in which the content of this book makes a great contribution from the approach of the data-driven city.

The city is not smarter by having more sensors and advanced technology but rather by being able to take advantage of the data it has by organizing the information in the most useful way to better manage urban services.

This book gathers input from a diverse group of experts who cover a full range of topics related to the smart city concept and implementation.

The first three chapters address the essential issues: the concept of a smart city and the role of data, the leadership of transformation, and finally an overview of data science for urban development.

Chapter 4 focus discusses how cities can build a realistic plan for building a data-driven city. Chapters 5 and 6 delve deeper by showing some examples of cities around the world that have been successful in this endeavor and debating on how to choose the right technology and processes for urban data visualization.

The last chapter brings all of the topics together with an overview of how policies can be evaluated and kept in check to ensure that cities are resilient and improving the lives of people, both residents and visitors. We have been fortunate in Barcelona to have a history of urban visionaries and a progressive resident population. We are still figuring out our best way forward, and I am excited that we have the ability to share what we have learned along the way through this publication and to continue the conversation every November at the Smart City World Congress.

As we have all become acutely aware during the COVID-19 pandemic, the situation is urgent and we need to keep sharing best practices and ideas so we can not only continue to build transparency and innovate but also so that we can help others who have fallen behind to make a leap forward. To deal effectively with future challenges, we need everyone to understand the role of data in their cities and be part of the conversation.

Acknowledgments

First and foremost, we are grateful to all the contributing authors for their time, effort, and understanding during the preparation of the book.

Didier would like to thank his boys, Arnau and Pol, for keeping him harmonious and happy along with his dearest Laura who has supported him throughout the entire process, listening carefully and providing him with a lot of useful encouragement. A lot of sleepless nights would have been impossible without thinking about all of you. He will be grateful forever for their love.

Carlos would like to thank Diana for being a compass in the middle of the fog, always side-by-side, and a source of support in countless moments. And to his family, who always supported him in his development, showing the value of work, and encouraging him to keep pursuing his dreams.

Finally, we would like to thank the staff of Elsevier, particularly Ruby Smith and Graham Nisbet. They were wonderful to work with.

Memoriam

All the authors of this book are sad that Manu Carricano, PhD, and contributor to Chapter 3 passed away in March 2021 and will not see the outcome of his dedication and effort. Manu was more than a great professional; he was a friend, and we will be ever grateful for his happiness, dedication, assistance, and constant advice. Rest in peace, Manu.

Chapter 1

From smart city to data-driven city

Didier Grimaldi[a], Kristi Shalla[b], Ignasi Fontanals[c], and Carlos Carrasco-Farré[d]
[a]*Ramon Llull University, La Salle Faculty, Barcelona, Spain,* [b]*Smart City Consultant, Washington, DC, United States,* [c]*Expert in Organizational and Urban Resilience and Director Europe at Rezilio Technologie, Beloeil, Canada,* [d]*Ramon Llull University—ESADE Business School, Barcelona, Spain*

1 Urban challenges

Global urban population exceeded rural population for the first time in history in 2008 (Crossette, 2010), and the United Nations forecast that 66% of the world's population will live in urban areas (United Nations Economic Commission for Europe (UNECE), 2014) by 2050. In Latin America, urban growth will be exceptional, and the forecast is even bigger, that is, 83% in 2030. Cities will consequently be the locus of major challenges like air pollution, traffic congestion, water, and waste management (DESA, 2009). They will also have to offer economic activity and good well-being for these immigrants coming from the rural zones looking for job opportunities. In this chapter, we develop the five major challenges we believe cities will face as corroborated by other authors (Assadian & Nejati, 2011). These are short-term issues related to the environment, economic competitiveness, and the quality of life offered but also long-term issues covering resilience and sustainability problems. At present, we are living through an overwhelming sanitary and financial crisis linked to the COVID-19 pandemic crisis. This book is not aimed at just discussing and measuring specific effects on the global economy and people health conditions. We have indeed embraced a wider and larger objective of reflection. Nevertheless, we have included in the following paragraphs the start of analysis of its possible effect.

1.1 Environment issue

Madlener and Sunak (2011) states that cities are responsible for around 75% of the overall resource consumption and thus environment problems, even if they occupy no more than 2% of the land (Miller & Hazel, 2007). The recent report of the World Bank (2017) corroborated it, estimating that metropolitan areas account for 70% of CO_2 emissions in the world. Cities are affected by global warming and climate change. Rising sea levels are one of the consequences that directly affect urban areas lying less than 10 m above sea level. As far as industrialized countries are concerned, a first estimation predicts 70% of Europe's largest cities (e.g., Paris, London, Amsterdam) or megacities like Tokyo or New York City will be affected. In emerging countries, Kolkata (formerly Calcutta, India), Shanghai, and Guangzhou (formerly Canton, China) are mentioned. Also, China alone has more than 78 million people living in vulnerable low elevation cities (McGranahan, Balk, & Anderson, 2007).

It is important to highlight that every year an estimated 8.8 million people worldwide die prematurely of air pollution, giving rise to an average reduction of 2.9 years in average global life expectancy. The climate crisis has further increased the number of premature deaths. Nevertheless, the drastic prevention measures against COVID-19 propagation have also caused a dramatic reduction in road traffic and industrial activity, which may in turn have resulted in significant reductions in CO_2 emissions and air pollution. The percentage differs depending on the countries, for example, between 70% and 80% in France or Spain, and up to 20%–30% in the case of China. This change has generated a reflection that another mode of production and consumption should exist that is greener and more responsible toward the planet. Nevertheless, it is too early to be able to measure if the effect will be long term and will decrease the air pollution levels.

1.2 Economic competitiveness

Cities usually have had a profound effect on the economic competitiveness of a country, performing better than the national indicator's average (Assadian & Nejati, 2011). The city of Tokyo is responsible for 40% of Japan's GDP while holding only 28% of the country's population. Similarly, Paris covers 30% of France GDP, with only 16% of the French population living there. Even among developing countries, similar examples can be found. The Nigerian capital, Lagos, forms 30% of the country's output, while only 8% of the country's population live there. However, the performance of a city cannot be disconnected to the general business situation of the country (Economist Intelligence Unit, 2004). The existence of transparent national business rules and regulations are among one of the most important economical motivations in attracting new investments to a city. They are conditions for the sustainability and competitiveness of the industry and service companies present in the city.

The financial crisis of 2007–08 also called subprime mortgage crisis was a severe contraction of liquidity in global financial markets. This crisis originated in the United States as a result of the collapse of the US housing market then spread to the rest of the world. The greatest effect of COVID-19 may be the economic downturn that includes job losses, although the evidence from the

2007 crisis was quite mixed, and outcomes may depend on the governmental measures taken to mitigate the recession. However, the current crisis appears to be much more severe and may lead to a total collapse of certain sectors, such as aviation, entertainment, and tourism, and will therefore have much more profound consequences for the urban economy.

1.3 Quality of life

Poverty, hunger, and sanitation problems drastically affect the lives of millions of people in the world. The last financial worldwide crisis initiated in, 2010 deteriorated the existing situation by pushing a lot of citizens into poverty (UNECE, 2014). In 2020, the situation was even worse after the COVID-19 sanitary crisis. A strong health system needs a strong economy, which is in real danger today. The quality of life is largely related to the economic conditions of living. Poverty remains one of the challenging and lasting problems in the city and provokes exclusion from society and social systems (World Bank, 2018). It causes also psychological deficiency among the people who feel they have failed to provide the essentials for themselves and their family (Mwenda & Muuka, 2004).

1.4 Sustainability

In common use, the "bottom line" refers to "benefits" or "losses" (depending on the company situation), which are usually recorded in a company's income accounts. Over the last 70 years, environmentalists and social justice lawyers have struggled to achieve a better definition of the "bottom line", seeking to introduce a more perfect accounting for the real effect of company business activities on the planet and society; for example, a company has a financial benefit, but its mining operations cause hundreds of deaths and contaminates a nearby lake. What real costs does this company have for society if the government ends up spending its money on public healthcare and cleaning the lake? To remain viable in the future, companies must focus on sustainability and pay attention to the effect of their actions on key three aspects: environmental, civic, and economic. Technologies enable cities to be prepared to these new risks while being eco-responsible and self-sufficient to a certain degree, which entails urban production and a local supply of food. The concept of sustainability in the urban domain has gained strong attraction due to the diffusion effort of the World Commission on Environment and Development (Brundtland, 1987). In early 2007, it became the dominant approach promoted by the United Nations for urban accounting and theorized by recent studies (De Guimarães, Severo, Felix Júnior, Da Costa, & Salmoria, 2020; Macke, Rubim Sarate, & de Atayde Moschen, 2019; Mora, Appio, Foss, Arellano, & Zhang, 2020). Scientist John Elkington (1994) in an exercise on synthesis defines sustainability according to three variables, each one of them beginning with the letter P: People, Profit, and Planet (Fig. 1.1).

4 Implementing data-driven strategies in smart cities

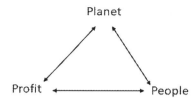

FIG. 1.1 Triple bottom line.

1.5 Resilience

Cities and societies are also vulnerable. Terrorist attacks such as those occurring in 2015 in Paris in a Media office ("*Charlie Hedbo*") or 2016 in Brussels or Munich and accidents due to technical failure or human error remind us of this, as do natural disasters that are more frequent today associated with climate change. A smart city needs to be "resilient" too and be prepared for major breakdowns. City resilience concepts need to be developed not only for the city infrastructure, but also for the whole city as understood as a network of services prepared to better cope with disruptions causing multiple cascade effects that affect the urban environment and life.

Etezadzadeh (2014) defines "resilience" as the ability to prevent actual or potentially adverse events from occurring, to take them, cope with them, and adapt to them more and more successfully. Resilience deals with the capacity of a community or organization to be prepared to cope with any kind of exceptional event (a storm like Katrina, a pandemic like COVID, etc.) and to be able to resist, absorb, and adapt. A resilient city then recovers its functions in a timely and effective manner, learns from such disruptions, and adapts to change its trajectory. This last point adds an important feature to the smart city definition. Attacks can be cyberattacks and resilience has to be digital as well, preventing manipulation of the critical infrastructure through the Internet.

Today, to apply this vision, a multitude of mature and emerging technologies are available. Data management will be a key to drive toward the vision of creating more resilient value chains, urban services, and local communities. To do so, we need the convergence of different data skills and knowledge to ensure and sustain the adaptation and operation of business continuity and resilience management frameworks supported by a judicious use of technology.

2 Definition of a smart city

2.1 Taxonomy of smart city

Over the last three decades, information and communication technologies (ICTs) have extensively influenced the nature, structure, and evolution of urban spaces. Cities that have chosen ICTs as part of their development strategy have been variously named as an intelligent city (Komninos, 2006), wired city

(Martin, 1978), or digital city (Toru & Isbister, 2000). The smart city concept can be considered as a consolidation of these various brands (Caragliu, del Bo, & Nijkamp, 2011; Hollands, 2008). Accordingly, Grimaldi and Fernandez (2017) defined a smart city as a technologically advanced city that can understand and manage its urban infrastructure, services, and forms to resolve any kind of problems and improve the quality of citizens' life. Moreover, they add two main approaches concerning smart cities that are described in the following two subsections.

2.2 Technology-oriented approach or top-down

There are top-down initiatives where priority is done on the urban infrastructure. This approach is also called an ICT-based smart city (Marsal-Llacuna, Colomer-Llinàs, & Meléndez-Frigola, 2015). Neirotti, De Marco, Cagliano, Mangano, and Scorrano (2014) explain that the concept usually combines different domains such as energy, environment, transport, healthcare, public security, and e-Government but managed as a separate silo. Technology's role is to optimize the use and exploitation of the natural resources, energy distribution, or the citizens' transport. As a common characteristic, these initiatives have to be governed by city hall in a unidirectional (top-down) approach and are ICT-oriented. Bakici, Almirall, and Wareham (2013) consider them as the foundation of smart cities. In the environmental domain, ICT allows better protection of environmental resources and controlling pollution as illustrated by the literature (Atzori, Iera, & Morabito, 2010; Chourabi et al., 2012; Inayatullah, 2011). e-Government and administration, where ICT promotes digitized public administration to enhance citizens' empowerment and involvement in public affairs, has also been analyzed in the literature (Correia & Wünstel, 2011).

2.3 People-oriented approach or social smart cities

This alternative approach encourages access to data and allows citizens to develop their own initiatives (Garriga, Salcedo, Vives, & Meseguer, 2015; Lorusso et al., 2014). New technology deployment is not the main objective here but rather citizens' cooperation to eliminate injustice; give (back) societal rights; mitigate inequalities while helping the integration of excluded people; give assistance to disabled, elder, or younger citizens; or provide access to culture and education to disadvantaged people. This approach considers the cities as not only a grid of intelligent sensors and a list of services but also having a unique character reflected in the citizens' daily life and culture. Cities are the people that inhabit them; their memories, stories, and concerns; and the experimentation developed through social interaction. The domains are related to education, culture, and healthcare(Grimaldi & Fernandez, 2017).

The term "sociable" is often added to smart cities suggesting that smartness is people-oriented, and ICT plays a limited role. Christopoulou, Ringas, and

Garofalakis (2014) say, "Sociable smart cities make the city different while (ICT) smart cities share the same modern infrastructure and offer similar functions. Technology issues are considered easy to fix as rapid corrective or enhance developments to solve issues of the present." The challenge is to foster a new collaborative attitude, a participatory approach to allow people to interact with their cities in novel ways, to enable them to design and decide the future of the city (Komninos, 2006), and to have a proper infrastructure that supports this social fabric (Mulder, 2014). This collaboration can take different forms, and in the next section we develop two important ones: social and urban entrepreneurship.

The cooperation between citizens may be organized inside what is usually called "living laboratories" (living labs), a shared physical space with the objective to engage users in a creative and collective perspective (e.g., the case of My City Project in Milan). Another interesting project is the so-called "smart citizen initiative" sponsored by FabLab of Barcelona. Based on "Arduino" open hardware (https://www.arduino.cc/), its objective is to allow citizens to develop small meteorological platforms equipped with Internet-connected captors that monitor NO_2, noise, humidity, temperature, and particles providing information about the atmospheric conditions of the city. All the data coming from these platforms are then shared on the smart citizen webpage (https://smartcitizen.me/kits/) and enabling citizens to make decisions to improve their conditions of living. For example, they can use these data to select the preferential road to use in the city according to the levels of pollution or particles rate reported for each street.

3 Smart city as an opportunity for innovation and entrepreneurship

3.1 Social entrepreneur

In the last years, the application of entrepreneurial approaches to social issues has been institutionalized in an innovative concept called social enterprise. Social initiatives that also meet financial value are usually described in the scientific literature as social entrepreneurship (Leadbeater, 2006). Neirotti et al. (2014) also coined the concept of social innovation as directly inculcated to it.

Nevertheless, to the best of our knowledge, the field remains largely limited to anecdotal case studies and instrumental analyses of efficiency and operational best practices (Leadbeater, 2006; Montgomery, Dacin, & Dacin, 2012). Moreover, the definition of social enterprise has been progressing while the debate concerning the business model was also evolving. Cornelius, Todres, Janjuha-Jivraj, Woods, and Wallace (2008), using the definition of the UK Department of Trade and Industry, described social enterprises as new ventures with social objectives, whereby profits are reinvested in the business or other initiatives to further support social purposes. Leadbeater (2006) proposes another way to define social entrepreneurship through its outcomes with the following definition: "Anyone who creates lasting social value through entrepreneurial activities."

However, it is paramount to understand how the objectives of social entrepreneurship may differ from the nonsocial firms. Jeff Skoll, co-founder of eBay, created a foundation and donated £4.4 million ($6.1 million) to establish a research center for social entrepreneurship. The Skoll Foundation comments that, unlike business entrepreneurs motivated by profits, social entrepreneurs seize opportunities or approaches to create sustainable solutions to change society for the better. Social entrepreneurs focus first on generating social value instead of maximizing profit for shareholders and other stakeholders. Alter (2000) analyzed the recipients of a social enterprise and clarified that "a social-purpose business is founded to support or create economic opportunities for poor or disadvantaged populations while simultaneously operating with reference to the financial bottom line". Bibri (2014) introduced the concept of "green entrepreneurs and ventures", that is, those that are not driven by mere commercial gains but by a concern for the environment and with a high desire to make the world more sustainable. Recently the concept has moved from social to urban entrepreneur.

3.2 Urban entrepreneur

Tax-financed urban services are monetarily constrained and are unable to respond effectively to rising societal needs (Hollands, 2008). Muñoz and Cohen (2016) introduced the concept of urban entrepreneurship as an alternative answer. They consider it as an advanced form of "social entrepreneur" who usually looks for traditional solutions to urban problems. They indeed categorize it as an person who seeks an "opportunity to venture", challenging the traditional market structure and institutions and looking for a broader solution than pure market failure. The entrepreneur is at the center of the stage, crosses the frontiers of the market rules, and develops a business solution capable of leveraging both the rigid rules of the formal economy with the flexibility that the informal economy offers. The city is considered as a whole system, and the solution exploits opportunities occurring outside formal institutional limits. It could look illegal somehow, but they are legitimate to a large group of individuals. We believe New York City is a fantastic example of how cities develop efforts to foster urban innovation and startup activity. We include in this chapter a deep analysis of its model (Box 1.1) and the full transcription of an interview realized to the Chief Analytics Officer (Box 1.2).

Good illustrations are Airbnb, Uber, Wallapop, or more recently Sitly in Spain, which is an initiative to create a community of babysitters to take care of young children while their parents are absent. These solutions cover more than a market deficiency and a social need as a social entrepreneur usually does (Sitly is the absence of secure solutions for parents who need to absence

Box 1.1 Case study: New York City Mayor's Office of Data Analytics (MODA).

As illustrated in the previous section, data-empowered entrepreneurship for smart city applications is usually split into two areas: social entrepreneurship, the application of new technological tools for social issues, and urban entrepreneurship, the use of new technological tools for the creation of new business models in an urban setting. New York City boasts a blossoming of both types of entrepreneurship due in large part to the city government's approach to empowering citizens with the tools to create change and their respect for the entrepreneurial process.

New York City has a dynamic business community that many global cities look to emulate in their efforts to grow local innovation sectors. But what is it about NYC that makes innovation flourish? In the 1960s, as the city's garment manufacturing business started to be gradually outsourced to lower cost regions both domestically and abroad, the finance industry started to gain importance and became the NYC's dominant industry in the late 1970s and early 1980s. When entrepreneurship and startup activity started to create an innovation sector in the global economy in the late 1990s, NYC became an integral part of the process but was not a driver of this development. Gradually, however, the city has become a major player in the creating and fostering the business of innovation over the past 15 years and, as global cities look to develop their own "homegrown" innovation sectors, they can look to the success of NYC as an example.

So what is NYC's secret sauce in producing a vibrant and dynamic ecosystem for innovative industries? There are many ingredients that have helped the city quickly develop into an innovation capitol including diversity and the historically dynamic "survival" culture of a large immigrant population, but there is also one city government-led initiative that has helped both the public and private sectors find and build innovative solutions to issues related to the welfare of city residents: open data.

The New York City government passed an Open Data Law in 2012. New York has long considered the benefits of openness in government with the first measures taken to combat corruption of the Tammany Hall era in the early 20th century. The results of those first reforms were basic measures created to build transparency in government: rules governing the awarding of public contracts and the creation of a modernized civil service. Many years later, the State of New York passed a series of Freedom of Information Laws that determined "that government is the public's business, and that the public, individually and collectively and represented by a free press, should have access to the records of government."[a]

With the onset of the Internet age, the city created the NYC Commission on Public Information and Communication (COPIC), which first set forth the idea that actual city government data should be accessible by the public. This idea matured and was more widely distributed throughout the public sector and business community during the 1990s and early 2000s, resulting in the 2012 "Open Data Law" (NYC Local Law 11 of 2012) mandating that data from city agencies be made available on a centralized Open Data Portal.

MODA has been working for nearly a decade and has played an integral role in ensuring that New York City policy-making is data-driven and that citizens of New York have easy access to public data. Much of their activity is dedicated to three

Box 1.1 Case study: New York City Mayor's Office of Data Analytics (MODA)—cont'd

principle areas: the open data program that ensures that public sector data is not only available but also understandable to most of the general population, facilitating data-sharing between city agencies for data that is not public due to privacy or sensitivity issues, and analytics projects dedicated to municipal issues such as tenant protection and emergency response. The objective of the open data program is to empower citizens to engage with the public sector. "Traditionally government engagement with the public has been top-down, but open data allows people to engage with the government on more even footing," explains Zachary Feder, the Open Data Manager at MODA.

It is especially noteworthy, considering the current boom in smart city development around the world, that the Open Data Program in NYC promotes both social and urban entrepreneurship in the city in three important ways: empowering communities, ensuring the quality and integrity of data, and enabling entrepreneurship with the creation of "home-grown" innovation.

Social Entrepreneurship
Inclusion and Empowering Communities through Data

New York City has historically had a much more diverse population than many global cities, so city policy-making has necessarily considered issues related to inclusion for decades. The city's Open Data Program has become an important tool for empowering diverse communities. Because of the city's long history of cultural diversity, the city boasts a dynamic business culture and a wealth of public interest groups and organizations. The dynamic business culture of the city has served as a base for which MODA has been able to partner with nonprofit organizations and public interest groups to empower social entrepreneurship in the diverse communities in New York City.

Since its creation in 2012, MODA has undertaken initiatives to not only make data available to all New Yorkers but also to educate the population on how to use the data and create a peer-to-peer community around open data in an effort to empower citizens to take a proactive approach to interaction with the city government and the rest of the society as a whole.

Open Data Week

Open Data Week is one such activity undertaken by MODA to educate citizens on how the Open Data Law contributes to transparency in city government and how they can use open data in their everyday lives. The first Open Data Week was launched in 2017 in collaboration with BetaNYC, a local civic tech group, and it has grown exponentially each year starting with 12 events across three boroughs and 900 participants in 2017. Three years later, the event had grown to include 39 events across all five boroughs and over 2000 participants.

Events during Open Data Week are focused on engaging the public through a variety of different formats. There are workshops such as "Open Data 101" in public libraries throughout Queens. Open Data 101 is an interactive workshop to help people get a basic understanding of how data is gathered and analyzed so that it can be used for policy-making. There are also community gatherings based on a specific kind of public data such as "Open Earth Happy Hour" in Brooklyn, an event focused on environmental data being gathered in New York City presented by professionals

Continued

Box 1.1 Case study: New York City Mayor's Office of Data Analytics (MODA)—cont'd

using that data for environmental monitoring. There were also more active events such as the "Data-Gathering Expedition" where participants were assigned to different NYC city parks to gather data on squirrels through observation and then handed their data over to organizers to create a new dataset. The offering of activities is diverse so as to showcase the various aspects of open data and to attract a large audience with varying interests throughout all five boroughs of the city.

But outreach is not just limited to one week out of the year. MODA also collaborates with BetaNYC and the Queens Public Library to train volunteer Open Data Ambassadors to teach Open Data 101 to the public throughout the year. The course is free for all participants and offers a basic overview on how open data contributes to government transparency, how datasets are created, and how to analyze data. During the fall and winter of 2019–20, there were 50 such workshops with 200 participants. Related to diversity and inclusion policies, it is noteworthy that this program has been undertaken in the Borough of Queens, often cited as one of the most ethnically diverse areas in the United States and sometimes the world. (A recent diversity study published by Lazaro Gamio showed that in Queens, NY, the probability of two random people having different ethnic backgrounds is 76.4%.)

All in all, *Open Data for All* is one of MODA's principle missions and their activities focus as much on the "for All" part of the statement as they do on the "Open Data" part. This focus on inclusion and citizen empowerment, they believe, is their raison d'être.

New Models for Empowering Communities through Data

As an extension of this duty to ensure inclusion and the empowering of communities through data, MODA also undertakes new initiatives to respond to specific needs of the city government and the public at large. A recent program launched in late July 2020, The NYC Recovery Data Partnership, is a partnership with community, nonprofit, and private sector entities to create complete datasets for COVID-19 response and recovery. This innovative program announced the partnership of the city with 11 public and private organizations and included an open call to potential partners who may have data relevant to the recovery effort and be interested in joining the program. The data included in this program is not part of the Open Data Program at this stage but undertakes to ensure that city agencies have a more complete picture of the effects of COVID-19 on all segments of society for more effective recovery policy-making.

The NYC Recovery Data Partnership is a new type of Public Private Partnership (PPP) in which the private sector provides data free-of-charge, and that data is made available to the city for use in emergency response efforts. At a time when much attention is being given to PPPs across all innovation sectors, from space exploration to transport and infrastructure, this type of multisector PPP based on city building (and in this case, emergency response) is new and noteworthy as it lays out a pathway for increasing collaboration in cities' functions beyond the limits of public entities. "This is the next frontier for city data-sharing beyond open data and hopefully will be the framework for further collaborative partnerships," added Feder.

Ensuring Quality of and Access to Open Data

Box 1.1 Case study: New York City Mayor's Office of Data Analytics (MODA)—cont'd

Under the Open Data Law, all city agencies in New York City are required to publish their datasets by default. The lawmakers knew what open data would mean for entrepreneurship and explicitly outlined the objective of creating economic opportunity in the language of the law:

For purposes of prioritizing public datasets, agencies shall consider whether information embodied in the public dataset: (1) can be used to increase agency accountability and responsiveness; (2) improves public knowledge of the agency and its operations; (3) furthers the mission of the agency; (4) creates economic opportunity; or (5) responds to a need or demand identified by public consultation.[b]

To ensure compliance with the law, each city agency has a designated Open Data Coordinator (ODC) who works with MODA and the Department of Information Technology (DoITT) to ensure that their data is published and updated on a regular basis. The ODCs not only work to make sure that their data is published but, as Feder explains, "they are also encouraged to work as ambassadors and translators for open data within their agency and community."

He goes onto say that, "continuing to bolster resources and training for ODCs was identified as a top priority in our 2019 strategic plan. This year, we held a virtual training for ODCs where the open data team and some more experienced ODCs shared best practices with newer ODCs."

So NYC's Open Data Program works to build a community of people within the public sector who are excited about open data and interested in ensuring that support for open data policies continues to grow.

Urban Entrepreneurship

Open Data as a Catalyst for Entrepreneurship and Local Innovation

One of the big questions for many cities as they look toward the future is how to build a stronger startup sector and promote "home-grown" innovation. New York is a global metropolis with a strong capital investment sector and has, over the past 15 years, developed into one of the centers of startup activity and entrepreneurship in the United States. Much of this growth has to do with the importation of talent from other parts of the world because the startup sector is composed largely of people in their 20s and 30s and New York City has a lot to offer people in this demographic. The public and private sectors have been dynamic in their approach to developing programs and solutions for these new, technology-based businesses, and this development was an important factor in the creation of the Open Data Program in the city.

As the science of city building becomes better understood and is moved to the forefront of city planning measures, the element of urban entrepreneurship is increasingly cited as an important ingredient to future success. New York City recognized relatively early that the creation and integration of innovative technology is key to long-term initiatives and that open data is necessary for the development of these initiatives. For this reason, the launch of the city's first Open Data Initiative was announced in conjunction with the NYC's first BigApps Competition, a competition launched by the city to encourage data scientists and developers to create mobile applications based on public data. For the first competition in, 2009, the city published 170 datasets, the first datasets made public citywide.

Continued

Box 1.1 Case study: New York City Mayor's Office of Data Analytics (MODA)—cont'd

This initial step in opening up public sector data to the general public was a success. The response to the competition for data applications was strong with 80 apps submitted for 10 prizes, and the BigApps Competition has grown in size every year since its launch in, 2009. Beyond the interaction between public and private entities on urban development issues, the launch of this initiative signified the beginning of a shift in the way that city business is conducted. Opening datasets to the public allows the people, who are the end users of city services, to identify areas of improvement in the city and take the initiative to fix them. City leaders saw that, simply by empowering the people of New York with the tools they needed to develop solutions, the city government could focus more on big picture issues and regulation and use less resources on the creation of solutions themselves.

MODA was a direct result of New York City's resolve to become a transparent, data-driven city and the first step in making sure smart, collaborative technology thrives in the city. A large part of MODA's contribution to enabling the growth of innovation in the city is very visible with initiatives such as the partnership with the Queens Library to offer Open Data 101 classes to the public, the organization of Open Data Week activities across the five boroughs, and their partnership with the NYC Department of Education and BetaNYC to promote the use of open data in middle and high schools throughout the city. But an important part of the MODA's support for entrepreneurship in the city is invisible: the lack of data they collect on open data. MODA does not specifically track the way in which open data is used, which offers urban entrepreneurs the discretion that they need to develop their business plans and carry out all of the activities necessary for effective product launch.

All in all, life around the world is changing rapidly, and cities are struggling to find the right mix of public-private collaboration for future success. For cities that are looking to increase citizen involvement, New York City can serve as a model of how open data policies lead to social and urban entrepreneurship and how data-driven policies can be used to improve quality of life across all demographics.

[a]The Freedom of Information Law of New York; https://www.dos.ny.gov/coog/foil2.html.
[b]Open Data Law section 23–506, part b: https://www1.nyc.gov/site/doitt/initiatives/open-data-law.page.

Box 1.2 Interview with Kelly Jin, Chief Analytics Officer for City of New York.

We had the great pleasure and honor to interview Kelly Jin (Fig. 1.2), the current Chief Analytics Officer for the City of New York and Director of the Mayor's Office of Data Analytics. In the following text, we share the main points raised during this interview.

Could you describe the vision/long-term objectives you have developed for your city?

As New York City's Chief Analytics Officer, my overarching vision is to institutionalize data and analytics functions across the city's government. Through our work at the Mayor's Office of Data Analytics (MODA), we manage, analyze, and transform

Box 1.2 Interview with Kelly Jin, Chief Analytics Officer for City of New York—cont'd

FIG. 1.2 Kelly Jin, Chief Analytics Officer for the City of New York and Director of the Mayor's Office of Data Analytics.

data into insight to help drive policy and operational decisions in the city. Each portfolio in our office works to improve the city's data infrastructure. Our analytics team of four data scientists work with city agencies on the most pressing issues facing the city and demonstrate best practices that we also work with agency analytics teams to build toward. Data scientists also need quality data to generate insights, which is where our two other portfolios come in. MODA manages the NYC Open Data program, which hosts more than 2000 city datasets, sets standards for the maintenance and documentation of those datasets, and is building a community of analysts inside and outside the city focused on using the city's data. MODA also supports citywide internal data-sharing efforts, including through the NYC Recovery Data Partnership, which launched July 2020 and is connecting city analysts with data from private organizations to inform the city's COVID-19 response and recovery efforts.

How do these objectives contribute to make your city more fair and equitable?

Building standards around data and analytics means having a better understanding of city agency operations and the lived experiences of New Yorkers, and then using that understanding to inform responsible decisions about policy and programming. Most recently, we've seen the power of data to drive decision-making in NYC in the response to the COVID-19 pandemic—granular information about cases and outcomes has driven the city's understanding of neighborhoods most in need and publishing the data has helped the public understand how the effects of this pandemic have been felt starkly along sociodemographic lines. MODA's vision for the NYC Open Data Program is "Open Data for All." The Open Data Program aims to connect New Yorkers to the administrative data that runs their city to answer important questions such as what services the city provides, how to access them, and how city agencies are performing. We

Continued

Box 1.2 Interview with Kelly Jin, Chief Analytics Officer for City of New York—cont'd

understand, however, that data and technology education and literacy can often be a barrier to entry; not everyone has the skills to manipulate and analyze a dataset. Over the last 5 years, we've developed strategies to break down these barriers, and in 2019, we co-designed a strategic plan built around these values of fostering data access for all with members of NYC's civic tech community. Through hackathons and curriculums that feature open data, NYC Open Data participates in the Computer Science For All initiative to bolster the city's computer science education efforts by connecting students to data that relates to their daily lives. We worked with our partner, the civic technology nonprofit BetaNYC, to pilot a new program called *Data Counts*, to similarly teach analytics skills using open data throughout the Queens Public Library system. Last but not least, our annual Open Data Week festival, with events across all five boroughs, aims to foster communities of people with all levels of technical skill to answer questions together using NYC Open Data. In recent years, this festival has featured a workshop on building your own app with open data, a data scavenger hunt, and data arts and crafts, as well as issue-specific hackathons and discussions on topics ranging from sustainability and urban planning to community health and transportation.

What are the urgent needs of residents? What are the services you have improved and you still want to improve?

Every year, residents, workers, and visitors in New York City have millions of engagements with the city's government. The urgent needs and priorities of NYC residents are similar to the residents of other major cities: affordable housing and childcare, access to a quality education, job stability, and more. MODA collaborates with agencies to analyze operational data and deliver recommendations to help the city better meet the needs of residents. For example, MODA has worked with the Department of Housing Preservation and Development and the Law Department to identify potential cases of tenant harassment to target inspection and enforcement resources. MODA is also working to integrate data from different agencies to identify how many vacant buildings and lots exist across the city and where those vacancies are to help policymakers target responses to housing market conditions. And after water main breaks this past winter, MODA began working to identify predictive conditions for future breaks. These examples highlight that MODA works across issue areas; where there is data and the potential to help better serve New Yorkers, we are prepared to assist. The COVID-19 pandemic has amplified some of these needs and created new ones in 2020. Some of the work MODA has done to support the city's response to COVID-19 has included tracking the supply chains and utilization rates for personal protective equipment (PPE) for city hospitals and other agencies, tracking city employee leave rates to support the continuity of government operations when cty workers and their families were hit hard by the pandemic, and prioritizing parks and neighborhoods for proactive outreach to encourage social distancing.

Is your decision-making process based wholly on data for the management of your city? Do you consider your city a data-driven city? Why?

We never work based wholly on data. Context matters. Our office collaborates with agencies across subject areas from education to transportation to sanitation,

Box 1.2 Interview with Kelly Jin, Chief Analytics Officer for City of New York—cont'd

meaning that every project comes with an initial learning curve. Talking to agency subject matter experts to understand the context of the project, the factors at play, and how they make decisions is an essential part of our process at the beginning and throughout a project. And we have learned that handoff of insights to a partner is more successful when we understand how they think about their work and how they will use what we share with them. There is no doubt in my mind that New York City is a data-driven city: during my tenure, top officials want people with analytics skill-sets in the room when there are important decisions to be made, and across the city's agencies there are emergent data and analytics teams doing critical work. MODA is working to create more opportunities for collaboration and responsible data-sharing across the city because we know that data-driven decision-making is impossible without comprehensive data assets, underlying technical architecture, and analytics talent.

What have been the key milestones in becoming data-driven?

MODA has been at the center of several important milestones in the development of both New York City's data landscape and the analytics community within the city's government. Over the last decade, NYC Open Data has accumulated a rich body of data with standards for documentation and timeliness. In 2012, NYC Open Data went from being an nascent program to being the law in New York City, making the datasets of city agencies "open by default," and compelling agencies to undergo an annual compliance process to find, document, and publish their data assets. Through MODA's work on compliance, technical standards, and community outreach, the Open Data Portal has become the first stop for both city analysts trying to better understand the operations of other agencies and New Yorkers trying to better understand how their city is serving them.

In recent years, data analytics teams have emerged in agencies across the city, from the Department of City Planning to the Taxi and Limousine Commission, with highly capable geographers, data engineers, and data scientists using advanced analytical methods to bolster the city's understanding of the lived experience of New Yorkers and drive operational improvements at their agencies. In 2017, our office established the Analytics Exchange (or AnEx, for short), a community of practice with over 600 data analysts and practitioners across more than 60 agencies. AnEx hosts quarterly meetings where everyone can share best practices and success stories, and discuss how to make the city a better environment for analytics talent. We're glad that MODA will continue to be at the center of this evolving ecosystem. In 2018, our office was enshrined in the New York City Charter, ensuring that it will continue to have a centralized role in data policy and in providing analytical insights for the city staff and leadership.

Which kind of data (structured or unstructured data) do you capture and use?

MODA works predominantly with administrative data captured by agencies in their standard course of operations. The NYC Open Data Portal provides a comprehensive view of the types of public administrative data that our data scientists use. One key example is NYC311 service requests, incoming correspondence from residents that is often asking how to access a service, or for the city to take action to respond to an on-the-ground phenomenon. 311 service requests are a unique,

Continued

Box 1.2 Interview with Kelly Jin, Chief Analytics Officer for City of New York—cont'd

dynamic indicator of conditions in the city and are often used as input for our models. Free-text submissions to 311 and images submitted to 311 are types of unstructured data that the city has yet to analyze for insights but are targets for future work.

Which mathematical models have you developed based on these datasets? Descriptive/Predictive/Prescriptive? Which services were in the scope of your models? (Transport, energy, education, security, etc.)

All of the above! MODA works with agencies that provide the full range of city services and the central question for our analytics work could range from describing what is happening, to diagnosing why it's happening, to predicting what will happen in the future, to prescribing what we should do about it. Regardless of who the end-user of analysis is or what the exact form of the question is, MODA's goal in analytics work is to provide actionable insight to improve city services and policy, which means we need to be able to explain what went into our models, why we made the choices we did, and ultimately to point to an action that an agency partner should take.

How have you resolved the problems of data privacy/security/confidentiality, especially when you collect personal data?

Whether it is in the management of NYC Open Data or in analytics projects, MODA takes its responsibility for protecting New Yorkers' information extremely seriously. Local legislation ensures that data in NYC is "open by default," but other laws and city policies are in place to protect the privacy of individuals' personal information. Balancing these mandates, agencies closely govern and manage their data, ensuring that any identifying or sensitive information about New Yorkers is not shared publicly, while seeing to it that datasets that should be made public are. When working on analytics projects, MODA also upholds a high standard of data minimization: in addition to adhering to any legal requirements, MODA does not access data containing personally identifying information when it isn't needed, and only allows the specific individual(s) working on a project to have access to this information, subject to compliance with stringent privacy and data security protocols. Both in our work on open data and on analytics projects, MODA benefits from the counsel of the City's Chief Privacy Officer, Laura Negrón, and her team at the Mayor's Office of Information Privacy, who have created and implemented high standards for data privacy protection citywide.

What are the main stakeholders (private or public or hybrid companies, citizens?) involved in your main projects/strategy?

MODA works closely both with agencies across the city government and with New Yorkers directly. Within the city government, MODA convenes data holders and analytics professionals both through our management of the NYC Open Data Program and through convening the Analytics Exchange (AnEx), the City's community of practice for analytics professionals. AnEx has over 600 members and meets quarterly to share success stories and best practices and discuss the environment for analytics in the city and how it could be improved. To celebrate the 10-year anniversary of NYC Open Data, in 2019, MODA conducted its most involved engagement of stakeholders to date to develop a strategic plan for the next decade of the

Box 1.2 Interview with Kelly Jin, Chief Analytics Officer for City of New York—cont'd

program. We conducted a 2-week public survey and 2-day co-design workshop connecting city agencies, community members, and private organizations who interact with the city's open data to set the priorities that will guide our management of the program going forward. Part of making data open to the public means not asking people how they are using it. Through conducting public engagement events like our annual Open Data Week celebration and co-design workshops like these, we hope to strengthen the feedback loop to make NYC Open Data more useful for all.

What are your recommendations/best practices based on your experience for future city managers that would like to transform their city and make it data-driven?

Making an analytics officer or data officer role permanent and connected to executive decisionmakers should be a priority for city managers. To be data-driven, cities need to create an environment for analytics that attracts top data science talent and upholds citywide standards for data that makes it easier to derive analytical insights and to work across agencies. Creating this environment takes time and buy-in from many different stakeholders, and for me it is pivotal that the Chief Analytics Officer role and MODA are organized within the Office of the Mayor. We have a talented analytics team with four data scientists. My advice for managers of civic analytics teams is to secure executive buy-in and engagement to target analytics where it is most needed and to be certain that there will be an audience for the analytics end-products before your team starts on a project. Once a project is over, analytics teams should strive to share their successes to continue to foster an environment for analytics and help with a future seat at the table when your agency, or your city, is confronting an important issue. Lastly, managers should invest in hiring strong communicators and translators between their organization's business needs and data analysis. MODA has a team of strong communicators willing to dive into complex topics with subject matter experts from any city agency; build strong relationships; and traverse the domains of analytics, policy, and operations on any given project.

themselves). It indeed offers a peer-to-peer and "self-organized" solution instead of an institutional or traditional one, which would be the creation of a private or public company hiring and training employees. The model goes beyond a public-private partnership and has a greater social and inclusion effect since it offers a job opportunity for many women who would have left the labor market and can reintegrate it through this community. The role of the citizen as an entrepreneur in the city takes a paramount interest. The discussion integrates the incipient debate regarding the model called Public-Private-People Partnerships (4Ps) promoted by the UNECE (2016) and that places the citizens as a fourth force of innovation.

When dealing with the topic of smart cities, it is relevant to also consider the evolution of cities toward models that value sustainable and resilient development by promoting sustainable and resilient objectives and governance. These are the focus of the next two sections.

4 Resilient city

Today, cities are all subject to different kind of disasters that would have a huge effect on the residing population. These can be classified from acute shocks such as floods, droughts, or earthquakes to chronic stresses such as climate change or environmental pollution (CSS, 2013; Weichselgartner & Kelman, 2015). The Organization for Economic Co-operation and Development (OECD) states consequently there is an urgent need to work on cities' resilience.

We repeat the definition of the 100 Resilient Cities movement (Agudelo-Vera, Leduc, Mels, & Rijnaarts, 2012) about the resilience of a city. They define it as the capacity of individuals, communities, institutions, businesses, and systems within the city to survive, adapt, and grow no matter what kinds of chronic stresses and acute shocks they experience. The stakeholders involved in the urban resilience building process may be individuals, groups, or organizations from different disciplines and with different needs, responsibilities, and resources.

Nevertheless, their integration and coordination are considered of paramount importance by international organizations focusing on building resilient cities (Rockström et al., 2009). They are recognized as the key drivers in carrying out effective policies and tools for ensuring the development of resilient cities ready to face disaster risks. Singh-Peterson and Underhill (2017) proposed a framework on how the different stakeholders of a city should work and collaborate together. Gimenez, Labaka, and Hernantes (2017) presented a maturity model and list of policies to foster the collaboration, awareness, training, and preparedness of the city stakeholders in the resilience building process.

In this regard, if the "how" is properly handled, there is still a little understanding of "why" the different stakeholders should work and collaborate. Indeed, metrics are missing to estimate a return on investment (ROI) of the actions aimed at improving city resilience. We believe the introduction of a data-driven philosophy in the management of cities will support to fill this gap, taking into the account the simple adage that "we can't monitor or fix what we can't measure". Many concepts like hazard, risk, vulnerability, mitigation, and resilience will be used consistently throughout this book. We consider it important to fix their definitions based on the current literature (Mendizabal, Heidrich, Feliu, García-Blanco, & Mendizabal, 2018; CSS, 2013; Vale, 2014) in Box 1.3.

If the traditional risk procedures are based on past experience and the science of statistics, an alternative is emerging based on the application of forecasting methods and data science. Singapore is an international leader in this

> **Box 1.3 Definitions related to resilience.**
>
> A hazard is an unexpected or uncertain event with the potential to disrupt society. Hazards may have natural (e.g., earthquakes or wildfires), technical (e.g., accidents in chemical production), or societal origins (e.g., riots or terrorist attacks). Hazards are the cause of disaster. So, logically, disaster occurs when a hazardous event or process has a major effect on a social system. A disaster thus has two dimensions: the actual hazard and the society it affects. An event that has no or only a minor effect on the society cannot be considered as a disaster. Finally, risk is the spatial or temporal probability that a hazard occurs. The risk is the product of a hazard's likelihood and its consequences.
>
> A disaster is a risk that has materialized. Although risk assessments are not a new field, the methods applied for urban planning and management have drastically suffered changes in the recent years. Today, risk assessments are frequently conducted quantitatively by internal urban staff or external consultancy team. This approach creates the possible bias that hazards that occur frequently (on a seasonal basis, like wildfire or flood) and that may have devastating consequences whenever they occur look like "more potentially disastrous" than a 1 in 100-year event (e.g., earthquake for example), which may have similar damages but is less frequent.

respect, having invested drastically in the development of predictive models and early warning tools in recent years (Wong & Brown, 2009). In this regard, an important instrument for proactive risk assessments is the use of scenarios. Scenarios engage different emergency management professionals including emergency agencies, infrastructure managers of private or public offices, government officials, and use of data science techniques. In terms of governance of these different stakeholders, we observe a trend toward the application of a centralized office that monitors, prevents, and applies technical solutions in case of disaster (CSS, 2013).

For example, Paris, Hamburg, Greater London Area, or Sydney are using offices of civil protection and disaster assistance (Turoff, Bañuls, Plotnick, Hiltz, & Ramírez de la Huerga, 2016). These techniques based on scenarios have nevertheless increased the complexity of the risk assessment process, which has led to the development of different standards, frameworks, and technologies to tackle urban resilience. Over the last few years, with several initiatives from research and multilateral organizations, the concept of resilience has opened up a range of theoretical conversations, which have often focused on building long-term resilience strategies to cope with stressors derived from climate change or social inequalities. Pioneer entrepreneurs and private investors aim at equipping the market with digital tools based on the operative side of the concept. In Europe, projects in the framework of H2020 are fueled with methods and tools with the capacity to operationalize resilience. From disaster risk reduction to climate change and critical infrastructures, these communities of users shared a common view of the city as a system of interconnected critical infrastructure where a disruption can put the city at risk due to domino effects. For example, COVID has shown how vulnerable our health systems were due to the interdependencies among the critical infrastructures and services.

The effects are calculated by simulating the city as interconnect systems (Grimaldi & Fernandez, 2017) and applying the cascading effects theory (Gonzva, Barroca, Gautier, & Diab, 2016) and interdependencies in sociotechnical networks methodologies. Sharing data between the different city stakeholders in charge of critical infrastructures affected by climate change becomes key. In summary, data science techniques help to identify the risks, probability, and effect and develop proactive actions to disrupt the cascading effect if a disaster occurs (Toubin, Lhomme, Diab, Serre, & Laganier, 2012). Nevertheless, a gap still exists to evaluate the effects and corresponding benefits if an effect is mitigated or even neutralized (Rose & Liao, 2005; Turoff et al., 2016; Tyler & Moench, 2012) that the continuous progress of the data science—we believe—could cover. Consequently, we believe resilience readiness should be part of a strategy of data-driven development of urban services.

5 Sustainable city

Cities are where most human beings live, so the concept of a sustainable city is linked to growing issue of increasing human well-being and making economic growth compatible with the use of scarce natural resources. The issue about sustainability has pervaded recent developments in urban planning. Urban planning aims to develop and design cities; it is about a rational use of urban land and a conscious design of the built environment. This latter includes not only buildings but also infrastructures of transportation, communication, and distribution networks (Handy, Boarnet, Ewing, & Killingsworth, 2002; Roof & Oleru, 2008). Urban planning has a long tradition, starting with the project of renovation of Paris by Georges-Eugène Haussmann to recent trends of urban design, where the arrangement of urban elements are intertwined with architectural interventions. The objectives of urban planning concerning sustainability are two-fold. First, urban planners seek to design an efficient city that provides services to citizens minimizing the use of natural resources. Second, they seek to make the city more effective for its inhabitants by improving the quality of services (Bibri, 2018). We can summarize these two objectives into one statement by saying that urban planning aims to design a sustainable city by making it more efficient and more effective at the same time.

In Bibri and Krogstie (2017), the sustainable city is defined as a city that "maximizes the efficiency of the energy and material use, looks for the achievement of a zero-waste system, supports production and consumption based on renewable energy, promotes carbon-neutrality, provides sustainable mobility services by encouraging walking and cycling, preserves the whole ecosystem, and finally fosters livability and community-based human conditions". Urban designers have adopted two approaches to build a sustainable city: the compact city and the eco-city (Jabareen, 2006).

The compact city model tries to reach sustainability by optimizing land use by incorporating a high density of population and a mix of living, working, and leisure buildings in the same neighborhood. This urban design allows the inhabitants of the compact city to work and have leisure in the same neighborhood they live. They can use environment-friendly means of transportation like biking, walking, or taking a bus to commute, thus achieving more sustainable transportation and a better quality of life because of shorter commuting times (Newman, 2000) and the reduction of noise and atmospheric pollution. The opposite of the compact city is the low-density city, with distant working and living spaces that require long commuting times, usually by car or train. The eco-city approach goes one step beyond the compact city; in an eco-city, the input of resources and the output of waste are minimized (Joss, 2011). This approach advocates incorporating infrastructures that minimize nonrenewable energy inputs and nonrecyclable waste. Those infrastructures are often called "green infrastructures" (Benedict & McMahon, 2002). An example of green infrastructure are photovoltaic or thermal solar panels, a source of renewable energy for urban infrastructures. An example of an eco-city practice is the promotion of the use of solar panels through tax reductions and subsidies (Owen et al., 2006). Another eco-city practice is the adaptation of architecture and urban design to local climatic conditions, projecting buildings and streets with the aim of reducing the need for artificial heating or cooling systems. On the waste reduction side, the eco-city approach advocates practices of waste recycling and waste reduction (Osmani, Glass, & Price, 2008) to reduce the ecological effect of city life, thus enhancing sustainability.

When examining the relationship between the concepts of a smart city and a sustainable city, we believe that the smart city techniques of gathering data from the city and transforming it into knowledge can be of significant help to attain the objectives of the sustainable city paradigm. We find, though, that the role of smart city technologies in social integration or sustainability is questionable and ambiguous. We will develop this idea in the two following subsections.

5.1 The risks of ICT to environmental and social sustainability

Emerging technologies related to the smart city paradigm have delivered the possibility of more effective processes or energy production and distribution, and therefore are expected to contribute effectively to sustainability objectives. This is the claim that IT corporations like Dell, HP, IBM, or Oracle make when they claim that they provide new technological solutions for a greener economy. But, as Bibri (2014) points out, there is no empirical evidence of a negative relationship between technological innovation in energy production and energy consumption. The empirical evidence is of the opposite sign: technological innovation increases energy consumption.

The main concern about ICT and sustainability comes from externalities arising in the market of ICT goods (computers, game consoles, mobile phones, tablets, etc.). On the supply side, technological development is governed by Moore's Law, the observation that the number of transistors in a dense integrated circuit is doubling every 18 months. This fast technological development implies that ICT goods become obsolete, as products with higher performance are offered at the same price. Fast technological improvement leads to price drops, making these goods available to more and more people. Another driver of demand is the generalized access to the Internet. The costs of telecommunications have lowered dramatically in the last few years, and as a result the number of people with access to the Internet has risen exponentially. In 2019, up to 2.3 billion people worldwide have access to the Internet. Internet access is a complementary good of ICT physical goods, making them much more appealing to customers. On the demand side, the attractiveness of ICT has risen dramatically. A computer or a mobile phone with access to the Internet substitutes habits of consumption, like buying records, buying newspapers, or going to movie theaters. The dynamic market of ICT goods has salient negative externalities: a large volume of technological waste coming from fast obsolescence and carbon emissions coming from the transportation of ICT goods from Asia, where most of them are produced, to the rest of the world.

The evidence of widespread diffusion of ICT has an important caveat, which is that this diffusion has been unequal, leading to a digital divide. The access to benefits coming from ICT may be hindered by motivational, skill, and material barriers (van Dijk, 2006). Motivational barriers consist of a lack of desire to access ICT, because of lack of knowledge of potential benefits. Even if we are motivated to use ICT, skill barriers may appear, if we are not able to manage the hardware and software. Even if we have the skills, we need to physically access ICT. Physical access can be prevented for economic reasons (we don't have enough resources to buy hardware or software) or if we have a disability. Developing countries can have large part of the population within the digital divide, because of lack of an adequate ICT infrastructure. This can be overcome, though, by the widespread use of mobile devices. In developed countries, the people affected by the digital divide tend to belong to socially excluded groups: disabled, unemployed, or retired people (Adams & Fitch, 2006). As more products or services like newspapers or movie theaters are being replaced by ICT and the Internet, the diffusion of ICT technologies can result in exclusion to these services for those groups, resulting in negative effects for social integration.

The digital divide in smart city initiatives can be tackled as a problem of diffusion of innovation. The model of technology adoption lifecycle (Rogers, 1995) defines five market segments related to any innovation: innovators, early adopters, early majority, late majority, and laggards. The diffusion in each segment is grounded in success in the previous segment. The most difficult step is going from early adopters to early majority, which is a chasm in the innovation curve (Moore, 2014). This is valid for any process of diffusion of innovation (in fact, Roger's model was considered previous to the appearance of the Internet and the explosion of ICT products) so it can be applied to smart city initiatives. Material barriers to diffusion of ICT cannot be overcome by marketing alone, as they are mainly associated with lack of financial resources or disability, but there is room for improvement in overcoming motivational and skill barriers. Technologies of big data and machine learning can help to motivate citizens to adopt smart city technologies, combining economies of scale with a very accurate segmentation, sometimes with segments encompassing only a single individual. This mass customization model of production (Duray, 2002) can find a way to motivate individuals of the early majority segment and provide them with the adequate skills, thus overcoming the chasm in the diffusion of smart city innovations.

5.2 The contribution of ICT to environmental and social sustainability

The concerns of the adoption of the smart city paradigm regarding environmental sustainability and social integration can be balanced with a focus of the potential benefits that smart city technologies can drive. The intensive use of ICT technologies like Internet of Things (IoT), cloud computing, big data curation, and automated learning can make life in the city more efficient, decoupling the increase of well-being and improvement of quality of life from the usage of fossil fuels, economic growth leading to the use of more resources, and an overall negative environmental effect (Chourabi et al., 2012; Shove & Walker, 2007). This decoupling is made possible as we move from an industrial economy to a knowledge-based one (Tseng, Pai, & Hung, 2011). Let us illustrate this with a piece of life in a smart city. I can use my mobile phone to buy a product from a large retailer like Amazon and pick it at a store that regularly sells completely different products. The retailer increases the efficiency of her store as she can get more revenue with the same labor and physical space. Months later, we can tire of the good we bought, so we resell it through apps like Vinted or Wallapop. To deliver the product to our buyer, we are again using the same channel of retailers that act as delivery points for the app product. When going to the retailer to pick up or deliver the product, I use an app like Cooltra that allows me to rent an electrical scooter. This service fosters mobility of citizens with fewer scooters but more intensely used.

The processes depicted are possible with the use of the smart city technologies we described. The paradigm of this new way of living in the city is doing more with less. We can access more services, enhancing human well-being with less use of resources and less waste. This paradigm is driven by increasing the efficiency of labor and capital through management of data and information linked to production processes. In the next section, we discuss the role of big data in enhancing sustainability in the smart city with more detail.

6 Augmented city

Practitioners from diverse professional fields, policymakers at diverse governance levels, and academics and scientists have shown large interest in the potential benefits of big data, data analytics, and machine learning. Understanding the cities as a source of data and a system that can be transformed by data analytics offers new and exciting possibilities regarding sustainability, social inclusion, and participation.

6.1 From small data to big data

The two last decades have seen a proliferation of sources of data about city life (Grimaldi, 2019; Grimaldi, Diaz Cely, & Arboleda, 2020; Grimaldi, Fernandez, & Carrasco, 2019). These sources have been public and private. Public sources have come from the creation of open data portals. In those portals, data retrieved by the government is put in the public domain in formats that make that data reusable and facilitate automatic retrieval. The initial motivation of open data portals was fostering government transparency and accountability, but in later stages, they have been used to foster entrepreneurship as anyone can use city data to develop their own app and start their own business. Private companies have also gathered data from the city, taking advantage of the city's infrastructures, as is the case of retail stores or banking, and later taking advantage of the geographic location services of mobile devices that most of us have by default. That data tells a lot about consumer habits, fostering strategies of consumer retention and raising sales (Manyika et al., 2011). In opposition to open data portals, data gathered by private corporations is kept private, as it is a relevant source of profits for these companies. It is the case of social media corporations, which are free for its users, which obtains revenues from targeted ads and from selling data to other companies. For example, apps like Google Maps or FourSquare are designed to gather data that later can be used to make decisions about the location of physical shops.

Before the technological expansion of ICT, there have been other sources of data available for a long time: population census, meteorological data (like temperature and rain for each day), maps, or property ownership and value (i.e., cadastre). Before implementing ICT for data management, data gathering and analysis were labor-intensive processes with serious limitations: massive retrieval of data, like a population census, had to be taken every 10 years because of the large amount of resources needed to obtain information from the entire population, the likelihood of making mistakes on data retrieval and of missing data was high, and it was time consuming and difficult to apply statistical analysis techniques to interpret and obtain information and knowledge from data. The cadastre, storing information about real estate, was one of the initial settings for implementation of ICT in the 1980s. The deployment of ICT technology on public administration and in the private sector in

1980–2000 allowed us to store data more safely and to analyze it through visualization and explanatory statistical analysis.

The exponential development of ICT technology for data management since the 2000s increased the possibilities dramatically, going from a situation of data scarcity to one of data deluge (Talia, Trunfio, & Marozzo, 2015). There was a qualitative and a quantitative transformation of available data. Data can be gathered and stored automatically at a lower cost and with lower probability of errors. Collected data was much detailed and granular, frequently incorporating precise geographical information. ICT technology also widened the possibilities of data analysis, allowing analysts to move from explanatory statistical analysis to predictive models automated in machine learning workflows (see Chapter 2). Scholars and practitioners refer to this new context as the big data era. There is no consensual definition of what big data is (Waller & Fawcett, 2013), although we can say that big data can be described by three v-words: the volume of data stored, the velocity at which new data is acquired, and the variety of data that can be acquired (Agarwal & Dhar, 2014; Woerner & Wixom, 2015). Concerning the source of acquisition, there are two broad categories of big data: automated and volunteered.

Automated data are obtained while the users are performing a task not explicitly linked to data gathering. Automated data requires connected sensors of IoT technologies, like sensors on parking spots connected to cars that can lead the driver to a free parking spot. We can also obtain automated information from transactions like buying goods in a supermarket or visiting a theater or museum from the infrastructure we use to perform the transaction, such as paying machines. Another source of automated data is CCTV, or any other device that can collect image, video, or sound. Machine learning techniques like neural networks have allowed an unprecedented use of image and sound data for predictive systems. There are two main approaches to deliver the capabilities of automated data. The traditional approach is cloud computing. In this system, all retrieved information is transferred to a centralized system, where storage, processing of data, and response to the user are performed. The emergence of IoT devices has favored the development of cloud computing solutions, distributed systems of analysis, and response to the customer. Those distributed intelligence systems allow improving the quality of service (e.g., less latency), also adding more safety because of redundancy.

Volunteered data are gathered from an explicit act of giving information by the user or even from a collaborative effort from a community of users. We give information explicitly when participating in a survey, either paper-and-pencil or web-based, or when we fill in data for a shopper's card from a retailer. These shopper's cards are a salient example of the value of data, as retailers offer discounts to customers in exchange of information to fed customer churn models. More evolved examples of volunteered data efforts are collaborative efforts. Grimaldi, Fernandez, and Carrasco (2019) present the eixos.cat initiative. It is an economic observatory that offers information to entrepreneurs, franchisers, or potential investors. They can find relevant intelligence for viability analysis for new ventures. The data of eixos.cat is obtained from fieldwork from volunteers and merged with databases from open data portals. Another salient example of collaborative building of big data is OpenStreetMap (OSM), an initiative for building an open-source, editable map of the world. The geodata of OSM is collected from free sources from volunteers through manual survey, GPS tracking, aerial photography, and even personal knowledge. OSM was inspired from the success of initiatives like Wikipedia (another example of volunteered data) and from the lack of nonproprietary sources of geographical information.

6.2 Big data applications for cities

The convergence of several streams of ICT development (increase of computing power, access to the Internet from mobile devices, etc.) with increasingly sophisticated data analytics techniques has led to a deep transformation of the business landscape. State-of-the art ICT makes the stages of a machine learning process available to an increasing number of businesses and government agencies. Thanks to these practices, decision-making today is less grounded on subjective expert judgment than on predictions of algorithms (Davenport & Prusak, 2000; Waller & Fawcett, 2013). A machine learning workflow starts with data acquisition from automated and sometimes volunteered sources. In this first stage, data are mined, scrapped, and aggregated. Then, data should be cleaned and preprocessed to be ready for model implementation. This stage consists of the deployment of predictive models either for a classification job (e.g., will this customer churn in the near future?) or for a prediction job (e.g., speech recognition). The most popular machine learning algorithms of the day are neural networks or deep learning through predefined architectures like PyTorch or TensorFlow. Those techniques have extraordinary results in tasks like image or speech recognition but require large amounts of data and large computing capabilities. The application of machine learning to the urban environment is known as urban informatics (Foth, Choi, & Satchell, 2011), and it is the technological backbone of a smart city project. Here we will summarize some applications of urban informatics that contribute to shape a smart city.

6.3 Smart mobility

Different vertical solutions have been deployed in cities to improve mobility. They include intelligent transport systems combined with smart parking services and solutions to share taxis (e.g., Mytaxi.com) and bikes (e.g., Cooltra). The data collected inform on the "health" of the city mobility services and allow proposal of alternative transport solutions in real time (Correia & Wünstel, 2011). In France, the city of Nancy, a medium-size city in the north-east of France offers to commuters a mobile application to know the status of the public and private transport to optimize their movement using the different mobility solutions of the city or to report infrastructure incidences during their transport. This project converges different existing solutions and provides an end-to-end vision about the status of the different mobility resources of the city (bike-sharing service, tramway, and bus geolocalization, and parking spots available) to assess the citizens on the best transportation mode for their need of mobility and to estimate the corresponding transport time.

As discussed, scholars commonly split the types of Big Data into two categories: automated and volunteered. In Nancy's case, data are automated, that is, without the formal consent of the user whenever they are collected (even if the user has to give general authorization the first time using the service, generally when he buys the mobility card). Contrasting with this approach, volunteered data are gathered with users' formal consent. In the next section, we illustrate this alternative model.

There is large room for improvement in the way we traditionally move around the city. If each family owns its means of transportation, they are used only when family members need it, remaining idle most of the time. Mobility solutions that put within reach a mobility solution when and where we need it, without the need of owning it, makes mobility more effective, reducing the number of needed transportation elements and the space they occupy in the city. A second order effect is that a smart, centralized management of city mobility resources helps to organize it more effectively through mobility data analysis. This is the economic logic behind bike-, motorbike- and car-sharing initiatives like Bicing, Cooltra, and Ubeeqo, respectively. The use of smart technologies can make the parking process more effective, indicating free parking spots, reducing traffic and therefore accidents and pollution (see Nice vignette in Chapter 4). Mobile technologies are also the trigger of the transformation of taxi services made by companies like Uber or Cabify. Smart mobility has also improved the user experience of public transportation. Companies like Moovit are making the use of public transportation smart, informing users about the best combinations of bus, metro, tram, or bike in real time. The most salient and evident effect of ICT developments like big data and mobile technologies is seen in the field of urban mobility.

6.4 Smart school

Education is suffering a big change with the nascent business of interactive online courses for workers like Coursera or ITunes Academy. Many universities propose their own MOOC solution: MIT and Harvard in the U.S., IESE in Spain, or HEC in France. Online platforms such as Zoom, Google Meet, MSN Teams, etc. allow for organizing virtual rooms and reproducing all the tools used by professors in classrooms such as white board, quizzes, small group' exercises, or reverse class mode. They complete the actual value chain of face-to-face plenary sessions providing an alternative or complementary solution. But during the recent COVID-19 pandemic, it became the main solution for students who were compelled to stay home. For example, many sophisticated solutions exist in Singapore universities. During a lecture, a video conference camera at the front of the room uses facial recognition and posture analysis to take attendance, check for student attentiveness, and assess the level of understanding based on gestures such as nodding, shaking one's head, and expressions of puzzlement.

All of this automated data—attentiveness and comprehension—are merged with volunteered data, which are generated by traditional exams, forms, or web-based questionnaires and go directly into the student's file.

Although not commonly associated with smart city technologies, ICT-driven education and leisure services transformation have a significant effect on city life. Schools, secondary education, and universities account for a significant volume of mobility and city resources. The COVID-19 pandemic has worked as a global experiment of alternatives of presential education. In countries like Spain with severe confinement periods, video conferences have been the main communication channel between students and teachers. The permanent effects of this experience are to be seen, but an increase of remote learning in university education it is to be expected, in a way paved by MOOC services offered by universities. As for leisure, streaming media services like Filmin, Netflix, and Spotify are significantly affecting how citizens develop their leisure activities in the city.

6.5 Smart energy

A smart meter is an IoT device, that is, a digital meter that measures electricity flowing in and out of houses at 5-min intervals. It communicates the home's energy use to the meter service provider. It also informs on incipient problems. High energy use times of households are usually weekday mornings, afternoons, and evenings. Unsurprisingly, low energy use times are overnight. Today, most utility companies are mainly dependent on carbon-based technologies for baseload and peaking generation. Aging transmission lines are constrained, distribution is one-way, yet at the same time customer demand is increasing since the population in cities is growing.

Utilities companies' answer to this growing demand is by implementing a smart grid, which is an intelligent electricity network that integrates multiple power sources: roofs equipped with solar cells, wind turbines, and strength of the tides. This converts the system to a bidirectional flow of energy. ICT collects all the events of the devices connected to it in the demand or supply side along with the actions realized by all the users. It allows for understanding the users' consumption behavior in real time and to reduce the peaks during the day (Chourabi et al., 2012; Correia & Wünstel, 2011). Indeed, beyond regular or flat-rate pricing tariffs, retailers offer flexible pricing plans or time-of-use tariffs to customers within intervals. Thus, smart meters can control and incentivize customers to use cheaper, off-peak energy (McAfee & Brynjolfsson, 2012).

In that way, the utility companies are able to produce more with less energy, increasing their number of clients with less environment effect; in other words, changing the business paradigm by providing MORE with LESS.

6.6 Smart facility management

The aim of facility management is to deliver support services to the built environment effectively. Facility management services deal with, among others, health and safety (control of temperature through heating or cooling, control of humidity, cleaning, waste management), operations (space allocation, office layout), safety (infrastructure for control of fires, and water or gas leakages, among other threats), and security (prevention of theft and intrusions). The requirements for services will depend upon the use of the building; it can be a warehouse, a store, a factory, or an administrative office. ICT technologies, mainly through IoT embedded in sensors, can help foster effectiveness of facility management in a variety of ways. Regarding energy consumption, facilities can use electrical accumulators to be loaded at hours of low tariffs and deliver electrical energy at peak hours. We can obtain data from sensors about temperature, humidity, and energy consumption in different parts of the building to monitor dysfunctions (e.g., power leakages, rooms with too high or too low temperature) and to reduce energy consumption in a continuous improvement process. Sustainability of buildings can be improved through installation of photovoltaic systems (Bibri, 2018). In some cities, the installation of photovoltaic systems is compulsory for new buildings, and there is the possibility to sell energy surpluses to the electrical grid. The use of more effective infrastructures, IoT technology to control inputs and outputs, and big data analysis can be extended to other facility management functions, like waste management, operations, safety, and security.

6.7 Smart hospital

Augmented and virtual reality (AR/VR) technologies also have different applications in cities. In the medicine sector, augmented reality is a new approach in executing detailed surgical operations. The development of augmented reality devices allow surgeons to incorporate data visualization into diagnostic and treatment procedures to improve work efficiency, safety, and cost and to enhance surgical training. A physician using an AR headset is able to see digital images and other vital data directly overlaid on the field of view. In such a scenario, the headset could display a hovering echocardiogram with vital signs and data on the characteristics of the patient's aneurysm directly above the surgical field. One of the main benefits is the doctor needn't look away from the patient to multiple displays to gather and interpret this information.

6.8 Smart security

AR/VR also allows a virtual modeling of dangerous environments and real-time situational awareness (Lehofer et al., 2016). It makes the training of first responders faster and better to get more accurate professionals. Second, in case of emergency situation or criminal pursuit, officers equipped with augmented reality glasses have a better understanding of the real-time conditions in the field and are aided in their task of law enforcement and citizens' protection. AR/VR also helps civic protection or fire fighters in the 3D vision of emergency situations and in the decision-making process, for example, to find the safest routes for search and rescue. With AR/VR, the vision of the city is enhanced, augmented by a digital vision that overlaps and extends the real one.

The advances of smart facility management developed inside buildings can be deployed on streets and urban environment. IoT sensors and cameras allow monitoring the city in real time and react effectively to safety and security threats. This has been tested empirically in Rio de Janeiro in the context of an IBM project (Kitchin, 2014). It must be noted, though, that the massive deployment of surveillance tools in the public space has strong ethical and political implications, and therefore values of safety and security must be balanced with values of privacy and human rights.

6.9 Smart public governance

The government of public affairs in most democratic countries has been carried out on a model of representative democracy. Given the high costs of information transfer and collective decision-making associated with direct participation of people in government, democracies have relied on representatives to make these decisions. A frequent claim in representative democracies is that the role of common people in government is limited to voting every 4 years. ICT technologies promise to lower the costs of people's participation on decision-making, so models of direct democracy can be economically viable. The first elements of a smart government have been open data portals that increase transparency and accountability. Another experience of direct participation of citizens are initiatives of consultation to citizens on decisions that affect them (Townsend, 2013). The Decidim Barcelona platform, an initiative of Barcelona city council, is a pioneering experience of smart government through direct participation.

Big data is affecting also how we design cities as a whole and how we want to manage them. Digital twin represents the cutting-edge model of smart governance. It is a data-informed model of a complex system like a city. It has the ability to make a virtual representation of all the physical elements and the dynamics of urban flows. In the past, cities have created isolated vertical models implementing IoT devices like smart meters to operate and optimize the distribution of energy between different fossil and green types via distributed or centralized sources. Digital twin is a combination of all existing and isolated models as a whole main process. It can be also seen as a further integration step, breaking silos from a vertical to a horizontal integration of the urban services. It is a digital version of a physical entity that is pinned to measurement data. It assumes the governance of a city as a transversal platform of services that aims at considering the needs of the citizens in a holistic way.

Digital twin is usually associated with the concept of a data thread. Assuming that all the elements of the city have a digital signature, the urban data thread is the data pipeline that covers them and tracks all the measurements of the urban processes. Digital twin and thread answers much more sophisticated questions about how the city operations run and possible correlations between urban concerns, for example, how quality issues of energy flows may effect telecommunication or water processes.

Another application of digital twin models is visualization and building information modeling. Accurate virtual representation of a city is a dynamic three-dimensional (3D) city model and a collaborative data platform for use by the public, private, and research sectors. It enables users from different sectors to develop sophisticated tools and applications for test-bedding concepts, planning and decision-making, and research on technologies to solve emerging and complex challenges related to urban security, historic heritage preservation, or conditions of living. Indeed, a digital twin model can be used in the analysis of light and temperature for solar energy potential. It calculates the percentage of light and shadow per building based on the position of the sun.

6.10 Smart economy

Companies selling consumer goods, like supermarkets and retail stores, are avid consumers of knowledge about consumer behavior. Big data technology has allowed the implementation of basket analysis, consisting of finding association rules between products that are frequently bought together (i.e., that are in the same basket). If a low-margin product is bought together with a high-margin one, sales of the later can be fostered with special offers of the former at a lower cost. Loyalty programs that reward customers using shopper's cards allow detecting customer churn based on recency, frequency, and monetary value of purchases (an RFM model). On the other hand, an extension of online commerce has not led to a reduction of physical shops in the city but to a transformation, now seen as a branch of a multichannel marketing strategy. The physical store can work as a showroom where consumers can see, touch, and try on products that can be bought later online, or can work as a pickup point of online purchases. In the multichannel strategy, the assets of companies add functionalities that make them more efficient and effective to serve customers.

7 Is a data-driven approach progress?

7.1 False promises of big data

Two major events explain the emergence of the data-driven approach. On one hand, it is the speed of the computer-based algorithms, when today CPUs of computers can quickly perform what was once performed by thousands of people (accountants, office people, militaries, etc.) in the past. On the other hand, the cost to get a data-driven answer has drastically decreased. Whatever the problem is (prescriptive or predictive), the algorithms of big data that learn by comparison of labeled data instead of the classic approach of expert systems are designed to solve more complex problems in a more efficient way than by reasoning through loops of "if-then-else" rules (Agrawal, Gans, & Goldfarb, 2017). However, such big data techniques are rarely present in university curricula, and a large gap of capability divides the group of citizens/students who has minimal knowledge to benefit from the technology (Grimaldi & Fernandez, 2017). This is the first false promise of big data to be able to quickly revolutionize the city.

Many ICT companies such as IBM or HP claim their big data solutions can help companies reduce costs and systemically minimize energy, water, carbon emissions, and waste. Their discourse is based on emerging technologies that help companies to become more energy efficient; implement new ways to source, manufacture, and distribute goods and services in a more sustainable manner; and enable safe and renewable sources of energy. However, since ICT evolution as previously discussed is still managed by Moore's Law (i.e., computing power or capacity doubles every 18 months), it has conducted two negative consequences as far as it concerns the sustainability of the planet. First, the cost of communication has largely decreased to fall toward zero. The main consequence was the emergence of a globalized market, a flat world where products are manufactured in China and delivered all over the world, thus increasing the distance between the supply and demand and having a bad effect on global carbon emissions.

Second, at the same thime, the estimated number of people connected to Internet has increased to reach 2.3 billion in 2019 worldwide. Consequently, a large global market of online sales has emerged where anyone can purchase technological goods or services from anywhere, anytime, and with the low unit costs associated with mass and outsourced production. This global market has exponentially increased where the consumption of goods and services becomes a desirable daily goal (as nutrition is) and artificially becomes connected to the person's well-being and happiness. This second effect has corresponding unsustainable environmental externalities and a huge negative effect on the planet's green ecosystem.

7.2 Potential benefits of big data

Some authors (Chourabi et al., 2012; Shove & Walker, 2007) have a different vision and highlight the critical role that ICT, especially the emerging ones

(Social Channels, Mobile, Analytics, Cloud, IoT), could play in a sustainable urban development by decoupling three variables considered strictly embedded so far: fossil resource, economic growth, and environmental effect (Derqui & Grimaldi, 2020). Tseng et al. (2011) add that this change occurs because we move from an industrial society to a knowledge-based (intensive) one where data is the new resource, the new oil. They all claim that the role of ICT is to invent solutions to share and reuse existing products, improving environmental sustainability. For example, using his mobile device, a citizen can buy a product on the Amazon app, and when he does not need it anymore, he can resell it again using his smart phone to another citizen through a variety of mobile applications such as eBay or Wallapop or also more specific ones for a vintage or niche (e.g., local) market. With the Ubeeqo app, he can also rent a car by the hour that he will geolocalize, unlocking or locking with his intelligent phone. ICT increases the lifecycle of manufactured things, improves its rate of use, and participates in a so-called circular economy. All these applications are possible by the use of big data and IoT technologies THAT are becoming essential to the functioning of the smart cities. We believe, moreover, they have the capacity to reconcile smart city and sustainable city objectives around the new and common paradigm of MORE with LESS: more service with less energy consumption, more clients served with less CO_2 emission.

8 Data-driven smart city architecture

8.1 Evolution of the smart city models

The maturity evolution of smart cities can be described in five phases. Fig. 1.3 shows this evolution and describes the journey that Cities have realized these last 40 years (from social smart city via resilient or sustainable city).

We define a data-driven smart city architecture as the most mature one, a model THAT we believe is able to respond to the citizens' needs and to provide an end-to-end service converging ICT, smart, resilient, sustainable, and social models. An alternative exercise can be to map the different types of smart citIES according to their ICT orientation in their DNA or origin as shown in Fig. 1.4.

8.2 The architecture of the solution

Our solution assumes a layered approach inspired by the literature on smart cities, sustainable cities, and resilient cities (Fig. 1.5).

A data-driven smart city is, first, the process of drawing all types of data associated with urban life. These urban (big) data are real time and come from physical sensors installed by the municipalities and spread all along the urban area. The result is a data infrastructure. The SENTILO project in Barcelona is a good illustration (https://connecta.bcn.cat/connecta-catalog-web/component/map). It is indeed a repository of data that gathers geolocalized information about the quality of air, water, pollution, pollen, or the noise of the streets.

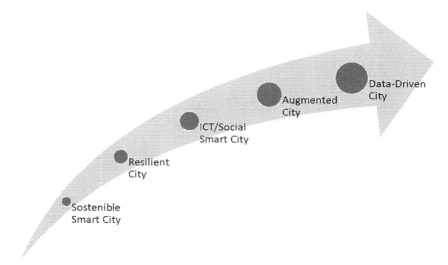

FIG. 1.3 Maturity evolution of the smart city.

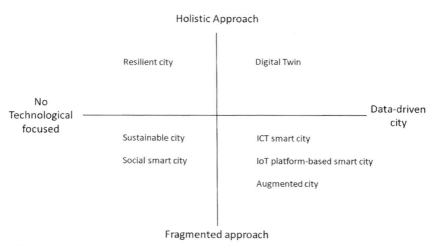

FIG. 1.4 Mapping of the smart city models.

It recently includes the humidity rate of green parks and traffic speed. Nevertheless, these (big) data can come also from the information that people reveal in social networks while chatting each other, participating in a social event (sport competition, music show, etc.), or commenting what they see or feel when living, commuting, or working in the city. In this way, they also become sensors who inform on what is happening in the city (Marsal-Llacuna et al., 2015).

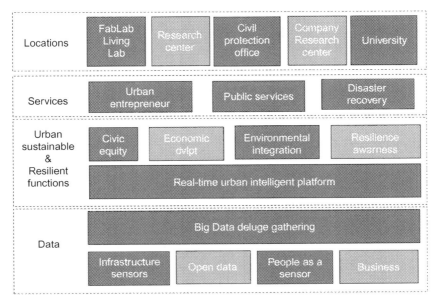

FIG. 1.5 Data-driven smart city architecture.

A data-driven smart city is also the result of the implementation of data-oriented competences integrating the discourse regarding the use of big data for urban services. Classifying labeled data could be useful to understand urban activities, for example, which part of the city generates the biggest interest for a temporal resident like a tourist. The data can come also from retail shops that, by unifying information about the purchasing behavior of the citizens, shows the rhythm of the business activities during the day and the possible day-to-day variation. Urban managers can leverage this information to detect undesired retailing closures. Intelligent urban platforms based on IoT and Cloud computing technologies intercorrelate this vast deluge of urban data providing an integrated and holistic view of the city by processing, storing, and analyzing the data coming from multiple sources. These platforms serve as a data analytic hub to support the decision-making process. Comparing with historical data, they can show positive or negative trends and help to set alerts to cover the three dimensions of sustainability, which are social/societal justice, environmental integration, and economic regeneration (Ramirez, Palominos, Camargo, & Grimaldi, 2021).

These platforms can also be connected to resilience platforms to notify alerts responding to long-term risks such as climate change, earthquakes, sea level rising, etc. The objective is to better understand systemwide cascade effects and their consequences to implement resilience preventive actions to impede or limit them. Finally, these platforms help private (urban or social) entrepreneurs, civic developers, researchers, and public managers to develop new public services. The city boosts this entrepreneurship process creating new information-sharing spaces like FabLab or Living Lab for startups/civic developers to present and sell their new products, apps, or innovative services.

8.3 Real-time urban platform

Using chatbots can be used to optimize customer support, part of the real-time urban platform. Chatbots and voicebots are, fundamentally, pieces of software that can replicate a human conversation. When a customer asks a question via a bot, natural language understanding (NLU) technology attempts to understand the intent of a user, find a response in the knowledge base, and return that response to the user. The result is that questions are answered immediately and without human intervention. These technology principles are being increasingly adopted by companies and organizations around the world to create operational efficiencies, speed up response times, boost customer satisfaction, and therefore positively affect the bottom line.

8.3.1 Collective intelligence

Natural language processing (NLP) is a branch of machine learning that enables computer systems to understand and comprehend human language (see Chapter 3 for more details). NLP training refers to the method in which developers train these systems using lots of data. When a user poses a question, the NLP system may or may not return an answer, depending on its level of comprehension. In the case when the system can't answer, the question is converted into data that are absorbed into the system via a training process. The objective is to ensure that when the question is asked again, the NLP system can more confidently respond. This process repeats itself over time as more data is obtained, resulting in an increased level of NLU.

Fundamentally, collective intelligence consists of pooling this training data to enable cities to exponentially improve the capacity of their chatbots to respond. Consider the following questions: How do I pay my council rates? How do I report an issue in my neighborhood? Where can I find electric vehicle chargers? Many cities get these questions all the time. The only thing that differs is the answer. The training data can therefore be pooled to help the chatbots improve.

For example, a user in The City of Adelaide might ask the question:

- *Where can I find electric vehicle chargers?*

A user in The City of London might ask the question:

- *Whereabouts can I charge my electric car?*

Both users are asking the same thing. Both of these queries can be used to train the model so that any time a user asks that question in the future, regardless of what city they are in, the chatbot will have a stronger chance of understanding their intention or request. A good way to sum this up is that *a rising tide lifts all boats*. The more cities that use the platform, the more training data we have to improve the natural language capabilities and the more intelligent all of our city-based chatbots become. The power of collective intelligence is to scale the model across thousands of cities worldwide, rapidly improving the level of intelligence as the deployment goes.

Driven by the power of collective intelligence and urban data, chatbot solutions like Hopstay's platform (see Box 1.4) helps cities optimize citizen support and improve access to urban services through smart digital assistants. Chatbots are an essential tool for cities to automate frequently asked questions so that customer service standards can be maintained and budgets managed, despite increased demand. Automating responses to FAQs allows customer service agents to focus on complex queries, speeding up response time and allowing a higher level of service by providing instant answers to customers.

8.3.2 Improving accessibility

For cities and councils, accessibility of the real-time platform is paramount. This is due to their responsibility as public bodies to ensure inclusiveness, that is, all citizens can access services. More than 1 billion people around the world have access to voice assistants today, which have the potential to unlock accessibility to both the elderly and disabled who may find it difficult to navigate a complex website or visit a customer service center. Via simple voice commands, customers can get answers to quick questions or receive status updates on services. This is a significant time saver for these people. Platforms like Google Assistant and Amazon Alexa are the leading voice platforms, but they don't come without their challenges.

Whilst the majority of the population are comfortable navigating a smartphone, voice platforms are a new frontier. Education is therefore key if cities are to successfully offer this service. One of these difficulties is how a user invokes a voicebot. In essence, this refers to the way in which a user accesses a particular voice skill or action. Or in simple terms, how do they tell their vocal assistant that they want to speak to their local council? One solution consists of invocating names for councils. Usually, place names are not allowed, but an exemption states that this does not apply to urban authorities, and the result is that the only organization allowed to register the invocation name of a city is the proper city. For example, only the City of Adelaide can register the name of Adelaide and all a user has to say is "Hey Google, can I speak to Adelaide?" to invoke the City of Adelaide voicebot. This simplifies this user experience for citizens, and it is expected to see greater uptake of voice assistants in councils down the track.

8.3.3 Service provided by modules

Advanced chatbot solutions develop a library of citizen service modules that address common city/local government processes and that have been precoded and designed for the conversational interface. These "plug and play" modules

> **Box 1.4 Hopstay solution.**
>
> Hopstay (https://www.hopstay.co/) believes in the potential of automation technology to play an important role in sustainable urbanization. The business argument is relatively universal—any technology that can save an organization more money than it costs, is, on the surface, worthy of investment. Although cities typically operate within the public sector framework (and therefore are not driven by the profit motive), this principle is still important when planning the distribution of resources and expenditure. A growing customer support burden operates as a budget distraction from citizen-centric sustainability and infrastructure projects. For a city to therefore be smart, they need to adopt a data-driven, efficient approach to operations to ensure they are maximizing the budget for more tangible initiatives. Hopstay believes that this is an underserved part of the smart city equation.
>
> Cities are using Hopstay's platform to integrate self-service modules into chatbots, thereby reducing reliance on customer service agents. A prime example of this is checking waste collection day. This is the most common query coming through many city-based customer service channels. Allowing citizens to self-serve via a chatbot removes this burden. A customer asks when their waste is being collected and the chatbot responds with a series of follow-up questions to obtain the correct response before delivering that response. In this case, this requires a simple API connection (either pre-existing or developed) so that the chatbot can recall the relevant waste collection day once it knows the user's address. Based on Hopstay's data, even partial automation can be beneficial. Cities are seeing frontline queries (the first question a customer asks) automated by 50%. In some cases, the follow-up question is too specific for the chatbot, but an effective handover protocol ensures that the customer gets their answer. Over time, as chatbots learn, the figure creeps closer to 60%, with approximately 40% of queries handed over to a human.
>
> Hopstay's NLP framework is consistently improving. At this time, the system can handle approximately 1000 of the most common queries passing through municipal customer service channels (numbers taken from across the entire client base; the average client stores 250 questions with fully trained models). These questions have, of course, been trained on thousands of different phraseologies (or, the technical term, *utterances*). Hopstay's analytics dashboard also tracks query frequency, enabling cities to see which questions are most common. The results show chatbots with larger clients typically observe the following usage metrics (taken as averages across top 20% of client base):
> - Approximately 2000–2500 monthly active users (citizens)—someone who has interacted with the chatbot within a 30-day period
> - Approximately 40,000 messages received per year
> - Chatbot response rate between 50% and 75%, indicating a handover rate of 25%–50% (handover meaning the percentage of queries that are handed over to a human because the bot could not respond).

seamlessly connect to both the backend system of the city and popular conversational platforms. They help improve accessibility to urban services whilst reducing reliance on traditional customer support channels such as email and phone.

Some of the more popular ones are described in the following. They are actually the capacities offered by the Hopstay platform:

Issue reporting

Prior to chatbots, there were a number of examples of cities adopting mobile apps that enable people to report issues in their neighborhood such as graffiti, potholes, or dumped rubbish. The specific issue reporting module enables citizens to report an issue directly through the chatbot, making use of inbuilt camera and location sharing. The chatbot takes the user through a series of questions to obtain the different elements of the issue report, such as issue type, location, description of the issue, and then any associated media (photos or videos of the issue). The report is then triaged to the relevant council department for immediate action. It provides a mobile-friendly way to report an issue without requiring citizens to download a new mobile app (depending on the geography of the city, we can identify the best messaging application by looking at usage metrics).

Waste collection

Waste collection module enables users to check waste collection dates and set up alerts to remind them when waste will be collected. To do so, the chatbot takes the waste calendar of the city and maps out the geography to obtain the waste collection dates of every address in the city. Sometimes this information is already available via API, otherwise it is a manual (but worthwhile) process. Users can then ask the chatbot when their waste will be collected. The chatbot will prompt them for an address before returning the relevant information. Then, the chatbot offers to set up an alert system that will notify the user every time their waste is being collected. This reduces missed waste collections and helps households manage their waste.

Parking management Smart parking module leverages available parking data to give citizens access to live parking availability via voice command. First, it connects citizens to live, up-to-date parking availability provided by smart parking sensors inserted into the ground. Then, it absorbs the data into a conversational framework and launches the smart parking assistant on leading voice platforms (Google Assistant, Amazon Alexa, etc.). Via a simple voice command, users can locate the nearest available car park to their destination.

For example, the user may say:

- *Hey Google, can you ask Smart Parking Rye where the nearest car park is to the Rye Hotel?*

The voice assistant will recognize the desired destination of the user and then return the nearest available car park using the available parking data. It will then offer the user the option to launch navigation. The beauty of this integration is that it is hands-free, offering users a convenient (and legal) way of obtaining this information whilst driving. This is an improvement on mobile app or website user interfaces that are challenging (and illegal in most countries) to operate while driving a car. On a global level, the combination of this technology has the potential to improve sustainability outcomes by reducing the average time that drivers spend searching for a car park. At scale, this will reduce traffic, congestion, and carbon emissions produced by cars on our roads.

8.3.4 Added value—ROI

Chatbot automation and NLP become an increasingly important operational pillar of the real-time urban platform as our cities continue to grow. The case for optimizing customer support is strong, and preliminary results disclosed by Hopstay suggest that a data-driven approach using chatbots and voicebots can create efficiencies of more than 50%. Reducing this operational burden will make cities more agile and allow them to redistribute valuable resources to high-ROI activities that tangibly benefit the citizen.

It's also important for cities to understand that accessibility standards require constant review. As our world shifts to social networks, messaging platforms, and voice assistants, cities must adapt. These shifts aren't just driven by emerging generations either. A nuanced approach should identify the best customer service channels for citizens of different ages and demographics. It is for this reason that best solution must remain platform-agnostic and capable of integrating into a number of third-party customer support channels.

References

Adams, C., & Fitch, T. (2006). Social inclusion and the shifting role of technology: Is age the new gender in mobile access? *Social Inclusion: Societal and Organizational Implications for Information Systems, 208*, 203–215.

Agarwal, R., & Dhar, V. (2014). Editorial—Big data, data science, and analytics: The opportunity and challenge for IS research. *Information Systems Research, 25*, 443–448.

Agrawal, A., Gans, J. S., & Goldfarb, A. (2017). What to expect from artificial intelligence. *MIT Sloan Management Review, 58*(3), 23–26.

Agudelo-Vera, C. M., Leduc, W. R. W. A., Mels, A. R., & Rijnaarts, H. H. M. (2012). Harvesting urban resources toward more resilient cities. *Resources, Conservation and Recycling, 64*, 3–12. https://doi.org/10.1016/j.resconrec.2012.01.014.

Alter, K. (2000). *Managing the double bottom line: A business planning reference guide for social enterprises*. P A C T Pub. https://www.bookdepository.com/Managing-Double-Bottom-Line-Sutia-Kim-Alter/9781888753172.

Assadian, A., & Nejati, M. (2011). Challenges faced by megacities in the future. *Information Resources Management Journal, 24*(2), 76–88. https://doi.org/10.4018/irmj.2011040106.

Atzori, L., Iera, A., & Morabito, G. (2010). The internet of things: A survey. *Computer Networks, 54*(15), 2787–2805. https://doi.org/10.1016/j.comnet.2010.05.010.

Bakici, T., Almirall, E., & Wareham, J. (2013). A smart city initiative: The case of Barcelona. *Journal of the Knowledge Economy, 4*(2), 135–148. https://doi.org/10.1007/s13132-012-0084-9.

Benedict, M. A., & McMahon, E. T. (2002). Green infrastructure: Smart conservation for the 21st century. *Renewable Resources Journal, 20*(3), 12–17.

Bibri, S. E. (2014). *The potential catalytic role of green entrepreneurship—technological eco-innovations and ecopreneurs' acts—in the structural transformation to a low-carbon or green economy: A Foucauldian discursive approach.* (Master's degree). https://www.lunduniversity.lu.se/lup/publication/4390551.

Bibri, S. E. (2018). Data science for urban sustainability: Data mining and data-analytic thinking in the next wave of city analytics. In *Smart sustainable cities of the future*, https://doi.org/10.1007/978-3-319-73981-6_4.

Bibri, S. E., & Krogstie, J. (2017). Smart sustainable cities of the future: An extensive interdisciplinary literature review. *Sustainable Cities and Society Journal.* https://doi.org/10.1016/j.scs.2017.02.016.

Brundtland, G. H. (Chairperson). (1987). *Our common future: World commission on environment and development.* Oxford: Oxford University Press.

Caragliu, A., del Bo, C., & Nijkamp, P. (2011). Smart cities in Europe. *Journal of Urban Technology, 18*(2), 65–82. https://doi.org/10.1080/10630732.2011.601117.

Chourabi, H., Nam, T., Walker, S., Gil-Garcia, J. R., Mellouli, S., Nahon, K., et al. (2012). Understanding smart cities: an integrative framework. In *Proceedings of the annual Hawaii international conference on system sciences* (pp. 2289–2297). IEEE Computer Society. https://doi.org/10.1109/HICSS.2012.615.

Christopoulou, E., Ringas, D., & Garofalakis, J. (2014). The vision of the sociable smart city. In *Vol. 8530. Lecture notes in computer science (including subseries lecture notes in artificial intelligence and lecture notes in bioinformatics)* (pp. 545–554). Springer Verlag. https://doi.org/10.1007/978-3-319-07788-8_50.

Cornelius, N., Todres, M., Janjuha-Jivraj, S., Woods, A., & Wallace, J. (2008). Corporate social responsibility and the social enterprise. *Journal of Business Ethics, 81,* 355–370. https://doi.org/10.1007/s10551-007-9500-7.

Correia, L. M., & Wünstel, K. (2011). *Smart Cities applications and requirements.* White Paper of the Experts Working Group. Works European Technology Platform.

Crossette, B. (2010). The state of world population, 2010. In *From conflict and crisis to renewal: generations of change.* New York, USA: UNFPA, United Nations Population Fund.

CSS. (2013). Preparing for disasters in global cities: An international comparison. *3RG Report.* ETH Zürich: Risk and Resilience Research Group, Center for Security Studies (CSS).

Davenport, T., & Prusak, L. (2000). *Working knowledge: How organisations manage what they know?.* Harvard, USA: Harvard Business School Press.

De Guimarães, J. C. F., Severo, E. A., Felix Júnior, L. A., Da Costa, W. P. L. B., & Salmoria, F. T. (2020). Governance and quality of life in smart cities: Toward sustainable development goals. *Journal of Cleaner Production, 253.* https://doi.org/10.1016/j.jclepro.2019.119926.

Derqui, B., & Grimaldi, D. (2020). Data on the sustainability profile and food waste management in primary and secondary schools: The case of the Catalonia region in Spain. *Data in Brief, 28,* 104825. https://doi.org/10.1016/j.dib.2019.104825.

DESA. (2009). World urbanization prospects. In *The 2009 revision. Proportion urban population.* New York: United Nations.

Economist Intelligence Unit. (2004).

Duray, R. (2002). Mass customization origins: Mass or custom manufacturing? *International Journal of Operations & Production Management, 22,* 314–328.

Elkington, J. (1994). Toward the sustainable corporation: win-win-win business strategies for sustainable development. *California Management Review, 36*(2), 90–100. https://doi.org/10.2307/41165746.

Etezadzadeh, C. (2014). *Smart city 2.0 as a liveable city and future market*. Igarss. https://doi.org/10.1007/s13398-014-0173-7.2.

Foth, M., Choi, J. H.-J., & Satchell, C. (2011). Urban informatics. In *Proceedings of the ACM 2011 conference on computer supported cooperative work* (pp. 1–8).

Garriga, M., Salcedo, J. L., Vives, N., & Meseguer, R. (2015). *An experimental methodology to promote and evaluate the use of community networks for civic engagement*. A: "ICTs for inclusive communities in developing societies" (pp. 45–72). Cambridge Scholars Publishing. http://www.cambridgescholars.com/icts-for-inclusive-communities-in-developing-societies.

Gimenez, R., Labaka, L., & Hernantes, J. (2017). A maturity model for the involvement of stakeholders in the city resilience building process. *Technological Forecasting and Social Change, 121*, 7–16. https://doi.org/10.1016/j.techfore.2016.08.001.

Gonzva, M., Barroca, B., Gautier, P. E., & Diab, Y. (2016). Analysis of disruptions cascade effect within and between urban sociotechnical systems in a context of risks. In *Vol. 7. E3S web of conferences*EDP Sciences. https://doi.org/10.1051/e3sconf/20160707008.

Grimaldi, D., Diaz Cely, J., & Arboleda, H. (2020). Inferring the votes in a new political landscape: The case of the 2019 Spanish Presidential elections. *Journal of Big Data, 7*, 58. https://doi.org/10.1186/s40537-020-00334-5.

Grimaldi, D., & Fernandez, V. (2017). The alignment of University curricula with the building of a Smart City: A case study from Barcelona. *Technological Forecasting and Social Change, 123*, 298–306. https://doi.org/10.1016/j.techfore.2016.03.011.

Grimaldi, D. (2019). Can we analyse political discourse using Twitter? Evidence from Spanish 2019 presidential election. *Social Network Analysis and Mining, 49*. https://doi.org/10.1007/s13278-019-0594-6.

Grimaldi, D., & Fernandez, V. (2017). The Road to School. The Barcelona case. *Cities, 65*, 24–31. https://doi.org/10.1016/j.cities.2017.01.013.

Grimaldi, D., Fernandez, V., & Carrasco, C. (2019). Heuristic for the localization of new shops based on business and social criteria. *Technological Forecasting and Social Change, 142*, 249–257. https://doi.org/10.1016/j.techfore.2018.07.034.

Grimaldi, D., Fernandez, V., & Carrasco, C. (2019). Heuristic for the localization of new shops based on business and social criteria. *Technological Forecasting and Social Change, 142*, 249–257. https://doi.org/10.1016/j.techfore.2018.07.034.

Handy, S. L., Boarnet, M. G., Ewing, R., & Killingsworth, R. E. (2002). How the built environment affects physical activity: Views from urban planning. *American Journal of Preventive Medicine, 23*(2 Suppl), 64–73. https://doi.org/10.1016/s0749-3797(02)00475-0.

Hollands, R. G. (2008). Will the real smart city please stand up? Intelligent, progressive or entrepreneurial? *City, 12*, 303–319.

Inayatullah, S. (2011). City futures in transformation: Emerging issues and case studies. *Futures, 43*(7), 654–661. https://doi.org/10.1016/j.futures.2011.05.006.

Jabareen, Y. R. (2006). Sustainable urban forms: Their typologies, models, and concepts. *Journal of Planning Education and Research*. https://doi.org/10.1177/0739456X05285119.

Joss, S. (2011). Eco-cities: The mainstreaming of urban sustainability–key characteristics and driving factors. *International Journal of Sustainable Development and Planning, 6*(3), 268–285. https://doi.org/10.2495/SDP-V6-N3-268-285.

Kitchin, R. (2014). The real-time city? Big data and smart urbanism. *GeoJournal, 79*, 1–14. https://doi.org/10.1007/s10708-013-9516-8.

Komninos, N. (2006). The architecture of intelligent cities: Integrating human, collective and artificial intelligence to enhance knowledge and innovation. In *IET conference publications, issue 518* (pp. 13–20). https://doi.org/10.1049/cp:20060620.

Leadbeater, C. (2006). *The rise of the social entrepreneur* (pp. 233–246). Springer. https://link.springer.com/article/10.1007/s11846-013-0104-6#citeas.

Lehofer, M., Heiss, M., Rogenhofer, S., Weng, C. W., Sturm, M., Rusitschka, S., et al. (2016). Platforms for smart cities—connecting humans, infrastructure and industrial IT. *2016 1st International Workshop on Science of Smart City Operations and Platforms Engineering (SCOPE) in partnership with Global City Teams Challenge (GCTC) (SCOPE-GCTC)* (pp. 1–6). https://doi.org/10.1109/SCOPE.2016.7515056.

Lorusso, S., Scioscia, M., Sassano, G., Graziadei, A., Passannante, P., Bellarosa, S., et al. (2014). Involving citizens in public space regeneration: The experience of garden in motion. In *Vol. 8580 (2). Lecture notes in computer science (including subseries lecture notes in artificial intelligence and lecture notes in bioinformatics)* (pp. 723–737). Springer Verlag. https://doi.org/10.1007/978-3-319-09129-7_52.

Macke, J., Rubim Sarate, J. A., & de Atayde Moschen, S. (2019). Smart sustainable cities evaluation and sense of community. *Journal of Cleaner Production, 239*. https://doi.org/10.1016/j.jclepro.2019.118103.

Madlener, R., & Sunak, Y. (2011). Impacts of urbanization on urban structures and energy demand: what can we learn for urban energy planning and urbanization management? *Sustainable Cities and Society, 1*, 45–53.

Manyika, J., Chui, M., Brown, B., Bughin, J., Dobbs, R., Roxburgh, C., et al. (2011). *Big Data: The next frontier for innovation, competition and productivity*. USA: McKinsey Global Institute.

Marsal-Llacuna, M. L., Colomer-Llinàs, J., & Meléndez-Frigola, J. (2015). Lessons in urban monitoring taken from sustainable and livable cities to better address the Smart Cities initiative. *Technological Forecasting and Social Change, 90*, 611–622. https://doi.org/10.1016/j.techfore.2014.01.012.

Martin, J. (1978). *The wired society*. Prentice-Hall, Inc.

McAfee, A., & Brynjolfsson, E. (2012). *Big data's management revolution*. Harvard Business Review.

McGranahan, G., Balk, D., & Anderson, B. (2007). The rising tide: Assessing the risks of climate change and human settlements in low elevation coastal zones. *Environment and Urbanization, 19*(1), 17–37. https://doi.org/10.1177/0956247807076960.

Mendizabal, M., Heidrich, O., Feliu, E., García-Blanco, G., & Mendizabal, A. (2018). Stimulating urban transition and transformation to achieve sustainable and resilient cities. *Renewable and Sustainable Energy Reviews, 94*, 410–418. https://doi.org/10.1016/j.rser.2018.06.003.

Miller, D., & Hazel, G. (2007). *Megacity challenges: A stakeholder perspective*. Retrieved from. http://www.siemens.com/press/pool/en/events/megacities/media_mrc_globe_170107_d_1431329.pdf. (Accessed 21 November 2020).

Montgomery, A. W., Dacin, P. A., & Dacin, M. T. (2012). Collective social entrepreneurship: Collaboratively shaping social good. *Journal of Business Ethics, 111*(3), 375–388. https://doi.org/10.1007/s10551-012-1501-5.

Moore, G. A. (2014). *Crossing the chasm: Marketing and selling disruptive products to mainstream customers*. New York: Harper Collins.

Mora, L., Appio, F., Foss, N., Arellano, D., & Zhang, X. (2020). Boosting urban sustainability through organizing collaborative ecosystems for smart city development. *Organization Studies*.

Mulder, I. (2014). Sociable smart cities: Rethinking our future through co-creative partnerships. In *Vol. 8530. Lecture notes in computer science (including subseries lecture notes in artificial intelligence and lecture notes in bioinformatics)* (pp. 566–574). Springer Verlag. https://doi.org/10.1007/978-3-319-07788-8_52.

Muñoz, P., & Cohen, B. (2016). The making of the urban entrepreneur. *California Management Review, 59*(1), 71–91. https://doi.org/10.1177/0008125616683953.

Mwenda, K. K., & Muuka, G. N. (2004). Toward best practices for micro finance institutional engagement in African rural areas: Selected cases and agenda for action. *International Journal of Social Economics, 31*(1–2), 143–158. https://doi.org/10.1108/03068290410515475.

Neirotti, P., De Marco, A., Cagliano, A. C., Mangano, G., & Scorrano, F. (2014). Current trends in smart city initiatives: Some stylised facts. *Cities, 38*, 25–36. https://doi.org/10.1016/j.cities.2013.12.010.

Newman, P. (2000). Changing patterns of regional governance in the EU. *Urban Studies, 37*(5–6), 895–908. https://doi.org/10.1080/00420980050011145.

Osmani, M., Glass, J., & Price, A. D. (2008). Architects' perspectives on construction waste reduction by design. *Waste Management, 28*(7), 1147–1158. https://doi.org/10.1016/j.wasman.2007.05.011.

Owen, A. M., Coleman, M. R., Boly, M., Davis, M. H., Laureys, S., & Pickard, J. D. (2006). Detecting awareness in the vegetative state. *Science, 313*(5792), 1402. https://doi.org/10.1126/science.1130197.

Ramirez, F., Palominos, P., Camargo, M., & Grimaldi, D. (2021). A new methodology to support smartness at the district level of metropolitan areas in emerging economies: The case of Santiago de Chile. *Sustainable Cities and Society, 67*. https://doi.org/10.1016/j.scs.2021.102713, 102713. In press.

Rockström, J., Falkenmark, M., Karlberg, L., Hoff, H., Rost, S., & Gerten, D. (2009). Future water availability for global food production: The potential of green water for increasing resilience to global change. *Water Resources Research, 45*(7). https://doi.org/10.1029/2007WR006767.

Rogers, E. M. (1995). Diffusion of innovations: Modifications of a model for telecommunications. *Die Diffusion von Innovationen in der Telekommunikation, 17*, 1453–1462.

Roof, K., & Oleru, N. (2008). Public health: Seattle and King County's push for the built environment. *The Journal of Environmental Health, 71*(1), 24–27.

Rose, A., & Liao, S. Y. (2005). Modeling regional economic resilience to disasters: A computable general equilibrium analysis of water service disruptions. *Journal of Regional Science, 45*(1), 75–112. https://doi.org/10.1111/j.0022-4146.2005.00365.x.

Shove, E., & Walker, G. (2007). CAUTION! Transitions ahead: Politics, practice, and sustainable transition management. *Environment and Planning A, 39*(4), 763–770. https://doi.org/10.1068/a39310.

Singh-Peterson, L., & Underhill, S. J. R. (2017). A multi-scalar, mixed methods framework for assessing rural communities' capacity for resilience, adaptation, and transformation. *Community Development, 48*(1), 124–140. https://doi.org/10.1080/15575330.2016.1250103.

Talia, D., Trunfio, P., & Marozzo, F. (2015). *Data analysis in the cloud: Models, techniques and applications* (1st ed.). Elsevier Science Publishers B.V., NLD.

Toru, I., & Isbister, K. (2000). *Digital cities*. Berlin Heidelberg: Springer.

Toubin, M., Lhomme, S., Diab, Y., Serre, D., & Laganier, R. (2012). La Résilience urbaine: un nouveau concept opérationnel vecteur de durabilité urbaine? Urban resilience: is it a useful concept for urban sustainability? *Développement Durable et Territoires, 3*(1), 0–18. https://doi.org/10.4000/developpementdurable.9208.

Townsend, A. M. (2013). *Smart cities: Big data, civic hackers, and the quest for a new utopia*. New York, NY: W.W. Norton & Company, Inc.

Tseng, C.-Y., Pai, D. C., & Hung, C.-H. (2011). Knowledge absorptive capacity and innovation performance in KIBS. *Journal of Knowledge Management*, *15*(6), 971–983.

Turoff, M., Bañuls, V. A., Plotnick, L., Hiltz, S. R., & Ramírez de la Huerga, M. (2016). A collaborative dynamic scenario model for the interaction of critical infrastructures. *Futures*, *84*, 23–42. https://doi.org/10.1016/j.futures.2016.09.003.

Tyler, S., & Moench, M. (2012). A framework for urban climate resilience. *Climate and Development*, *4*(4), 311–326. https://doi.org/10.1080/17565529.2012.745389.

United Nations Economic Commission for Europe (UNECE). (2014). *Human development report*.

United Nations Economic Commission for Europe (UNECE). (2016). *Promoting people first public-private partnerships (PPPs) for the UN SDGs*. Special Issue, Bref series.

Vale, L. J. (2014). The politics of resilient cities: Whose resilience and whose city? *Building Research and Information*, *42*(2), 191–201. https://doi.org/10.1080/09613218.2014.850602.

van Dijk, T. A. (2006). Discourse and manipulation. *Discourse & Society*, *17*(3), 359–383. https://doi.org/10.1177/0957926506060250.

Waller, M. A., & Fawcett, S. E. (2013). Data science, predictive analytics, and Big Data: A revolution that will transform supply chain design and management. *Journal of Business Logistics*, *34*, 77–84. https://doi.org/10.1111/jbl.12010.

Weichselgartner, J., & Kelman, I. (2015). Geographies of resilience: Challenges and opportunities of a descriptive concept. *Progress in Human Geography*, *39*(3), 249–267. https://doi.org/10.1177/0309132513518834.

Woerner, S. L., & Wixom, B. H. (2015). Big data: Extending the business strategy toolbox. *Journal of Information Technology*, *30*(1), 60–62. https://doi.org/10.1057/jit.2014.31.

Wong, T. H. F., & Brown, R. R. (2009). The water sensitive city: Principles for practice. *Water Science and Technology*, *60*(3), 673–682. https://doi.org/10.2166/wst.2009.436.

World Bank. (2017). *World development report* (p. 2017). http://www.worldbank.org/en/publication/wdr2017.

World Bank. (2018). *World bank*. https://openknowledge.worldbank.org/bitstream/handle/10986/29801/9781464812576.pdf (Retrieved 11 September 2018).

Chapter 2

Governance, decision-making, and strategy for urban development

Didier Grimaldi[a], Eula Bianca Villar[b], Laurent Dupont[c], Jose M. Sallan[d], and Carlos Carrasco-Farré[e]

[a]Ramon Llull University, La Salle Faculty, Barcelona, Spain, [b]Asian Institute of Management, Manila, Philippines, [c]Université de Lorraine, ERPI Laboratory/Lorraine Fab Living Lab, Nancy, France, [d]Universitat Politècnica de Catalunya, BarcelonaTech, Barcelona, Spain, [e]Ramon Llull University—ESADE Business School, Barcelona, Spain

1 Data-driven approaches for smart city

This chapter starts with a systematic review of the academic state of art about the trending topics that deal with data-driven approaches in an urban environment. Then, we select a specific example and analyze recent progress in the use of data to improve the urban process, which is as strategic and a priority as the resilience process. In this vein, we then use the case of the Philippines and show their data-driven policy to cope with disasters that drastically affect their urban areas.

1.1 A systematic literature review

Tran, Dupont, and Camargo (2019) conducted a systematic literature review on decision-making in the smart city. Based on a bibliometric process using Scopus database (from the years 2005 to 2018), this study contributes to a general mapping of the different decision-making methods applied during the design and implementation phases of a smart city project. This previous work underlines that smart city planning and decision-making are not only a data-driven multilevel scaling practice but are also a collective learning procedure supported by advanced ICT-based technologies and visualizations of available data, constant processes, and local history and stories (Eräranta & Staffans, 2015). Starting from this bibliometric methodology supported by an original "big data analysis" of a bibliography database, we decide to update the data and push the analysis exploring complementary information (Tran et al., 2019).

According to the approach described by Tran et al. (2019), this new study starts with two complementary search equations, which are composed of keywords, period of time, database, and type of documents (Table 2.1). The first equation aims to update the initial research and see how scientific productions have evolved. Thus, we are not only including the publication of a new full year (2019), but we also integrate those of the current year 2020 (the Scopus consultation being carried out on Sep. 15, 2020). The two complementary keywords are "decision-making" and "smart city." The previous study revealed the importance of big data and data management (Tran et al., 2019). Thus, the second equation aims to explore the data-driven trend on a smart city. In the second option, the two complementary keywords are "data-driven" and "smart city." Furthermore, "smart urban" and "urban" were included to complete the bibliometric approach for the first and the second equations, respectively. Indeed, some authors or practitioners used the terms "smart urban system," "smart urbanization," etc. instead of "smart city." For the second equation, we used the term "urban," because it takes on a "smart" connotation when associated with "data-driven." We only focus on articles and conference papers. Unpublished articles, working papers, and magazine articles were therefore excluded during the data purification process.

Fig. 2.1 shows a notable increase in published studies regarding decision-making (DM) processes or data-driven (DD) approaches in smart urban system or smart cities over the past 15 years. To compare this trend, we normalized the data collected from the Scopus database to the actual number of publications per year that were published at https://dblp.uni-trier.de/statistics/publicationsperyear. Indeed, since 2007, the total number of journal articles and conference papers (all fields) has been increasing annually by 5%. For each year until 2019, we took the data of the total number of publications, and we computed their Increase Rate (IR_y). Thus, the normalized data for 2005 is

TABLE 2.1 Two search equations focusing on hot topics for smart city.

Field	First introduced option	Second introduced option
Keywords	"decision making" AND ("smart city" OR "smart cities" OR "smart urban")	"data-driven" AND ("smart city" OR "smart cities" OR "urban")
Search in	Title, abstract, keywords	Title, abstract, keywords
Explored period	All years	All years
Type of documents	Articles and conference papers	Articles and conference papers
Database	Scopus	Scopus

Governance, decision-making, and strategy for urban development Chapter | 2 49

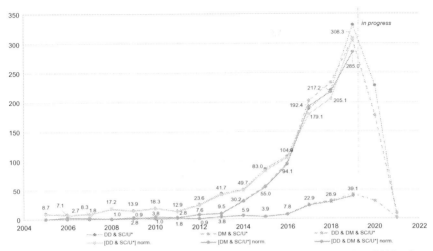

FIG. 2.1 Distribution of articles or conference papers focusing on DD or DM from 2005 to September 2020 (collected and normalized data).

the initial data from the Scopus database multiplied by $(1\text{-}IR_{2005\text{-}06})$ and so on until 2019. Since the year 2020 is not yet finished, we have not included its data. In Fig. 2.1, gray curves represent initial data, and the curves represent the normalized data. With the first search equation, 1139 scientific publications were found in Scopus database, i.e., 533 more publications between January 2019 and September 2020 (green curve, dark gray in print version, with normalized data ((DM & SC/U*)norm.) in Fig. 2.1). In fact, in just over a year and a half, the number of publications on the subject has doubled. This confirms the interest of the scientific community in the decision-making (DM) processes related to the smart city (SC). The second search equation allows us to identify research equation in 1351 articles or conference papers in the same database. It is interesting to note that both curves follow the same trend (yellow curve, light gray in print version, with normalized data ((DD & SC/U*)norm.) in Fig. 2.1). Data-Driven (DD) approaches represent a growing interest for the scientific community (Grimaldi, 2019; Grimaldi, Diaz, & Arboleda, 2020; Grimaldi, Fernandez, & Carrasco, 2019; Grimaldi & Fernandez, 2017). The development of technologies and their democratization also has increased the fields of application and feedback since 2014/2015. It is important to point out that we do not have a full year for 2020. Finally, Fig. 2.1 also includes a blue curve (dark gray in print version) ((DD & DM & SC/U*)norm.) based on the search equation merging Data-Driven (DD) and Decision-Making (DM) keywords to study the smart city concept (Matheus, Janssen, & Maheshwari, 2020). This last topic does not seem to be as dynamic as the themes taken individually.

The two groups of publications coming from equations 1 and 2 were transferred as bibliographical data to the VOSviewer software. These bibliographical data were used to develop two networks of keywords by co-occurrence links. The whole networks of keywords and their links are mapped out in Figs. 2.2 and 2.3. In these networks, the circles are a representation of the keywords, and the diameter of the circles represents the frequency of the occurrence for each keyword. The distance between two keywords indicates their relatedness in terms of co-occurrence links that were determined based on the number of documents in which keywords occur together. Thus, the closer two keywords are located to each other, the stronger their relatedness.

In the networks, a collection of keywords having strong relationships creates clusters, and these are tagged by different colors. By integrating all the keywords of each search equation in the Scopus database, we have identified a set of papers that represent the research trend of each cluster. The 11 and 10 main clusters generated by the VOSviewer software are described in Table 2.2, which includes the color, the main keywords, and the components of the clusters. The order of the groups depends on the number of items it contains.

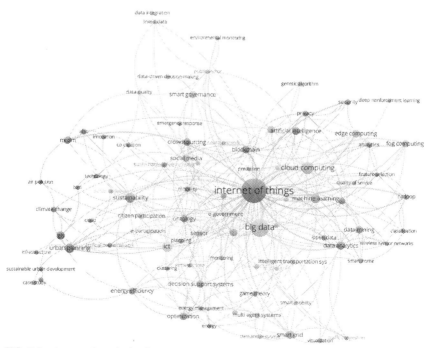

FIG. 2.2 A network analysis of 1139 publications focusing on decision-making, by VOSviewer software.

Governance, decision-making, and strategy for urban development Chapter | 2 51

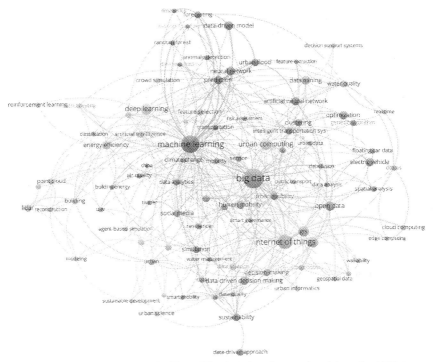

FIG. 2.3 A network analysis of 1351 publications focusing on data-driven, by VOSviewer software.

Table 2.2 shows that three main keywords stand out on both sides: "big data", "internet of things" and "sustainability." Furthermore, 39 keywords out of 95 can be found in both corpuses, i.e., 40% of the terms. Figs. 2.2 and 2.3 show the diversity of the links according to the adopted approach. The analysis of the clusters and keywords reveal that specific concepts linked to computer science are particularly used: data, ICT, artificial intelligence, etc. There even seems to be predominant technologies. However, other topics are emerging. These are more applicative.

The cluster network analysis also shows the distribution and the evolution in time of the keywords in the network. Using the overlay and the density visualization of VOSviewer, the same network could display the total frequency and length in research of each keyword. In Figs. 2.4 and 2.5, lines are defined by the average publication per year of each keyword (with different colors in the print version), with yellow for the most recent and dark blue for the oldest. Most of the recent themes are again related to technological aspects or linked to computer science. Nevertheless, the first equation related to decision-making processes shows that "citizen participation" and "co-creation" are emerging themes

TABLE 2.2 Clusters analysis.

Search equation	"decision making" AND ("smart city" OR "smart cities" OR "smart urban*")		"data-driven" AND ("smart city" OR "smart cities" OR "urban*")	
Figure	2.2		2.3	
Cluster	Main keywords	Other keywords	Main keywords	Other keywords
1 (Red)	urban planning	air pollution, artificial neural network, BIM, case study, climate change, cloud, GIS, infrastructure, policy making, sustainable urban development, technology	machine learning	anomaly detection, artificial neural network, data visualization, data-driven model, forecasting, neural network, prediction, random forest, support vector regression, time series, transportation, urban flood
2 (Green)	sustainability	decision support systems, energy, energy efficiency, energy management, fuzzy logic, game theory, monitoring, optimization, planning, semantic web	big data	data, data quality, data-driven decision-making, decision-making, mobility, public transport, sensor, smart governance, urban, urban data
3 (Dark Blue)	crowdsourcing & MCDM & ontology	AHP, clustering, co-creation, emergency response, innovation, mobility, sustainable development	intelligent transportation system	clustering, data analysis, data fusion, electric vehicle, floating car data, genetic algorithm, open data, optimization, spatial analysis, urban mobility
4 (Yellow)	big data	anomaly detection, data visualization, intelligent transportation system, sensor, simulation, smart mobility, urban mobility	deep learning & urban computing	big data analytics, crowd simulation, data science, modeling, sustainable development, traffic flow prediction, urban informatics, urban science, urban sustainability

5 (Purple)	data analytics	classification, data mining, feature selection, hadoop, open data, smart home, wireless sensor networks	human mobility	air quality, China, climate change, land use, mobile phone data, remote sensing, resilience, risk assessment, social media, twitter
6 (Light blue)	smart governance	data integration, data quality, data-driven decision-making, environmental monitoring, linked data, neural network, public sector	lidar	agent-based simulation, autonomous vehicles, building, classification, feature selection, point cloud, reconstruction, segmentation, UAV (unmanned aerial vehicle)
7 (Orange)	machine learning	deep learning, genetic algorithm, prediction, situation awareness, social media, social networks, twitter	internet of things	cloud computing, data mining, DDDAS (dynamic data driven applications systems), decision support systems, edge computing, feature extraction, real-time, water quality
8 (Brown)	internet of things	analytics, artificial intelligence, big data analytics, blockchain, privacy, security	sustainability	building energy, data analytics, data-driven approach, ontology, simulation, smart mobility, water management
9 (pink)	smart grid	demand response, multi agent systems, traffic congestion, visualization, waste management	GIS & urban planning	decision support, geospatial data, urban development, walkability
10 (Light red)	cloud computing	deep reinforcement learning, edge computing, fog computing, quality of service	energy efficiency	artificial intelligence, district heating, reinforcement learning, smart grid
11 (Light green)	ICT	citizen participation, e-government, e-participation		

54 Implementing data-driven strategies in smart cities

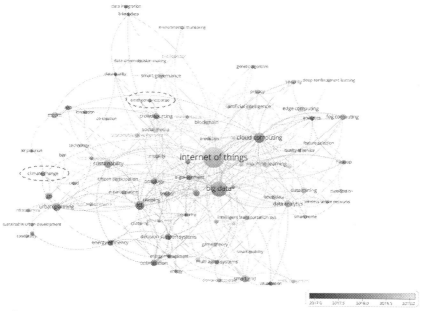

FIG. 2.4 Evolution over time of the keywords for the first search equation, by VOSviewer software.

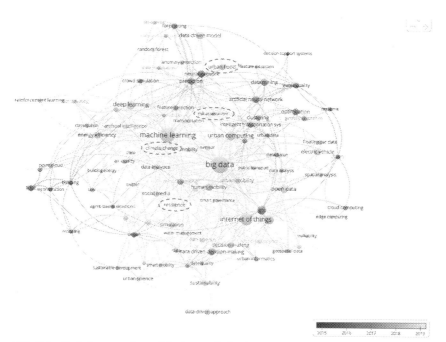

FIG. 2.5 Evolution over time of the keywords for the second search equation, by VOSviewer software.

Governance, decision-making, and strategy for urban development Chapter | 2 55

(Fig. 2.4). The second equation, focusing on data-driven approach, shows that, in 2019, "resilience" and "climate change" are new trends for the community (Fig. 2.5). By extension, we can see that "risk management" and "urban flood" are subjects of interest already addressed about a year before. Data-driven approach seems to converge with the environmental issues we are now facing. On the other hand, it seems that the academic communities focusing on decision-making process have already studied these topics. They focused on "emergency response" and "climate change" issues around 2017 (Fig. 2.4).

Furthermore, considering the complexity of the urban systems, the climate system, and the risk induced by climate change on cities, it seems relevant to consider all the possible sources of data, including that of the private sector (Derqui & Grimaldi, 2020; Grimaldi, 2020; Ramirez, Palominos, Camargo, & Grimaldi, 2021). Indeed, many companies are involved in the generation, processing, and storage of data. The rest of this section proposes a review of publications on these topics. Table 2.3 present three new specific search equations to specify how the terms "disaster," "resilience" or "resilient," and "private (sector)" are studied with a data-driven approach.

Fig. 2.6 illustrates the current trend in September 2020 for the three keywords. Gray curves represent the initial data and colored curves (in the print version) represent the normalized data. It seems that, since 2017/2018,

TABLE 2.3 Search equations focusing on "Disaster," "Resilience," "Private sector."

Keywords	"data-driven" AND "disaster" AND ("smart city" OR "smart cities" OR "urban*")	"data-driven" AND "resilien*" AND ("smart city" OR "smart cities" OR "urban*")	"data-driven" AND "private*" AND ("smart city" OR "smart cities" OR "urban*")
Search in	Title, abstract, keywords		
Explored period	All years		
Type of documents	Journal articles and conference papers		
Database	Scopus		
Number of publications	44	40	33
Shared papers	9		
	1		

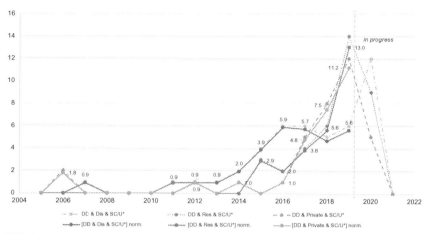

FIG. 2.6 Distribution of publications focusing on "data-driven" (DD) and "disaster" (Dis) or "resilience" (Res) or "private sector" from 2005 to September 2020 (collected and normalized data).

the data-driven scientific community has become increasingly interested in "resilience" ([DD & Res & SSC/U*] norm.) and "Private sector" ([DD & Private & SSC/U*] norm.) issues. After an apparent stagnation, the projections for "disaster" publications (DD & Dis & SSC/U*) are already very high for 2020. A total of 107 unique articles have been published since 2005. It should be noted that one publication is common to the three groups of publications (Pastor-Escuredo, Torres, Martínez-Torres, & Zufiria, 2020) while nine publications are common to groups 1 and 2 (Anonymous, 2012; Gandini, Garmendia, & San Mateos, 2017; Petrini, Gkoumas, & Bontempi, 2015; Rodríguez-Gaviria, Ochoa-Osorio, Builes-Jaramillo, & Botero-Fernández, 2019; Wang & Taylor, 2018, 2019; Wang, Taylor, & Garvin, 2020; Xu, Wang, Huang, & Chen, 2018; Yang, Su, & Chen, 2017).

Finally, Fig. 2.7 also shows the low density of the issue of "resilience" and "climate change" that reflects the low level of interest in this topic compared with the other topics. Therefore, we believe it would be interesting to deepen the knowledge on these fields, which nowadays are at the heart of the urban systems challenges. In the coming section, we analyze how a data-driven approach can help to face disasters. Concretely, in the next section, we present the recent advances that the data science offers to the urban resilience theme.

1.2 Evolutionary path to data-driven resilience in a private sector network

Resilience amid an uncertain and complex environment requires collaborative effort across multiple sectors (Davidson, Nguyen, Beilin, & Briggs, 2019; Smith & Stirling, 2008). Uncertainty and complexity manifest in emergencies,

Governance, decision-making, and strategy for urban development Chapter | 2   57

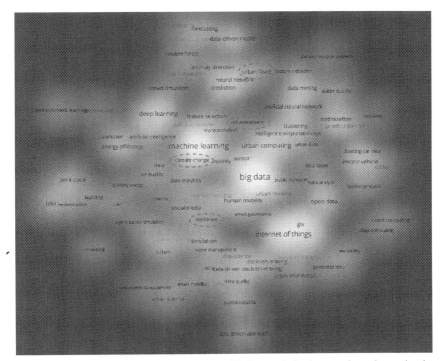

FIG. 2.7 Visual diagram of density distribution of the keywords for the second search equation, by VOSviewer software.

crises, and disasters that affect a multitude of actors and disrupt social and economic systems. Some examples include global pandemic, tropical cyclones and earthquakes, civil unrest, and related problems. Data is central to navigate this kind of environment, so that decision-makers can extract actionable information as they manage crises and disasters. Two important questions arise in relation to achieving resilience: first, in what ways can data be engaged to achieve resilience? Second, who can spearhead such programs for resilience? In Box 2.1, we use the case of the Philippine Disaster Resilience Foundation (PDRF), a Philippine-based private sector network, to surface some key points on a plausible evolutionary path to achieve data-driven resilience, as well as the role of the private sector in becoming an ally of the public sector to champion resilience.

2   Smart urban governance

The final objective of any government is to provide a service to the citizens at quality. Operational-wise, it means improving the well-being of the people, the security of their basic rights (equality, liberty, justice), their education, and their

BOX 2.1
Lessons on data governance from the Philippine Disaster Resilience Foundation

PDRF: A curious model of private sector initiated data-driven resilience

The Philippine Disaster Resilience Foundation (PDRF) is a private sector network that brings together many of the leading private sector firms in the Philippines. Its origin dates back to 2009, when a national executive order was passed to create the Special National Public Reconstruction Commission (Public Commission) in the aftermath of two successive weather-related disasters, Typhoon Parma and Tropical Storm Ketsana. The Public Commission was mandated to spearhead postdisaster reconstruction of affected communities, and one of its action points was to enjoin the private sector to be active partners in the reconstruction process.

As a result, some of the country's largest firms worked alongside nongovernment organizations to establish the *Philippine Disaster Recovery Foundation*. The partnership was formally established through the signing of a cooperation agreement, which strengthened the private sector involvement in the reconstruction programs of the Philippine government. In 2013, the country experienced large-scale disasters, including the Zamboanga siege, the 7.2 magnitude earthquake in Bohol and Cebu, and the deadliest typhoon recorded in the country's history, Typhoon Haiyan. This became a precedent for PDRF to reorganize as a private sector network that develops programs across all thematic areas of disaster management. In 2015, the organization was renamed to *Philippine Disaster Resilience Foundation*, to capture a proactive approach to disaster risk reduction and management.

PDRF has since set a steady path toward the institutionalization of coordination processes among various private sector firms in the development and implementation of programs related to disaster resilience. It specifically leverages two characteristics as anchor points of its role in advocating for resilience across the country. First, it is technology-driven. The initial vision of PDRF was to build a technology complement to the coordination process of the network members, which translated to the creation of a facility that allows them to collate, analyze, and coordinate data that will be useful in emergency response. To date, PDRF has built an Operations Center (hereafter referred to as the center), which can be considered its data hive. Much of the information collated has helped inform the coordination and decision-making processes during disaster response, as well as the roll-out of programs designed for resilience.

Second, it harnesses the capabilities of the private sector, considering that many of the members provide disaster critical services. This provides an interesting angle to explore as far as models of governance are concerned. In particular, it surfaces a model where the private sector plays an active, complementary role to the government in espousing data-driven resilience, given that utility services such as water, electricity, healthcare, and telecommunications, among others, are privatized. These characteristics make PDRF a unique case through which we could more closely understand how the private sector can initiate data-driven resilience and unpack a model of smart urban governance that is led by a network of private sector firms that aims to complement and reinforce the public sector's efforts in making cities disaster resilient.

BOX 2.1—cont'd

The succeeding sections are organized in three parts. The first part describes the operations center of the PDRF, including the kind of data it stores, the purpose of such data, how it is managed and used, and the network approach for overseeing data management. The second part demonstrates the capability of data in driving resilience during disasters. By outlining the engagement of PDRF across a number of big disasters/crises, we surface the process by which PDRF has evolved from merely collecting and coordinating data during disaster response into a proactive body that builds the capacity to analyze and distill data into various forms that can lead to action across all phases of disaster management. Finally, we discuss some key lessons from the case of PDRF that can inform readers on key considerations for data-driven resilience using a governance model that highlights a proactive role from the private sector. Specifically, we articulate the role that the private sector can play to complement and reinforce public sector advocacy on resilience. We also raise some points on how and why the private sector can act as a conduit across critical stakeholder groups in achieving data-driven resilience, namely the public sector and the local communities. Finally, we point out in which contexts such a governance model can work, specifically developing countries.

PDRF's Emergency Operations Center (EOC): The data hive
PDRF is comprised of some of the largest conglomerates in the country, whose lines of business include critical infrastructure, e.g., telecommunications, electricity, water, and health facilities. As mentioned earlier, the lines of business that PDRF members are engaged in manifest the importance of the role that they play in disasters. In the case of the Philippines, they automatically become partners of the public sector during disasters and crises, as they are gatekeepers of critical services. Note also that a unique characteristic of PDRF is how the private sector firms come together collaboratively despite being traditionally considered to be economic competition of one another. This is due for the most part to the acknowledgment that a grand challenge such as vulnerability to disasters and crises requires forging sustained cooperation and partnership that included information and resource coordination during times of calamities. As of 2020, there are approximately 64 private sector members, which are primarily large enterprises.

The nature of their engagement with one another is founded primarily on the ability to coordinate and share information, which in turn allows for more efficient response and recovery activities. Noting that information sharing and coordination are central to the relationship of these private sector members, it was inevitable that the next phase of their partnership included the establishment of a facility that provides a central platform where information exchange could be managed. For a network with a large membership, and whose services are either overlapping or complementary, questions of management surface, such as *"where do we deploy our resources," "which of our facilities are affected, and how can we manage that,"* and *"what does the overall picture of response look like."* As a result, a prototype Operations Center was established in Makati City, Metro Manila, in 2016, with the primary objective of addressing concerns of information management and coordination across a network of private sector firms.

Continued

BOX 2.1—cont'd

In 2018, an official Operations Center was launched in Clark, Pampanga. Clark is less than 100 km from Metro Manila, where the headquarters of majority of the member organizations are based. Clark was selected as a site for the center because of its low-risk to hazards (in comparison to Metro Manila), but at the same time accessible to air and land transportation. The facility is also located in a building that is specifically retrofitted for multihazard resilience, with stand-alone power and water systems. As seen in Fig. 2.8, the facility uses advanced communications software and technology, which allows them to put together information from multiple vetted sources and integrate them into a useable and actionable information that the member organizations can act on.

FIG. 2.8 PDRF Emergency Operations Center located in Clark, Pampanga. *(Photo source: PDRF Website. From* Philippine Disaster Resilience Foundation. *(c. 2020). https://www.pdrf.org/eoc/functions/.)*

The center is considered as a foundational pillar of the PDRF and has acted as a central space to coordinate information for more effective response across some of the biggest calamities that happened in the Philippines, including the recent Taal Volcano Ashfall in 2020 and the COVID-19 Pandemic. It should be noted, however, that the way that the data has been used over the years since the establishment of the facility has also evolved. During the facility's establishment in 2016, the primary use of the center was as a central repository of data that the private sector members can use in ensuring that their response activities were not redundant, that the resources being mobilized were a fit in the area that they were targeting, and that they were able to have an overview of the likely effect of certain calamities on their organization through site mapping. However, in recent years and in seeking better alignment with the essence of "resilience," PDRF is starting to leverage the data at their disposal to provide information and analysis that can help private firms develop proactive programs to create stable systems and processes amid disruptions arising from natural and anthropogenic hazards.

BOX 2.1—cont'd

PDRF has an information management system called HANDA (short-form for Hazard and Disaster Analysis for Business Resilience),[a] which features incident reporting, incident monitoring, incident management, and hazard monitoring. The kinds of data that the center collects, stores, and analyzes include warnings, disaster evacuation, asset inventory, and emergency services integration. PDRF also has a human resource complement in charge primarily of managing, integrating, and uploading the data for consumption of the private sector members primarily, but also as a potentially helpful information for the public sector. Once such data have been uploaded and made accessible to the network members, they have a more complete picture of disaster response coordination. As mentioned earlier, this includes having a more straightforward and evidence-based approach to the questions, *"where does the private sector work, and how can the private sector best mobilize its resources?"* Another use for the data from the center is for public sector consumption. Most reports from the center are sent to the National Disaster Risk Reduction and Management Council (NDRRMC) of the Philippines, with the objective of highlighting the interoperability between the government and the private sector.

The journey toward data-driven resilience: The evolution of data use beyond coordination

As mentioned earlier, the founding principle of PDRF is the ability to coordinate data for a more effective disaster response. While the center as a facility came about much later than the establishment of the network, PDRF already leveraged the use of data right at the beginning. Interestingly, it is also evident how the manner in which data is used has evolved over the years parallel to the various types of disasters that PDRF has been engaged in.

As an example, the history of involvement of PDRF in the response and recovery process from the 2013 Typhoon Haiyan provided a benchmark for showing the various ways that data can be used beyond coordination. While, indeed, the primary objective was to provide actionable information to help in responding to and recovering from the disaster ex-post facto, this has evolved to using the data more proactively to help inform future-oriented programs before a disaster of the same kind could occur.

A deeper analysis of the data that they already collated from previous disaster response operations of PDRF have shaped the way their other programs are designed. To this end, they follow a *cluster system*, where they bring together private sector members that are engaged in similar intervention areas to address sector-specific needs across all the thematic areas of the disaster management cycle. Some of these clustered organizations include power, fuel and energy, telecommunications, water and sanitation, emergency supplies (food and nonfood), logistics, health and medical services, and finance to support early recovery. Corollary to these clustered sectors, specific recovery and rehabilitation programs have been designed in the areas of livelihood, education, shelter, environment, and water, infrastructure, sanitation, and health (WISH).

From Typhoon Haiyan in 2013 to other emergencies that occurred over the recent years in the country, including more recent ones (as of this writing) like

Continued

BOX 2.1—cont'd

the 2020 Taal Volcano Ashfall and the COVID-19 pandemic, PDRF has steadily evolved to use the data at their disposal beyond coordination. As mentioned earlier, their programs on recovery, rehabilitation, and to some extent disaster preparedness are ultimately grounded on close reading of data, which helped them identify where gaps are present, and what advocacy programs are most needed and most impactful in certain areas. Still, PDRF as a private sector network that advocates for resilience has a long experimental and iterative process to go through to see what the evolutionary path of their data use might look like. Touchpoints with the organization suggest that their journey might involve using data for predictive analytics as a way of promoting resilience amid an uncertain environment.

Note though that this evolutionary path will also depend on how fast the organization can become *data fluent*. Data fluency requires building an ecosystem with expertise at both levels of data consumption and data production, which in turn reinforces a data-driven culture and where data can be distilled into actionable decision items (Gemignani, Gemignani, Galentino, & Schuermann, 2014). In the case of PDRF and similar organizations that are leading the way toward data-driven resilience, achieving data fluency implies two critical points. First, data consumers need to have high data literacy. This requires buy-in from the data consumers, which in the case of PDRF, will include a multitude of actors, i.e., the private sector members, the public sector (which it engages), the local communities, and the society-at-large. It is important that the data consumers understand how data can provide value in their programs on resilience and how it can help them in their decision-making process. For a network organization like the PDRF, bringing the network members and their related stakeholders on the same level of understanding on what data can do is critical. The level of maturity that the data consumers have in using data will determine how advanced the evolutionary path on data-driven resilience will be.

Second, as data producers, PDRF needs to articulate and demonstrate the potential use of their data. How can data be used to manage resilience? Dunn-Cavelty and Suter (2009) describe two frameworks that policymakers have in using science to manage resilience. On the one hand, data may be used for predictive scenarios, in which policymakers use statistical techniques, risk modeling, and other predictive modeling tools to have a good grasp of risks that their organizations face. In this regard, data is used retrospectively to answer the question, *how likely are those risks to occur and what is the likely effect?* In this scenario, which Dunn-Cavelty terms *predicting scenario*, policymakers aim to populate their risk registers with as much precision as possible. This works when organizations aim to manage imminent threats within the short and mid-term period.

However, being that the concept of resilience is future-looking and largely deals with uncertainty, Dunn-Cavelty argues that an overemphasis on prediction may constrain the ability of organizations to look beyond the risk register, and in turn, fail to manage that which is not listed in their risk register. Hence, a second framework that policymakers resort to in managing resilience is what she terms as a *forecasting scenario*. A forecasting scenario focuses on narratives of possible futures, given existing signals from data. In this regard, data is used prospectively to ask the questions, *what might our future look like given the signals that the present data is giving us?* A forecasting scenario requires not just interpreting the metrics and the numbers but also engaging nonnumerical data that can be transformed into convincing narratives of possible futures. To get to this point, a private sector network like PDRF should steadily set the tone toward reflexive engagement with the data.

BOX 2.1—cont'd

Fig. 2.9 postulates a potential evolutionary path that private sector networks advocating for data-driven resilience may follow. It specifically shows that as data fluency increases, the maturity of data engagement (or data use) will also increase over time. As a result, an organization's evolutionary path may go through four levels. Each level has variation points in terms of the time when it is used (i.e., phase in the crisis/disaster management), extent of integration across the actors involved, whether the information is complementary or a prerequisite to decision-making, and the capabilities necessary.

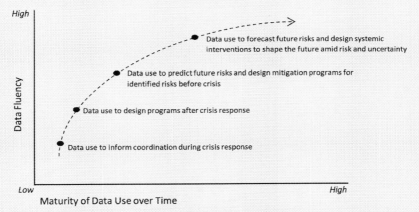

FIG. 2.9 Levels of data engagement toward data-driven resilience.

The points of variation in terms of data engagement per level are described as follows:

Level 1: Data use to inform coordination during crisis response At this level, the organization has both the technological and human resource capacity to collect the data. In the case of PDRF, they have a devoted facility to integrate fragmented information that can be used to provide an overall picture of the crisis response. Likewise, the data generation and engagement peaks during crisis response. The main objective is to provide information that can complement the decision-making and coordination processes of the actors involved. Note as well that, as demonstrated by the PDRF case, the data they produce is also provided to the public sector for reference. This means to say that while data production aims to help decision-making process, it is not necessarily a prerequisite for action to take place. Hence, at this level, data is there primarily to inform how help may best be mobilized during response. At best, the data serves as complementary information that can support a decision-making process. This is due in part to different factors, which can include low data fluency of the consumers and producers (i.e., they are only beginning to discover how to leverage data) but also because of the low integration between the stakeholders involved in managing data-driven resilience. As emphasized earlier, resilience requires multisectoral and multistakeholder engagement, as well as an alignment in vision on how to achieve data-driven resilience. In a way, it could be argued that this is the level wherein all the stakeholders go through a trial-and-error process of how they can

Continued

BOX 2.1—cont'd

complement one another's action during crisis response. From a governance perspective, this is the stage when the lead actor in crisis response (i.e., public sector) heeds the call for help or call to action of another actor (i.e., the private sector) who has the capacity to do it (i.e., data provision), or when an actor who has the capacity to help (i.e., private sector) will pitch ways where it can provide support (i.e., data provision) to the lead actor during crisis response.

Level 2: Data use to design programs after crisis response At this level, the organization maintains its technological capabilities, but the human resource complement levels up and learns to understand how the technological ability to collect data can be used to design recovery and rehabilitation programs. This implies that the organization engages with the data retrospectively and undergoes a reflective process in identifying what sustained actions can be undertaken in the recovery and rehabilitation stages of disaster/crisis management. The questions that they ask include, *what have we learned about the needs of our stakeholders from the response phase,* and *how can we sustain their ability to recover?* As a result, organizations at this level are expected to engage with the data *during* and *after* the crisis/disaster. Similarly, it is expected that organizations at this level have tighter integration with the primary actors in disaster management (e.g., public sector) and other network actors, so that there is alignment and consistency in the programs. Partnerships and collaboration are deeper at this level in comparison to level 1 and are often manifested in formal partnerships like *Memorandum of Agreements*. During this stage, data produced by the organization (i.e., private sector network) becomes the favored information[b] used by decision-makers in designing programs for resilience.

Level 3: Data use to predict future risks and design mitigation programs for identified risks before crisis At this level, the network organization evolves into a more forward-looking organization that aims to reduce risks. There is a conscious shift in mindset from response-oriented practices toward a proactive mitigating practices. The organization then starts to engage the data beyond descriptive techniques and starts to use more sophisticated statistical techniques and models to ascertain the kinds of risks that the ecosystem may be faced with. As mentioned earlier, this *predicting scenario* aims to create a comprehensive risk register which lists the probability and impact of all potential risks. Hence, the organization engages data retrospectively to determine future risks, and ultimately design programs that will mitigate such risks. At this level, data is engaged during the mitigation phase of the disaster management. Note also that the guiding question for the private sector network here is, *how can the data inform us of the risks we need to pay attention to, so that we can design programs to mitigate their likelihood?* The integration required among the stakeholders of the private sector network is high. Specifically, the stakeholders should have a common language in dealing with the risk and also a shared understanding of the effect of the risk. During this stage, data produced by the network becomes prerequisite to decision-making, as it forms a foundational block to the design of mitigation programs. In more ways than one, the collaboration between the private sector network and the public sector is starting to emulate a public-private partnership model (Wang, Xiong, Wu, & Zhu, 2018), in that long partnerships occur, and there is shared risk and benefit between the two sectors. In this regard, the mitigation programs have mutually reinforcing effects on each sector, and the success of the programs become dependent on how well both sectors can work with one another.

BOX 2.1—cont'd

Level 4: Data use to forecast future risks and design systemic interventions to shape the future amid risk and uncertainty At this level, the organization enters the *forecasting scenario*, wherein the private sector network starts to engage the data beyond the metrics and numerical measures they provide but also engage in discursive and deliberative processes to imagine possible futures, and how these might be useful in designing systemic interventions to shape the future amid risk and uncertainty. At this level, the question evolves from being risk-oriented (i.e., level 3) to being proactive amid the uncertain. As a result, the question here becomes *how can the data help us imagine what the future will look like, so we can design systemic interventions to navigate, and ultimately shape the future?* The data is engaged not just for performative metrics but also for peering into signals that may enable the data producers to imagine future scenarios. At this level, an exercise of *disciplined imagination* (Weick, 1989, 2002) occurs among the stakeholders (albeit in the context of practitioners),[c] where they go through a reflexive process on *"the things [they] forget, the values [they] slight, the facts [that] they avoid, and the questions that they fear"* in identifying and reckoning future possibilities. Ultimately, organizations who have reached this level of data engagement are also active across all phases of disaster/crisis management—they are engaging the data before the crisis occurs, during the crisis, and after the crisis. Likewise, there is fluidity in their temporal orientation, in that whatever decision arises to design systemic interventions to manage the uncertain will have some effects on preparedness, mitigation, response, recovery, and rehabilitation efforts. It is thus expected that the level of integration between the private sector network and the public sector is high, that the private sector network is considered an ally and a champion of the public sector in advocating for resilience, and that there is shared vision among the stakeholders (Weber, Sailer, & Katzy, 2015). It is also possible that the type of governance that occurs here is a more integrated form of PPP, where the public sector devolves the role of data provision to the private sector network. Depending on the level of cultural acceptance, of course, the private sector network can also be the supplier and manager of data that are necessary for decision-making in relation to designing programs for resilience. Somehow, this kind of model has worked in developing countries where critical infrastructure has been privatized, e.g., the Philippines. A more liberal form of governance that can also occur is a *metagovernance* (Dunn-Cavelty & Suter, 2009), where the public sector creates a nurturing environment for networks to self-organize and accomplish a service that will aid them in managing resilience-oriented programs. Of course, this more advanced set-up prompts bigger questions such as, *"can a private sector network that manages data-driven resilience programs be considered critical services,"* and *"can the provision of data in relation to crisis/disaster resilience be considered critical service?"*

Among the levels described previously, PDRF is somewhere between Level 2 and Level 3. As emphasized before, reaching level 4 is a conscious choice that the private sector organization needs to make and will also involve forging of partnerships that can only be cultivated and deepened over time.

Continued

BOX 2.1—cont'd
Conclusion: Lessons on data-driven resilience
The context that we are currently navigating is heavily characterized by the presence of multiple hazards that require concerted effort from multiple sectors (Ferraro, Etzion, & Gehman, 2015; George, Howard-Grenville, Joshi, & Tihanyi, 2016; Kuhlmann & Rip, 2018). Indeed, in a time when crises can potentially compound to bigger ones or otherwise have affiliated crises (e.g., COVID-19 being a health crisis that compounded into multiple crises, including economic, social, and political crisis), organizations need to develop capabilities that can help the society-at-large become resilient. An ideal way to manage resilience is to leverage data to ground decision-making. If we engage (quality) data in designing programs and systemic interventions to advocate for resilience, then the concept of resilience becomes much more than a policy rhetoric—it becomes evidence-based, action-oriented, strategic, and sustainable.

Traditionally, the salient governance model in the management of data-driven resilience follows a government-centric model, considering that disaster management and crisis management policies fall within the purview of the government (Kusumasari & Alam, 2012), and therefore efforts and strategic vision are orchestrated by the government (Kusumasari & Alam, 2012). Consequently, data-driven resilience in the face of risk and uncertainty can be misconstrued as a burden that must be solely carried by the public sector. However, this view has changed over the years, with collaborative networks being a favored set-up for more efficient disaster response (Weber et al., 2015).

The PDRF case provides a demonstrative example of how a private sector network can complement the initiatives of the public sector in achieving and managing resilience by leveraging technology and the private sector to champion resilience programs. At the time of writing, PDRF is the only private sector network in the Philippines known to have the technological (in the form of their operations center), human resource (in the form of hired data specialists, geographers, hazards, and learning and development specialists), and network (in the form of wide membership, including critical infrastructure organizations) to champion resilience. The reach of PDRF is promising in that they work as a central node that is linked with large conglomerates (which also happen to be providers of critical infrastructure), who in turn are linked with suppliers (which also include small and medium enterprises), and ultimately members of the society-at-large (who consume the products provided by the private sector network). In the same vein, the PDRF has cultivated a social capital with the public sector, and other related stakeholders, including higher education institutions. As PDRF evolves in the way it uses its data, and the way that it charts resilience programs in partnership with the public sector, key learnings emerge:

1. Private sector plays an important role in advocating for resilience

Certain factors, as demonstrated by the PDRF case, reinforce this. First, considering that some private sector organizations provide essential infrastructure and services in disaster and crisis management are supplied by private sector, they are, by virtue, critical partners of the public sector. Second, private sector firms are argued to have advantage of technology and innovation, as those are important components of

BOX 2.1—cont'd

organizational competitiveness. Third, the private sector can scale resilience to a multitude of actors (e.g., consumers, small and medium enterprises, any actor engaging in economic activity). The third point is specifically important as it can act as the private sector can act as a conduit among multiple sectors.

2. **Data-driven resilience can be achieved through various governance models, including private-public partnerships, network governance, and more liberal ones such as metagovernance, and there are parameters for success**

There are various ways to mobilize the private sector to become champions of data-driven resilience—but the defining points for their success include high level of data fluency, and a shared vision across the stakeholders.

3. **Private sector network model for achieving data-driven resilience can work, but trust, transparency and public confidence are prerequisite**

Private sector networks mobilize data-driven resilience not merely as an act of goodness, but primarily because of the positive effects it can have on the business environment. Ultimately, having a resilient society equates to good business. In effect, good social practices will translate to good business results. However, in tackling the case of the PDRF, we capitalized on the positive outcomes to demonstrate the potential of data-driven resilience initiated by the private sector. On that note, it is also important to emphasize that this form of governance needs to have established trust, transparency, and public confidence. When these are absent, there is a danger of commodifying data that is a prerequisite to designing resilience programs, and in effect, data-driven resilience can inevitably become a commodity afforded only by selected groups of people. It is extremely important that when private sector is mobilized to provide a service that affects the public (i.e., resilience programs), it is important that everyone gains equitable access to the service.

[a]HANDA is also a Filipino term for "ready."
[b]Note that Karl Weick's arguments on *disciplined imagination* was written in the context of theory construction among organizational scholars. However, the process by which the theorist (or the practitioner in this context) undergoes "thought trials" to assess plausibility of scenarios and goes through an iterative learning process from artefacts surrounding the unknown or unsolved puzzle that they are seeking to address (i.e., in the case of practitioners, achieving resilience amid uncertainty), can be transferrable to private sector networks advocating for data-driven resilience.
[c]Examples of critical infrastructure or critical services are telecommunications, hospitals, water, and energy distribution services, among others.

healthcare. Harith and Rahayu (2018) coin a government system using web and mobile applications as an e-government and argue the coordination between the user requirements and the lead-time to implement the solution can result in an important showstopper for its development.

We believe as other authors (Maciejewski, 2017) that big data can act as a game-changer to do it better, faster, and more cheaply. Public administrations in many countries are tackling big data strategies like in the United Kingdom, United States, and China (Lee, 2018; Agnellutti, 2014; UK Department for

Business Innovation and Skills, 2013). In spite of the efforts of reform, studies (Gerrish, 2016) show little effect has been produced thus far. See Chapter 7 for more information. So, big data emergence generates high expectations.

Johnston (2015) defines policy informatics as the "study of how computation and communication technology is leveraged to understand and address complex public policy and administration problems and realize innovations in governance processes and institutions." He suggests that "computational methods"—which we consider to be both use of computerized technology to capture large-scale data sets in the first place and computation-intensive efforts to analyze those data sets—are necessary to deal with the increasing governance complexities the public sector is facing. Cardone et al. (2013) argue that big data place the citizen in the center of government action while asking them to cooperate in the production of the policies and services.

Maciejewski (2017) adds the use of big data for public governance could be classified into three categories: public supervision, public regulation, and public service delivery. Public supervision aims at identifying irregularities, e.g., fraud or legal incompliance and helps to take the corresponding corrective actions. The French taxes department has proved how the use of Facebook and Instagram could identify citizens who have declared revenues that do not match the level of travel and holiday expenses they are describing in the social media. Public regulation aims at incorporating alerts in the different systems (or systems of systems—see Chapter 1) that monitor the city. The Catalan social department in Spain has developed a Social big data system that identifies population at risk or already excluded in the region, which could have asked for assistance or financial subsidiaries but did not know their rights. The tool permits the local government to provide aid offering them specific "proactive"/anticipative assistance. The experience shows this fragile population is usually eligible but does not receive the support that they have never requested. Most of the time, the reason is due to lack of information about their civil rights, fear of stigmatization, or lack of digital skills. Finally, regarding service delivery, big data collects and analyzes different sources of urban data (as described in Chapter 5 of this book) and can actively support the resolution of urban governance issues related to transport, health, emergency, or environment management in a top-down approach, i.e., led by the urban government. This approach is usually ex-post, i.e., analyzing the effect of the urban governance decisions on the citizens' life afterward. Big data reveals information that was previously impossible to seize, and this new knowledge can be converted into preventive or corrective actions for improving the public service delivery and the well-being of the citizens.

The challenges that reside in their mode of actions are related to the cooperation that requires the resolution of city issues. But today, the evidence shows departments of the same public organization usually work in solo mode (Grimaldi & Fernandez, 2017), and each government department or agency typically manages its own project and data warehouse. It is therefore hard for them to pursue a common objective, which explains why it usually results in a long-term decision-making process because they need time to converge and harmonize their thoughts and analysis (Kim, Trimi, & Chung, 2014). Smart city governance using big data analytics has the objective to improve this current situation. Moreover, few scholars add that big data can offer more benefit to the citizens. Indeed, it can also participate to give them more visibility of the governmental action, increasing their participation, even engagement in the public affairs.

2.1 Definition of a big data citizen-centered approach

A citizen-centered urban governance is more than a bottom-up approach of smart city governance. As a reminder, a bottom-up strategy promotes the citizen's participation but usually collects relatively small amounts of data compared with the rest of the urban population. They have different forms like a survey released in a very popular or touristic location in the city, a questionnaire to users on the bus, or an online campaign. They have the limitation to consider the answers as a homogeneous collective. As an illustration, the "decidim" platform designed in Barcelona (Spain) to ask opinions to citizens do not filter the responses by gender, localization, or family status. In some cases, a clustering analysis is possible to give a stratification inside the collective answers received, but it is very difficult to know if each group of a population represents the whole. This strategy actually has not been designed to encourage a big participation of the citizens (Shepherd & Sutcliffe, 2011).

Nevertheless, their conclusions, validated by a small group of citizens, is usually considered through statistical justification, missing other ways to execute their task. This approach addresses the audible and the digital community but not the majority of the citizenship. It can't be considered as inclusive (Ju, Liu, & Feng, 2018). A citizen-centered urban governance considers each single citizen at the same time and all of them as a customer and applies practices of open innovation and co-design for the co-creation of smart city services (Bugshan, 2015). The co-creation process is based on the requirements and preferences of the inhabitants and, once delivered, includes the assessment based on citizens' satisfaction about its quality and responsiveness. A citizen-centered public service delivery has to build a governance where any co-creation must be accessible for all citizens as co-producers, whatever their personal characteristics are. It has to be inclusive focusing not only on citizens willing to participate but also considering the rest of stakeholders of the service. Citizen-centered big data analysis may predict the percentage the citizens willing to respond and suggests corrective actions to enhance the extent of public participation.

A citizen-centered urban governance requires a real-time analysis of the urban services also a capacity of immediate reaction in case of emergency needs (Kitchin, 2014). This type of governance needs the use of big data, artificial intelligence, IoT, and mobile and social channels technologies. In the next section, we will present the different items of a citizen-centered big data architecture. But since its implementation is not easy, we first highlight hereunder the issues usually faced. Meijer (2015) identifies two main challenges for a big data citizen-centered approach. He relates the first one to the capacity of real and massive mobilization. He argues the government has to take the corresponding actions to give a reasonable context to the citizen for asking their participation showing the value of the innovation and a positive and immediate return. He calls it the "framing" strategy, which considers the citizens as a customer, a receiver of a service, who balances the benefit received against the time spent during its engagement. We could make a parallelism here between private versus public and add the citizen can be considered as a standard customer receiving a product from an organization through a transaction. The product has to go further than the gratitude regarding the civic aspect of participation but has to be a real deliverable that the citizen receives and brings home. As an example, it could be that they can share their contribution to friends through different social channels and becomes a reference/champion in the domain and attracts recognition and digital status.

The second barrier that Meijer (2015) defines is related to the problem usually known as the digital divide in the citizenship, which impedes the massive citizen's participation. He suggests a so-called "fixing" strategy developing among the citizenship the use of technological tools through the invitation to participate to "familiarization" classes that can occur in public university, FabLab, or Living Lab. We believe therefore reducing the digital divide present between poor and well-eased class or even between young and older generation participates into a citizen-centered strategy.

If these challenges are overcome, Mergel, Rethemeyer, and Isett (2016) state the resulting service is mass-adapted, tailored, and personalized according to the conditions and preferences of each and all citizens instead of a mass and normalized one. Dawes (2008) adds it drastically improves the transparency/visibility of the urban governance and therefore the trust between the administered (i.e., citizens) and the government. Nevertheless, literature is scanty to evaluate the performance of these new forms of government (e-government) in terms of service quality or improvement of the citizen engagement process (Cleland, Wallace, & Black, 2018) and we will address it in the last chapter of this book.

3 Big data citizen-centered organization change

In this section, we detail the organization change that supposes a big data citizen-centered organization and describe the new roles and responsibilities generated. A Data Governance department needs to be created to manage the big data citizen-centered organization. It aims at coordinating, promoting, and operationalizing an efficient management of data across the whole public administration organization. Its main goals are to make the organization

Governance, decision-making, and strategy for urban development **Chapter | 2** 71

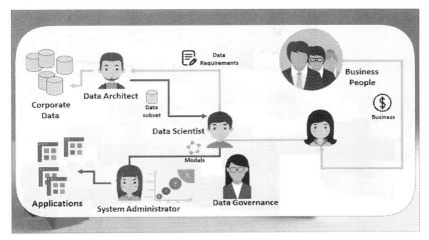

FIG. 2.10 Big data organization model.

consider the data as a strategic asset, to redesign and roll out new processes to capture, clean, store, and analyze data to take data-driven decisions, while ensuring data privacy and confidentiality for the citizens, and complying with the ethical and local legal regulation. It will be in charge of training public sector employees to develop digital capacities and also, of the processes related to the implementation of the Master Data Model (MDM) or the data quality policy. The level of change required is so high than this function has to be inserted inside the existing organization reporting to the maximum level of authority to ascertain its success. This department has three main roles: data governance manager, data architect, and system administrator for technical purpose (Fig. 2.10).

The main functions of the Data Governance Manager are:

- Ensure the full implementation of the integral model of governance engaging the largest and more inclusive citizen participation
- Keep the legal, privacy, and confidentiality regulations and normative updated
- Define a periodic reporting system
- Assign responsibilities for the different roles involved during the data life cycle
- Certify the functional departments that have been converted into big data citizen-centered
- Ensure the identification and the training of the professional of each domain involved in the datafication

The main functions of the System Administrator are:

- Ensure that data access permissions are aligned with the technological framework and or information security framework

- Coordinate the resolution of MDM issues in terms of accuracy, consistency, completeness or uniqueness
- Analyze, in collaboration with the different functional managers the results of the data quality control

The main functions of the Data Architect are:

- Coordinate the different professionals of the functional areas to carry it out the capture of the data-based process requirements
- Define and approve reputable data sources and collaborate on the traceability of the data
- Define and coordinate processes of control and methodologies to evaluate and manage the MDM

The existing and legacy departments have to participate into this transformation naming a business translator who will liaise with the central unit.

The main functions of the business translator are:

- Promote the maintenance and management of a common glossary of business terms
- Define mechanisms of supervision, coordination, and monitoring of the quality plan
- Establish training program inside the department to enable the transformation
- Ensure the process of continuous improvement of the quality

4 Architecture of a big data citizen-centered urban governance

Wang, Kung, and Byrd (2018) name a big data citizen-centered urban governance as a combination of three major components: an MDM, which defines the critical data of an organization and supports decision-making; a data lifecycle model, which describes the flow of the data in the organization; and finally a policy of data security and privacy for a responsible use of the information gathered. Our recent research orientate us to add a fourth and a fifth element: a technological platform, which collects the necessary data to get a real-time and complete insight of citizen's behavior, and a data quality plan for the efficiency of this data-based governance.

Many frameworks exist for a bottom-up and collective action (Ben Letaifa, 2015; Bibri, 2018; Jin, Gubbi, Marusic, & Palaniswami, 2014; Joshi, Saxena, Godbole, & Shreya, 2016; Salerno, Nunziante, & Santoro, 2014); our model shown in the searches places the citizen in the center of our model. We compose this framework based on five pillars corresponding to the five elements described previously. We present and develop them in the following lines.

Moreover, we put this model in practice by describing the Swiss response to fight the 2020 Coronavirus pandemic (Box 2.2).

BOX 2.2
Swiss response to COVID-19: Case illustration of science-focused and data-driven response to a global pandemic
Switzerland is one of the countries to have first felt the brunt of COVID-19. The first COVID-19 positive cases appeared in the country as early as February 2020, even prior to the World Health Organization's declaration of COVID-19 as a global pandemic. On February 25, 2020, one case was reported in Ticino, the southern canton of Switzerland that borders with Italy,[d] and days later, new COVID-19 positive cases were recorded in the cantons of Geneva, Graubünden, Basel, Vaud, and Zurich.[e] The number of cases continued to rise within a matter of weeks, with a count of approximately 333 new cases per day as of March 11,[f] a day just before the World Health Organization declared COVID-19 a global pandemic, and subsequently announced Europe as the new epicenter of the virus.[g] On March 16, 2020, the Swiss Government declared "extraordinary situation," where it imposed social distancing measures, ordered the temporary closure of shops (except food stores and healthcare institutions), restaurants, bars, entertainment, and related leisure activities, and also introduced border controls to Germany, Austria, and France. Similarly, the Federal Government authorized the deployment of about 8000 members of the armed forces to provide help to the cantons on matters pertaining to health, logistics, and security. The preventive policies that the Swiss government has taken were largely complemented by data-driven and science-focused approaches to addressing COVID-19. Some of these measures are highlighted as follows:

1. Science task force as central advisory body

The Swiss government immediately set up the Swiss National COVID-19 Science Task Force (SN-STF) to advice the government on policies and interventions necessary to slow down the spread and eventually *flatten the curve* of COVID-19 positive cases. This group is comprised of researchers across the Swiss scientific community. On that note, gaps between COVID-related policy and scientific developments are anticipated to be low.

2. Growth and containment simulation through agent-based modeling

Consistent with a science-focused approach and with the resources directed to the scientific community, laboratories in Switzerland have been working on various facets of containment and forecasting models for COVID-19. The Laboratory for Energy Conversion of the Swiss Federal Institute of Technology (ETH), which pioneered the development of *Enerpol* (Marini, Brunner, Chokani, & Abhari, 2020), an in-house an agent-based modeling framework, demonstrated how the framework[h] could be applied to the COVID-19 context by simulating the growth of the pandemic, and subsequently drawing up containment strategies (Marini et al., 2020).

3. Swiss COVID app to detect movements and influence behavior

The Swiss government began the process of relaxing lockdown measures in June 2020, which was also the time when they launched the Swiss COVID app. The contact tracing app was co-developed by multiple stakeholders in Switzerland including scientific institutions, the Federal Institutes of Technology in Zurich (ETH) and Lausanne (EPFL), government institutions, the Federal Institutes of Public Health, as well as Information Technology, and private company, Ubique. The aim of the app is to break transmission chains through contact tracing. In more ways than

Continued

BOX 2.2—cont'd

one, this is reminiscent of a big data citizen-centered governance, considering that the citizen's movement and data consent are central to efficiency and efficacy of the contact tracing app. Once a resident in Switzerland has downloaded the app, the app automatically exchanges credentials with other residents who have downloaded the app through Bluetooth and alerts the user in case it has been in contact with another user who tested positive for more than 15 min. Needless to say, the app depends on the volume of users (i.e., the more users, the better), as well as the diligence of those who tested positive to input the unique ID that is provided to them by the health institution that carried out the test. As of July 2020, 3 weeks after its release, the app has been downloaded 2 million times,[i] which is approximately one-fourth of the total population in Switzerland.

4. Integration of health announcements in the public transportation system

The Swiss government also maximized its reach to the public through the public transportation system, SBB. As of 2019, the number of commuters who use the Swiss public transportation system averaged at 1.32 million passengers per day.[j] A majority of these commuters have a Swiss ID that is also integrated in the SBB Mobile app. The app is rated as the number 1 travel app in the country in Apple's App Store and Google Play.[k] Many informative health-related announcements have since been circulated in the app, complementary to the information campaign found in train stations regarding social distancing and hygiene measures. Likewise, when the Federal Office of Public Health required the wearing of masks in public transportation, the app was also one of the main media used to disseminate the information.

The measures described before illustrate the ways in which data can be central to the management of a crisis, i.e., a global pandemic. It also demonstrates how citizens can be engaged so that policies and government interventions are grounded on the experience, movement, and general behavior of the citizens. Likewise, it also shows the potential for a bottom-up model of data governance. Of course, this does not discount that a narrow focus on the dynamics of data integration into decision-making and policy-making should be studied more carefully, including the establishment of causalities and a more detailed unpacking of the mechanisms at play. On a related note, it must also be emphasized that certain characteristics unique to the context of Switzerland may be contributing to their data-driven approach. Some of these characteristics include the following: first, a strong scientific tradition, and research support. As of September 2020, the Swiss government mobilized resources for the scientific institutions to undertake COVID-19-related research. In fact, the Swiss School of Public Health (SSPH+) brought together 12 Swiss universities to undertake coordinated research, and subsequently coordinated response to the pandemic. Likewise, the Swiss National Science Foundation records about 94 active projects related to COVID-19.[l] Other characteristics that may be at play include the democratic model of the country, as well as high level of development and the digital readiness of the country. Note that the Swiss political system is a direct democracy, which allows the electorate to play an active role in expressing their views on decisions of the parliament, as well as to propose amendments to the federal constitution. It is possible that the culture of engagement as a result of their political system has a ripple effect on the sense of citizen responsibility and accountability that they carry in remaining engaged as far as crisis management is concerned

BOX 2.2—cont'd

(and may consequently play a role in the population's maturity to adopt a big data citizen-centered model of governance). Similarly, the political system of the country may also have some implications on the level of public trust. To this point, Transparency International reported in 2019 that the Corruption Perceptions Index in Switzerland is very low (garnering a score of 85/100, and ranked as fourth least corrupt in the world) (Transparency International, 2020). OECD also reported in 2017 that the public confidence in the government was at 80% and is considered to be the highest among OECD countries. Finally, Switzerland is one of the most advanced economies in the world, with technological infrastructure, skilled workforce, and advanced frameworks for data protection and privacy (Tucci, Gautschi, & Viscusi, 2016). All these factors may play critical roles in shaping Switzerland's data-driven approach to crisis management and ultimately city governance.

[d]Report from the Swiss Federal Office of Public Health (2020): https://www.bag.admin.ch/bag/en/home/das-bag/aktuell/medienmitteilungen.msg-id-78233.html.
[e]Swiss coronavirus cases rise to nine as children placed in precautionary quarantine https://www.reuters.com/article/us-china-health-swiss-idUSKCN20L167 (February 27, 2020).
[f]COVID-19 Statistics in Switzerland: https://covid-19-schweiz.bagapps.ch/de-2.html.
[g]Detailed timeline of actions, information, and related announcements are consolidated by the World Health Organization in this link: https://www.who.int/emergencies/diseases/novel-coronavirus-2019/interactive-timeline.
[h]Note that the framework has been used in various contexts and sectors aside from COVID-19, and in various country case studies, including the United States, countries across Europe, Japan, South Korea, and sub-Saharan countries in Africa.
[i]Report from the Swiss Federal Office of Public Health (2020): https://www.bag.admin.ch/bag/en/home/das-bag/aktuell/news/news-23-07-2020.html.
[j]Report from SBB: https://reporting.sbb.ch/en/home?scroll=100.
[k]Rating culled from Google Play and App Store charts as of September 2020.
[l]Data from COVID-19 Project Registry of the Swiss National Science Foundation as of September 2020: https://data.snf.ch/covid-19.

4.1 Data life cycle management

Data Life cycle management is comprised of different steps: data collection, data visualization, analysis, modeling, and close-down. We will examine these in more detail in Chapters 3 and 6 of this book. What differs a data-centered governance from other top-down or even bottom-up approaches is the data are automatically collected in the course of citizens' operations and immediately processed for action. It will be therefore the focus in this section. After analysis, the citizens' operations can be split into five different levels, each of them corresponding to a grade of citizen's engagement: observation, participation, interaction, transaction, and co-creation.

Regarding the first level, it is comprised of data automatically generated from sensors when the citizens walk on the streets, drive, work, go to the hospital, or participate in leisure or sport activities (Bates, Saria, Ohno-Machado, Shah, & Escobar, 2014; Kim et al., 2014; Song, Fisher, Wang, & Cui, 2018).

The citizens' behavior can be also tracked through commercial apps that all citizens have downloaded in their mobile companion. They usually correspond to different business services they receive from private companies for electricity, gas, telephone provision, shopping (Amazon), or mobility solutions (Uber, Blabla car, etc.). Citizen's behavior can be also watched using social media open discussion (Twitter, Instagram, Facebook, etc.). Moreover, many companies such as Fidzup, Shyhook, Near, Gimbal, Tamoco, Foursquare, Teemo, and Safegraph are working in the location of data business and are analyzing citizen's movement with the tracking of their GPS position that usually users leave in active mode (with or without a formal consent) while downloading business or entertainment mobile applications. Their objective is to identify patterns of citizens' movement, knowledge that they will sell for commercial purpose.

As a second level, the active participation of the citizens in the civic life of their urban area can be registered through specific collaborative platform (like www.decidim.cat) or also in a more traditional way with paper-based formularies, while the interview is released on the streets (usually the interviewers are placed in very famous or touristic spots in the city). As a third level, the citizen interacts with the institutions, residents, or other stakeholders. They can meet the department representative related to the nature of their request directly in the city hall office. Cities provide them with alternative solution, i.e., web- or mobile-based formulary to prevent them from displacing. These web forms allow them to interact, to ask for an information or a support request, to report a claim, to tell an experience, or even to show the grade of satisfaction for a past service received. As a fourth level, the city hall authorizes and enables citizen to manage online transactional, administrative, or financial tasks (e.g., pay a parking, taxes, fines, or respond to a census inquiry).

As a last and fifth level, the urban co-creation consists of citizens informing or providing local service directly to other urban residents in a citizen-to-citizen mode. Diverse initiatives and co-design platforms already exist. They are government platform such as www.chicagoshovels.org in Chicago (Linders, 2012) or citizen ones with more recently initiative such as https://tienes-sal.es/ in Spain. Previous discussions of citizen-centered urban co-creation show the progress is slower than many hoped and especially if we compare with the progress of the private sector and the expansion of transactional websites that allow, with a mobile app, creation of articles customized or designed by clients and ship them directly at home (Cleland et al., 2018). Moreover, Thiel and Ertio (2018) add gamification tools that can really boost and improve public co-creation in the tasks related to urban design and planning.

The participation of private sectors is key in this context. Anyway, two issues need to be fixed. A private company that shares its data can do it due to a condition defined in its contract that allows to operate in the city. When this clause is not present, private company can be motivated by a special interest, which is based on exchange conditions, i.e., to be able to get access to more data by a mutual exchange with other providers and to therefore get a wider vision (till 360 degrees) of its clients/users. The second issue is related to the source format of the data. Today, there is no standard of data format and all the stakeholders involved in the city are using per se different formats of data. A European project exists to fix this issue.

4.2 Real-time urban platform

A big data citizen-centered governance requires a real-time platform that facilitates intelligence based on five main principles. The first one is that citizen or the business are considered as a whole, and the administration interacts with them with a 360-degree perspective that includes elements about their social, education, justice, financial, taxes, health, real estate, and family status along with data related to the belonging assets: house, vehicle, etc. It means also that all the personal data are consolidated into a unique database to be managed and analyzed later on. However, this database centralization adds new risks of losing the context and the origin of the request. The technical contingency plan exists to enrich the database with new types of data, usually called metadata. These latter are collected along with the data and contain information that permits the traceability of the business/functional concepts, the follow-up of the transformations made between the different systems, and determines the level of data confidentiality.

As a step further, the second principle is to be able to ask only once the same information to the citizen. The effectiveness of a citizen-centered big data governance requires that the architecture supporting the collection of the data instead to be soloed by department, which may be centralized. This integration of the different departmental information systems can happen if the transactional web/mobile-based formulary moves from many to a general one and for any requests issued by the citizen. A similar approach has to be done also for the companies/business/professional requests and the different administrative formularies they have to fulfill according to the type of information they need. Finally, it has to cover also the "offline" requests, i.e., when a citizen or a company is received physically face-to-face by a public agent who manually enters the information in the systems from his desk.

In an operational perspective, this approach needs a mapping of all the existing formularies with their different concepts and terminology. Indeed, besides the generic or "core" data related to the citizen's identification (such as gender, nationality, ID number, etc.), each public department owns specific data related to its type and sector of activity. Then, a homogenization of the functional concepts and terminology have to be proceeded and an agreement has to be reached to consolidate all of these forms into a unique one. By making converging all the requests, the city council improves the service offered to the citizens resolving one of the historic and common service complaints that reports the citizen is usually compelled to repeat the same information many times while they address different municipal departments.

The exploitation of this information quickly requires a platform with an artificial intelligence solution able to automatize responses and deliver them in real-time increasing the service window to a 24 h/24 and 365 day a year coverage (see Chapter 1 and the case of the HOPSTAY). This solution uses Natural Language Processing algorithm (type Apple Siri or Google Alexia), and the database of responses is initially preloaded with past requests and their respective answers developed and written by the business translators. This preconfiguration can train the intelligent platform, i.e., the machine and to improve the algorithms used by the chatbot since the start of the service. These previous requests and their respective answers also contribute to a cross-departmental catalogue of services that will be the responsibility of each business translator to maintain and keep updated. We believe that at the beginning of this service, this machine will need human supervision that will decrease all along the transition period to a minimum that will depend on the complexity, the reproducibility of the requests placed into the system, and the accuracy of the answers given by the machine.

The ethical issue that this solution raises if the resolution of a new request requires the use of information owned by the city council but not included in the formulary placed by the citizen. The system needs to resolve this issue by acceding to a repository of formal consents provided by the individuals and authorizing the access to personal or sensitive information if it is necessary. The question becomes more arduous if the access to this information is not motivated by the request of the proper individual (bottom-up) but is part of an action plan led by the city council to target specific group of population (top-down). As an illustration, the question to resolve could be: *if I declare my monthly wages and the nationality of each member that composes my family, would it be ethical to be incorporated in the next seminar for the social integration of foreigners and linguistic classes and be proposed this service by default? Is the information provided to one department be used by another department for a different need, i.e., a different origin?* Actually, the question becomes more critical with the integration of information coming from other sources like social media, business app, etc. As an example, is the government of my country authorized to use information regarding my private discussion with friends about my recent summer or winter holidays to know my travel and accommodation expenses and determine my costs of living to correlate them with the yearly incomes claimed to the Treasury during the tax recovery campaign or to validate possible subventions granted to low-income families.

The third and fourth principles of our platform really describe the big change of paradigm we suggest, i.e., the move from a collective action to a citizen-centered one and from an analysis ex-post (afterwards) to ex-ante (beforehand).

Ju et al. (2018) believe the quality of the service provided to the urban residents can be improved by collecting information from the citizen beforehand and with the objective to design the services that will be implemented afterward for them. They call this approach "ex-ante," i.e., analyzing the characteristics/

needs of the person/collective who will be the client of the service that is supposed to be built. They argue this mass-customized service design provide better results: first, the transparency/the trust of the decision-making process is increased; second, the citizen is seen in the center of the government action, which improves the service provided and their overall satisfaction rate.

Many studies in the past were afterward analyzing clients or citizens to understand patterns and propose predictive or even prescriptive actions. They had in common to consider the citizens as a whole and were "postmortem" analytics. As an example, Bates et al. (2014) show how big data allows the US Healthcare department to determine future possible readmissions, decompensation, adverse events, or lack of treatment adherence among their patients. Their analysis aims at seeking opportunities to reduce costs among clients already identified as high-risk or high-cost. Grimaldi and Fernandez (2017) show how data science can reduce the traffic congestion, accidents, and urban contamination considering all the cars circulating in the city of Nice (France) as identic in terms of technical characteristics, CO_2 footprint, and urban traffic impact. Moreover, their analysis is done after the situation of congestion in Nice becomes reality.

Citizen-centered big data is a completely different approach and consists first not to consider citizen as a whole, a homogeneous population, but instead to identify citizen group profiles and persona, which both determine the specific actions that will be directed to each single person. Second, it aims at analyzing and defining actions before the situation happens, i.e., ex-ante analytics to predict phenomenon and prescript preventive actions for the current present state. The effectiveness of a citizen-centered big data governance goes through providing a complete profile for an individual or a homogeneous citizen group. It pushes information directly to the citizen through the use of a mobile companion and can call them to action if necessary. So, this governance combines pull-and-push modes regarding the governance of the urban residents.

Commercial exploitation of public sector information is limited; 35% of the use is geographical, but only 12% is for economic or social purpose (Capgemini Institute & European Commission, 2015). The open data philosophy has not succeeded, and public-owned information has not proliferated or been distributed in the form of large datasets. Ojo, Curry, and Zeleti (2015) suggest, however, that these datasets could enable collaboration between local, central governments and other city stakeholders like software developers, residents, and SMEs, and largely respond to issues related to governance, economy, and transport (Abella, Ortiz-de-Urbina-Criado, & De-Pablos-Heredero, 2017). It is our fifth and last principle because we believe it will drastically accelerate the effect and benefits of a citizen-centered governance. As an example, the localization of food markets and supermarkets is information owned by the census public administration. These data correlated to the population density, gender, and age can reveal how the lack of healthy food in a specific district leads to problems of traffic or obesity of the young generation. In that specific

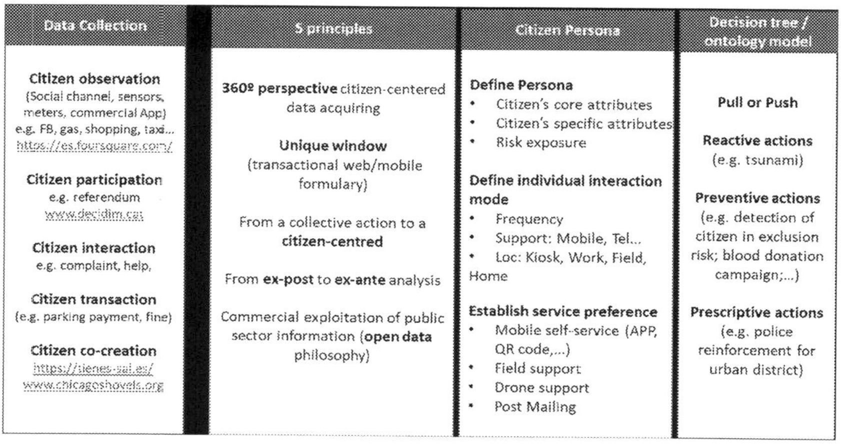

80 Implementing data-driven strategies in smart cities

Data Collection	5 principles	Citizen Persona	Decision tree / ontology model
Citizen observation (Social channel, sensors, meters, commercial App) e.g. FB, gas, shopping, taxi... https://es.foursquare.com/	360º perspective citizen-centered data acquiring	**Define Persona** • Citizen's core attributes • Citizen's specific attributes • Risk exposure	Pull or Push Reactive actions (e.g. tsunami)
Citizen participation e.g. referendum www.decidim.cat	Unique window (transactional web/mobile formulary)	**Define individual interaction mode** • Frequency	Preventive actions (e.g. detection of citizen in exclusion
Citizen interaction e.g. complaint, help,	From a collective action to a citizen-centred	• Support: Mobile, Tel... • Loc: Kiosk, Work, Field, Home	risk; blood donation campaign;...)
Citizen transaction (e.g. parking payment, fine)	From ex-post to ex-ante analysis	**Establish service preference** • Mobile self-service (APP,	Prescriptive actions (e.g. police
Citizen co-creation https://tienes-sal.es/ www.chicagoshovels.org	Commercial exploitation of public sector information (open data philosophy)	QR code,...) • Field support • Drone support • Post Mailing	reinforcement for urban district)

FIG. 2.11 Real-time platform.

example, we believe a large opportunity resides if the exploitation of Public Sector Information (PSI) could be integrated and leveraged in a citizen-centered approach to determine specific action at individual level to propose alternative supply solutions to offer fruit and vegetable provision.

However, today, the diffusion of the open datasets is scarce and with a low level of quality. The possible reason of this situation is the policymakers responsible of e-government strategies see Web 2.0 and onwards failing to generate meaningful interaction with the citizens (Bolivar, 2018). Moreover, their configuration based on flat excel files suppose high efforts of extraction and cleaning, consistency, and integration. So, our approach would be possible if they are accessible via API technology and supposes a marginal or free cost for it. However, this condition may generate an ethical debate if we can consider fair to acquire at low-cost quantities of public data and resell it maybe at an expensive price (Janssen, 2011). The resolution of this debate is still open.

Fig. 2.11 shows the mode of running of the real-time urban platform.

This real-time platform provides sustainable and resilient functions as described in Chapter 1 of this book. It runs well and has a strong dependence on the reliability and the robustness of the data stored in the systems. It is the reason for the creation of a Master Data Model.

4.3 Master Data Model

An MDM is a consistent and uniform set of extended identifiers and attributes that describe central government entities, including citizens, companies, procedures regarding specific events, departmental master data, and hierarchies. It defines and manages the critical data of an organization to provide a single point of reference. Jörg, Ralf, and Jens (2009) describe an MDM as an artifact that aims at solving the problem of data management of a wide organization providing an as-is situation status and identifying actions for improvements. The process that culminates in an MDM is called the Master Data Management, a technology-based process in which the administration and IT department work together to ensure frequency, unicity, accuracy, consistency, and responsibility to maintain the master data officially stored and used by the administration.

We consider that the following points should be considered when planning a Master Data Management strategy:

- Identify the candidate sources that will provide a reference point and eliminate the costly redundancies that occur when administration depends on multiple conflicting sources of information.
- Establish a method for distributing trusted data to systems throughout the whole administration. For example, make sure that when a citizen informs their contact information changes to one department (health for instance), the whole administration acknowledges this input and another department (justice for instance) will not try to contact them using the old and obsolete one. Having multiple sources of information is a widespread problem, especially in large organizations, and the associated costs can be very high
- Elaborate rules for precisely combining and merging the unit systems into a single large one
- Incorporate rules to eliminate incorrect data spread in the system and create an authoritative source of data
- Establish an approach to identify mismatched data and restore the data merged in an unappropriated way
- Include reference data, i.e., a set of permissible values

The MDM includes metadata that contain all the internal necessary information for the provision, the sharing, and the analysis of the data between different departments. They participate in the resolution of conflicts in case of redundancies or inconsistencies between information describing the same citizen. They are, for example: logs of information load, history of extractions, logs of errors, the volume of data and usage, the data cleaning criteria, the criteria of data expurgation, or the service level agreements (SLAs) with other parties. They provide the name and localization of the systems in which the data is stored and, more specifically, the physical names of the tables and columns of the different datasets. They can be functional, providing back-up and recovery rules, a data dictionary with the definition of the used concepts, the data update frequency, a data clustering description, the business rules and algorithms for calculation, or even the known issues with this type of data. They can be related to security and privacy issues, determining the level of data confidentiality (is it public information, or is it internal, restricted, or confidential?) or also covering privacy and sensibility issues (is it personal-level data, an anonymized one, an aggregated one?). Finally, they can be related to the access log history for auditory purposes.

4.4 Data quality management

The effectiveness of the data-based governance is strictly linked to the full implementation of a Master Data Model while its efficiency is linked to the quality of the data managed by the organization. If the data is of bad quality, it does not represent the reality of the citizenship and the decision is delayed or can't be data-proven, and a large debate inside the organization starts. The problem in this case is the efficiency of the decision-making process. To mitigate this risk, each functional department needs to establish a clear quality plan for the data to meet the quality requirements that the governance requests. The management of the data quality needs to be largely present during the data capture process (see Chapter 4). The urban quality plan is comprised of three items: a control plan with its corresponding list of evidence to be considered during the life cycle of the urban data, a reporting model/dashboard where the measures of data quality are compared with quality criteria, and finally a model of a continuous improvement plan that lists the necessary procedures to fix potential deficiencies of quality in a reasonable time. We describe each of the three in the following text.

A plan of control consists of defining the checks that will allow evaluation of the quality of the data. For each control, the plan defines the data that will be measured and the different values of criticality according to the measures picked, even if these values always consider a tolerance window. Once the controls have been selected, a model of reporting or dashboard is necessary to follow the evolution of the data quality and the execution of possible action plans. The dashboard includes technical and functional data quality measurements and feeds the continuous Improvement Plan, which consists of improving the quality of the data once the deficiencies have been identified. It is composed of different phases from the identification of the root cause of the problem to the approval of the necessary solution.

4.5 Data security and privacy

Emerging technologies, like artificial intelligence, IoT platforms, and geosurveillance aim at analyzing human attitudes offline and online to predict future behaviors or prescript corrective actions to avoid undesired possible situations in the future. They may create a number of potential harms against privacy laws and other principles concerning the fair use of citizen's information. On one side, our consent could be converted as an empty exercise (e.g., if you want to access a website, you usually need to accept its cookies in a global way). On the other side, our consent is not asked, expressed, and thus absent as, for example, when we get the results of a request from a search platform (i.e., Google, MSN, Yahoo, etc.). The providers delete possible answers without our authorization. To respond to this concern and to conform to legal and privacy aspects, we recommend issuing a legal normative, i.e., a set of technical and functional conditions along with a certification process that accompanies its implementation and that culminates with a final certificate confirming the possible use of data to the city department. This issue will be largely more developed in Chapter 4 when we present a roadmap to implement a data-driven city.

References

Abella, A., Ortiz-de-Urbina-Criado, M., & De-Pablos-Heredero, C. (2017). A model for the analysis of data-driven innovation and value generation in smart cities' ecosystems. *Cities, 64*, 47–53. https://doi.org/10.1016/j.cities.2017.01.011.

Agnellutti, C. (2014). *Big data: An exploration of opportunities, values, and privacy issues*. Nova Science Publishers, Inc. 191 pp https://public.ebookcentral.proquest.com/choice/publicfullrecord.aspx?p=3024547.

Anonymous. (2012). *3rd international conference on flood recovery, innovation and response, FRIAR 2012. WIT transactions on ecology and the environment*.

Bates, D. W., Saria, S., Ohno-Machado, L., Shah, A., & Escobar, G. (2014). Big data in health care: Using analytics to identify and manage high-risk and high-cost patients. *Health Affairs, 33*(7), 1123–1131. https://doi.org/10.1377/hlthaff.2014.0041.

Ben Letaifa, S. (2015). How to strategize smart cities: Revealing the SMART model. *Journal of Business Research, 68*(7), 1414–1419. https://doi.org/10.1016/j.jbusres.2015.01.024.

Bibri, S. E. (2018). The IoT for smart sustainable cities of the future: An analytical framework for sensor-based big data applications for environmental sustainability. *Sustainable Cities and Society, 38*, 230–253. https://doi.org/10.1016/j.scs.2017.12.034.

Bolivar, M. P. R. (2018). User centric services under the web 2.0 era. Coproduction, execution and efficiency of public services. In *User centric E-government* (pp. 137–158). Springer, Cham. https://link.springer.com/chapter/10.1007%2F978-3-319-59442-2_8.

Bugshan, H. (2015). Co-innovation: The role of online communities. *Journal of Strategic Marketing, 23*(2), 175–186. https://doi.org/10.1080/0965254X.2014.920905.

Capgemini Institute & European Commission. (2015). *Creating value through open data: Study on the impact of re-use of public data resources*. https://doi.org/10.2759/328101.

Cardone, G., Foschini, L., Bellavista, P., Corradi, A., Borcea, C., Talasila, M., et al. (2013). Fostering participacion in smart cities: A geo-social crowdsensing platform. *IEEE Communications Magazine, 51*(6), 112–119. https://doi.org/10.1109/MCOM.2013.6525603.

Cleland, B., Wallace, J., & Black, M. (2018). The "engage" system: Using real-time digital technologies to support citizen-centred design in government. In S. Saeed, et al. (Eds.), *vol. 39. User centric E-government. Integrated series in information systems* Springer International Publishing AG, doi:10.1007/978-3-319-59442-2_11.

Davidson, K., Nguyen, T. M. P., Beilin, R., & Briggs, J. (2019). The emerging addition of resilience as a component of sustainability in urban policy. *Cities, 92*, 1–9. https://doi.org/10.1016/j.cities.2019.03.012.

Dawes, S. S. (2008). The evolution and continuing challenges of e-governance. *Public Administration Review, 68*, S86–S102. https://doi.org/10.1111/j.1540-6210.2008.00981.x.

Derqui, B., & Grimaldi, D. (2020). Data on the sustainability profile and food waste management in primary and secondary schools: The case of the Catalonia region in Spain. *Data in Brief*. https://doi.org/10.1016/j.dib.2019.104825. In press.

Dunn-Cavelty, M., & Suter, M. (2009). Public-private partnerships are no silver bullet: An expanded governance model for critical infrastructure protection. *International Journal of Critical Infrastructure Protection, 2*(4), 179–187. https://doi.org/10.1016/j.ijcip.2009.08.006.

Eräranta, S., & Staffans, A. (2015). *From situation awareness to smart city planning and decision making*.

Ferraro, F., Etzion, D., & Gehman, J. (2015). Tackling grand challenges pragmatically: Robust action revisited. *Organization Studies, 36*(3), 363–390. https://doi.org/10.1177/0170840614563742.

Gandini, A., Garmendia, L., & San Mateos, R. (2017). Towards sustainable historic cities: Adaptation to climate change risks. *Entrepreneurship and Sustainability Issues, 4*(3), 319–327. https://doi.org/10.9770/jesi.2017.4.3S(7).

Gemignani, Z., Gemignani, C., Galentino, R., & Schuermann, P. (2014). *Data fluency: Empowering your organization with effective data communication*. John Wiley & Sons. https://www.wiley.com/en-ao/Data+Fluency%3A+Empowering+Your+Organization+with+Effective+Data+Communication-p-9781118851012.

George, G., Howard-Grenville, J., Joshi, A., & Tihanyi, L. (2016). Understanding and tackling societal grand challenges through management research. *Academy of Management Journal, 59*(6), 1880–1895. https://doi.org/10.5465/amj.2016.4007.

Gerrish, E. (2016). The impact of performance management on performance in public organizations: A meta-analysis. *Public Administration Review, 76*(1), 48–66. https://doi.org/10.1111/puar.12433.

Grimaldi, D. (2019). Can we analyse political discourse using Twitter? Evidence from Spanish 2019 presidential election. *Social Network Analysis and Mining, 12*. https://doi.org/10.1007/s13278-019-0594-6. In press.

Grimaldi, D. (2020). Factors affecting big data analytics based innovation processes. A Spanish evidence. *International Journal of Innovation and Technology Management*. https://doi.org/10.1142/S0219877020500364. In press.

Grimaldi, D., Diaz, J., & Arboleda, H. (2020). Inferring the votes in a new political landscape: The case of the 2019 Spanish Presidential elections. *Journal of Big Data*. https://doi.org/10.1186/s40537-020-00334-5. In press.

Grimaldi, D., & Fernandez, V. (2017). The alignment of university curricula with the building of a Smart City: A case study from Barcelona. *Technological Forecasting and Social Change, 123*, 298–306. https://doi.org/10.1016/j.techfore.2016.03.011.

Grimaldi, D., & Fernandez, V. (2017). The road to school. The Barcelona case. *Cities*. https://doi.org/10.1016/j.cities.2017.01.013. In press.

Grimaldi, D., Fernandez, V., & Carrasco, C. (2019). Heuristic for the localization of new shops based on business and social criteria. *Technological Forecasting and Social Change, 142*, 249–257. https://doi.org/10.1016/j.techfore.2018.07.034. In press.

Harith, A.-Y., & Rahayu, A. (2018). The concept of user participation in the development process of E-government system. *International Journal of Scientific Research in Computer Science, Engineering and Information Technology*, 44–49. https://doi.org/10.32628/cseit1183790.

Janssen, K. (2011). The role of public sector information in the European market for online content: A never-ending story or a new beginning? *info, 13*(6), 20–29. https://doi.org/10.1108/14636691111174234.

Jin, J., Gubbi, J., Marusic, S., & Palaniswami, M. (2014). An information framework for creating a smart city through internet of things. *IEEE Internet of Things Journal, 1*(2), 112–121. https://doi.org/10.1109/JIOT.2013.2296516.

Johnston, E. (2015). *Governance in the information era: Theory and practice of policy informatics*. Routledge.

Jörg, B., Ralf, K., & Jens, P. (2009). Developing maturity models for IT management. *Business & Information Systems Engineering*, 213–222. https://doi.org/10.1007/s12599-009-0044-5.

Joshi, S., Saxena, S., Godbole, T., & Shreya. (2016). Developing smart cities: An integrated framework. In *Vol. 93. Procedia computer science* (pp. 902–909). Elsevier B.V. https://doi.org/10.1016/j.procs.2016.07.258.

Ju, J., Liu, L., & Feng, Y. (2018). Citizen-centered big data analysis-driven governance intelligence framework for smart cities. *Telecommunications Policy, 42*(10), 881–896. https://doi.org/10.1016/j.telpol.2018.01.003.

Kim, G. H., Trimi, S., & Chung, J. H. (2014). Big-data applications in the government sector. *Communications of the ACM, 57*(3), 78–85. https://doi.org/10.1145/2500873.

Kitchin, R. (2014). The real-time city? Big data and smart urbanism. *GeoJournal, 79*(1), 1–14. https://doi.org/10.1007/s10708-013-9516-8.

Kuhlmann, S., & Rip, A. (2018). Next-generation innovation policy and grand challenges. *Science and Public Policy, 45*(4), 448–454. https://doi.org/10.1093/SCIPOL/SCY011.

Kusumasari, B., & Alam, Q. (2012). Bridging the gaps: The role of local government capability and the management of a natural disaster in Bantul, Indonesia. *Natural Hazards, 60*(2), 761–779. https://doi.org/10.1007/s11069-011-0016-1.

Lee, K. F. (2018). *AI superpowers: China, silicon valley, and the new world order*. Boston, MA: Houghton Mifflin Co.

Linders, D. (2012). From e-government to we-government: Defining a typology for citizen coproduction in the age of social media. *Government Information Quarterly, 29*(4), 446–454. https://doi.org/10.1016/j.giq.2012.06.003.

Maciejewski, M. (2017). To do more, better, faster and more cheaply: Using big data in public administration. *International Review of Administrative Sciences, 83*(1), 120–135. https://doi.org/10.1177/0020852316640058.

Marini, M., Brunner, C., Chokani, N., & Abhari, R. S. (2020). Enhancing response preparedness to influenza epidemics: Agent-based study of 2050 influenza season in Switzerland. *Simulation Modelling Practice and Theory, 103*, 102091. https://doi.org/10.1016/j.simpat.2020.102091.

Matheus, R., Janssen, M., & Maheshwari, D. (2020). Data science empowering the public: Data-driven dashboards for transparent and accountable decision-making in smart cities. *Government Information Quarterly, 37*(3). https://doi.org/10.1016/j.giq.2018.01.006.

Meijer, A. (2015). E-governance innovation: Barriers and strategies. *Government Information Quarterly, 32*(2), 198–206. https://doi.org/10.1016/j.giq.2015.01.001.

Mergel, I., Rethemeyer, R. K., & Isett, K. (2016). Big data in public affairs. *Public Administration Review, 76*(6), 928–937. https://doi.org/10.1111/puar.12625.

Ojo, A., Curry, E., & Zeleti, F. A. (2015). A tale of open data innovations in five smart cities. In *Vol. 2015. 2015 48th Hawaii international conference on system sciences* (pp. 2326–2335). IEEE Computer Society. https://doi.org/10.1109/HICSS.2015.280.

Pastor-Escuredo, D., Torres, Y., Martínez-Torres, M., & Zufiria, P. J. (2020). Rapid multidimensional impact assessment of floods. *Sustainability (Switzerland), 12*(10). https://doi.org/10.3390/su12104246.

Petrini, F., Gkoumas, K., & Bontempi, F. (2015). From resilient—And towards antifragile—Design: Considerations from a civil engineering point of view. In *SHMII 2015—7th international conference on structural health monitoring of intelligent infrastructure*.

Ramirez, F., Palominos, P., Camargo, M., & Grimaldi, D. (2021). A new methodology to support smartness at the district level of metropolitan areas in emerging economies: The case of Santiago de Chile. *Sustainable Cities and Society, 67*. https://doi.org/10.1016/j.scs.2021.102713. In press.

Rodríguez-Gaviria, E. M., Ochoa-Osorio, S., Builes-Jaramillo, A., & Botero-Fernández, V. (2019). Computational bottom-up vulnerability indicator for low-income flood-prone urban areas. *Sustainability (Switzerland)*, *11*(16). https://doi.org/10.3390/su11164341.

Salerno, S., Nunziante, A., & Santoro, G. (2014). Competences and knowledge: Key-factors in the smart city of the future. *Knowledge Management and E-Learning*, *6*(4), 356–376. http://www.kmel-journal.org/ojs/index.php/online-publication/article/view/393/238.

Shepherd, D., & Sutcliffe, K. (2011). Inductive top-down theorizing: A source of new theories of organization. *Academy of Management Review*, *36*(2), 361–380. https://doi.org/10.5465/amr.2009.0157.

Smith, A., & Stirling, A. (2008). *Transitions social-ecological resilience and socio-technical transitions: Critical issues for sustainability governance*. Available at: www.steps-centre.org.

Song, M. L., Fisher, R., Wang, J. L., & Cui, L. B. (2018). Environmental performance evaluation with big data: Theories and methods. *Annals of Operations Research*, *270*(1–2), 459–472. https://doi.org/10.1007/s10479-016-2158-8.

Thiel, S. K., & Ertio, T. (2018). Play it to plan it? The impact of game elements on usage of a urban planning app. In S. Saeed, et al. (Eds.), *vol. 39. User centric e-government. Integrated series in information system* (pp. 203–229). Springer International Publishing AG. https://doi.org/10.1007/978-3-319-59442-2_12.

Tran, G. T. H., Dupont, L., & Camargo, M. (2019). Application of decision-making methods in Smart City projects: A systematic literature review. *Smart Cities*, 433–452. https://doi.org/10.3390/smartcities2030027.

Transparency International. (2020). *Corruption perceptions index 2019*. Berlin: Transparency International. Available at: www.transparency.org/cpi. (Accessed 30 September 2020).

Tucci, C. L., Gautschi, H., & Viscusi, G. (2016). *Switzerland's digital future: Facts, challenges, recommendations*. Lausanne. Available at: https://www.egovernment.ch/files/6614/6425/3280/epfl-study-switzerland-digital-future.pdf. (Accessed 30 September 2020).

UK Department for Business Innovation and Skills. (2013). *Seizing the data opportunity: A strategy for UK data capability*. London: The National Archives.

Wang, Y., Kung, L. A., & Byrd, T. A. (2018). Big data analytics: Understanding its capabilities and potential benefits for healthcare organizations. *Technological Forecasting and Social Change*, *126*, 3–13. https://doi.org/10.1016/j.techfore.2015.12.019.

Wang, Y., & Taylor, J. E. (2018). Urban crisis detection technique: A spatial and data driven approach based on latent dirichlet allocation (LDA) topic modeling. In *Vol. 33. Construction research congress 2018: Construction project management—Selected papers from the construction research congress 2018* (pp. 250–259). American Society of Civil Engineers (ASCE).

Wang, Y., & Taylor, J. E. (2019). DUET: Data-driven approach based on latent Dirichlet allocation topic modeling. *Journal of Computing in Civil Engineering*, *33*(3). https://doi.org/10.1061/(ASCE)CP.1943-5487.0000819.

Wang, Y., Taylor, J. E., & Garvin, M. J. (2020). Measuring resilience of human-spatial systems to disasters: Framework combining spatial-network analysis and fisher information. *Journal of Management in Engineering*, *36*(4). https://doi.org/10.1061/(ASCE)ME.1943-5479.0000782.

Wang, H., Xiong, W., Wu, G., & Zhu, D. (2018). Public–private partnership in public administration discipline: A literature review. *Public Management Review*, *20*(2), 293–316. https://doi.org/10.1080/14719037.2017.1313445.

Weber, C., Sailer, K., & Katzy, B. (2015). Real-time foresight—Preparedness for dynamic networks. *Technological Forecasting and Social Change*, *101*, 299–313. https://doi.org/10.1016/j.techfore.2015.05.016.

Weick, K. (1989). Theory construction as disciplined imagination. *Academy of Management Review*, 516–531. https://doi.org/10.5465/amr.1989.4308376.
Weick, K. (2002). Puzzles in organizational learning: An exercise in disciplined imagination. *British Journal of Management*, *13*(S2), S7–S15. https://doi.org/10.1111/1467-8551.13.s2.2.
Xu, G., Wang, J., Huang, G. Q., & Chen, C. H. (2018). Data-driven resilient fleet management for cloud asset-enabled urban flood control. *IEEE Transactions on Intelligent Transportation Systems*, *19*(6), 1827–1838. https://doi.org/10.1109/TITS.2017.2740438.
Yang, C., Su, G., & Chen, J. (2017). Using big data to enhance crisis response and disaster resilience for a smart city. In *2017 IEEE 2nd international conference on big data analysis, ICBDA 2017* (pp. 504–507). Institute of Electrical and Electronics Engineers Inc. https://doi.org/10.1109/ICBDA.2017.8078684.

Chapter 3

Data Science technologies

Carlos Carrasco-Farré[a], Manu Carricano[b,*], and Didier Grimaldi[c]
[a]Ramon Llull University—ESADE Business School, Barcelona, Spain, [b]Department of Operations, Innovation and Data Sciences, Universitat Ramon Llull—ESADE Business School, Barcelona, Spain, [c]Ramon Llull University, La Salle Faculty, Barcelona, Spain

In this chapter, we will present how data science and its different domains have recently opened new forms to handle urban issues. In particular, we will see how science can help us understand urban situations by describing the process of collecting and analysis of data related to the problem encountered and the definition of a model (prescriptive, predictive, etc.). Moreover, we will debate how recent advances (ML, AI, Big Data, etc.) allow us to include more dimensions (metadata), more volume, and more variety. Finally, we will provide a guide to start your own data-driven project providing an urban data canvas model, a description of the team needed and an example about retail data.

1 What is data science?

The way we define things is important because it shapes how we understand and interact with the world. However, as Juliet told Romeo in Shakespeare's masterpiece, "A rose by any other name would smell as sweet." That is to say, we may find many data science definitions, but the important elements will remain there (explicitly or not). In general, data science is not only about processes and techniques for understanding our world through analysis of data but also decision-making. While on one side of the equation we will have the most obvious interpretation (data gathering, analysis, and so on), we should not forget about the human factor. Both are two sides of the same coin because, ultimately, the goal of data science is to improve decision-making.

The reason we have so many definitions for data science is that the field is moderately new. It has roots in the vast amount of data, computational power,

---

*All the authors of this book are sad that Manu Carricano, PhD, and contributor of the Chapter 3 passed away on March 2021 and will not see the outcome of his hard dedication and effort. Manu was more than a great professional, he was a friend, and we will be ever grateful for his happiness, dedication, assistance, and constant advise. Rest in peace Manu.

and statistical techniques available. We say "moderately" new because, although we have access to more data and computational power than ever, many of the statistical techniques used in data science have been around for decades.

During World War II, before Operation Overlord (the codename for the Battle of Normandy), the Allies had to know the operational power of their enemy to assess whether an invasion of the European continent could succeed. Among the information needed, knowing the number of German tanks in the western front was vital for calibrating the force (in terms of troops and equipment) needed to effectively liberate Europe. By that time, German Panzers V were scary machines with high velocity, long-barreled 75 mm/L70 guns, and heavy armor, so the Allies needed to be certain how many tanks they would face before the D-Day. However, the allied forces knew nothing about how many tanks the enemy was able to produce. This is known as the "German tank problem."

To determine German tank capacity, the Allied forces relied on gathering information from intelligence services infiltrated in enemy territory. The informants started to report the output of German factories or simply counting tanks on the battlefield. Using this information, the Allied intelligence estimated a German tank production of around 1400 units a month between June 1940 and September 1942. If true, those numbers would mean that an invasion would have low chances of succeeding. However, statistical intelligence had another approach.

Each German tank had a serial number, and the idea was to use these numbers to estimate the tanks produced in a given moment. The idea was pretty simple: take the maximum serial number, subtract 1, multiply by sample size plus 1, and divide by the sample size. Applying this formula, the statistical estimate of monthly German tank production was 169 in June 1940, 244 in June 1941, and 327 in August 1942. In contrast, intelligence estimate figures were 1000 in June 1940, 1550 in June 1941, and 1550 in August 1942. The Allied forces had a hard decision to make: Should they trust the informants' estimates and forget about a land invasion or should they trust the formula output and risk their troops into a potentially deadly trap?

Confident about their statistical estimates, the Allies decided to attack the Western front in 1944. The number of German Panzers they found was below the estimated numbers of their intelligence services, which demonstrated the superiority of the data-driven approach. After the war, once the Allies had access to real German records of tank production, data showed that the statistical estimate was much more accurate than the intelligence estimate. The German records showed that Nazis were producing 122 tanks per month in June 1940, 271 in June 1941, and 342 in August 1942. The solution for the "German tank problem" was found.

As we have seen with this example, many of the statistical tools were in place decades ago. However, there is a main difference between then and now: the availability of data. To get the information needed to be plugged into the statistical formula, the Allied forces had to capture German tanks and collect their serial numbers. Of course, this has a huge cost not only in economic terms but in human lives. Thankfully, nowadays, data is everywhere at (almost) no cost. Data is everywhere, and even when we do not know or think about it, data is being generated because we are surrounded by technology. Therefore, we have the opportunity to leverage data science to make better and more informed decisions in cities. However, we have not provided an exact definition for data science. In contrast, we do believe that, since data science is a relatively new field, it is easier to understand by defining the type of problems that data science deals with using the descriptions provided by Provost and Fawcett (2013).

Classification problems. In this set of problems, data science helps us to estimate the probability of a given observation to belong to a set of classes (usually, mutually exclusive). For example, we may want to deliver a new social program for citizens in danger of falling below the poverty line. Since resources for the program are scarce, we may want to prioritize for those more in danger. Through data science, we can answer the question, "Among all our citizens, who are more likely to fall below the poverty line in the next year?" In this example, we can classify citizens among those who are likely and not likely. This is similar to procedures known as scoring. Typically, banks and financial institutions perform risk analysis on people asking for a mortgage and, based on these analyses, they calculate a probability of default. If the probability is above a certain threshold, the bank will deny the mortgage. If it is below, the mortgage will be approved. That is a classification problem. In our example, the city council can calculate the probability of a citizen to face financial problems in the next year and offer a subsidy (or the desired type of program) to those with a probability higher than a given threshold.

Value estimation problems. In this set of problems, we are interested in finding a specific number for a given observation/individual in a given variable. Usually, this type of problem is solved using regressions to try to answer questions like, "How much traffic are we going to have in this specific street next Sunday?" or "How many employees do we need to deploy a given policy in a given neighborhood?" By analyzing historical traffic or historical workload, we can find the value for our target variables: the number of cars or number of employees. As you can see, it is a similar problem as the previous classification problem, although with a big difference. While in the first problem we tried to identify a specific class (in a finite set of options), in value estimation problems, we face potential infinite options. In value estimation, we care about *how much*, while in classification we care about *probability*.

Similarity matching problems. Many recommendation systems are based on matching products based on similarity. For example, think about Netflix or Amazon. When Netflix recommends a new movie or Amazon a new product, they are matching your preferences (based on previous behavior) or the characteristics of a product with similar preferences (other people with similar behavior) or similar characteristics (other products with shared or complementary features). Usually, this similarity matching is done using value estimation methods or classification methods.

Clustering problems. Data science techniques aimed at solving clustering problems are used to group people, services, or products based on their similarity. Especially in preliminary analysis, cluster analysis can help to identify potential causes/opportunities or discern among citizens and allow greater personalization. For example, think about public transportation tickets. We may want to incentivize the usage of public transport to reduce the noise and pollution generated by private cars. Instead of reducing the price of the ticket for all citizens, we may want to personalize the price based on behavior. To do so, we use clustering technics. Through them, we may observe that certain citizens with specific characteristics (i.e., young people) use public transportation more often during weekdays than weekends. To incentivize them, we may think about a discount program for weekends, so they keep using it during their free time instead of using their private vehicle.

Association problems. This type of problem is concerned with identifying co-occurrence of events. Usually, supermarkets tend to place complementary products next to each other to incentivize people to buy the second product once they have seen the first one. For example, if we are buying soft drinks, we may also be interested in snacks. Therefore, placing snacks near soft drinks is a good idea. Similarly, we may use association rules for detecting people who may need public support. Usually, public administrations have many social programs to help citizens in need. However, due to bureaucratic inefficiencies or lack of information, many of these programs are unknown for their potential beneficiaries. If we know that somebody that has been approved to receive program A has also the characteristics to apply for program B, we may advise them to do so or may suggest visiting another link on a webpage.

Data reduction problems. Sometimes, due to the huge availability of data, we face problems dealing with too much information. However, many of the information contained in a myriad of variables is sometimes overlapping. In other words, it is not adding extra signal but instead extra noise. Or it could be the case that some variables just add a little bit of signal. In these cases, we may want to reduce the data for better understanding or easier processing (always being aware of the potential trade-off between quantity and richness of information). Data reduction techniques are used to replace a large set of data with a smaller one thus minimizing the amount of information lost.

Causality problems. "What causes what" is one of the main challenges that the scientific method deals with. If I hit a ball, the ball will move. In this case, the causal effect is easy to establish, and our ability to do so has been one of the main drivers behind human evolution. However, establishing causality in social sciences is a much harder task. For example, if we observe an improvement in our local economy, how do we know if it is due to our economic policy or due to another reason (like our competitors performing worse or a supralocal policy)? Or is a crime increase in a specific neighborhood caused by poor lighting in the street or because we reduced the amount of police officers? What if it is a combination of both? What matters more, lighting or police presence? Answering this type of question often involves complicated causal models (especially if we use observational data) or running experiments to collect data to isolate a specific cause (A/B testing).

After seeing problems being solved with data science, it is tempting to think about it as merely a subfield of statistics or even a job performed only by statisticians. Obviously, statistics is a fundamental part in data science but is not the only one. The ocean of data that is drowning every organization in the world needs many more skills and one of the most prominent is computer science. The ability to collect, gather, store, or query large (often messy) databases requires some knowledge of, at least, one programming language. In other words, a data scientist is somebody who knows more statistics than a computer scientist and more computer science than a statistician.

2 Organizing for data science

Data Scientist is the sexiest job of the 21st century. That is how Harvard Business Review titled an article published by Davenport and Patil (2012). According to them, it is a high-ranked professional with the training and curiosity to make discoveries in the world of big data. The huge amounts of data generated and stored by any type of organization plus the results obtained by companies like Google, Netflix, or Amazon are behind the popularity of this type of professional and their high demand in many industries. As an example of the importance of data scientists, we can check how the term has a skyrocketing trend in Google searches (Fig. 3.1).

The concept reflects the fact that organizations were starting to face an amount of data without precedents. Soon, new technologies (like Hadoop or MongoDB) started to appear to make the life of data scientists easier. Following these new developments, data scientists started to specialize in programming languages (like Python or R) and specific software. It is a field in constant

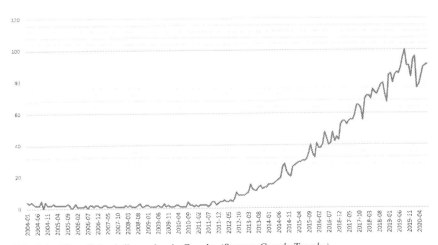

FIG. 3.1 "Data Scientist" searches in Google. *(Source: Google Trends.)*

change as data scientists keep finding novel solutions for old and new problems, helping the industry in developing new tools, processes, and methods to solve them. This is why many data scientists, like those working in Google, Amazon, or Facebook, also conduct academic research. Davenport and Patil define them as a rare combination of data hacking, analytical, communication, and advising skills. In other words, we can define a data scientist as somebody who has some mastering in computer science, statistics, visualization, and domain knowledge.

Computer skills are necessary for gathering, storing, and analyzing data (as we will see in Chapter 5); statistics skills are important because analyzing data without a minimal knowledge of what is going on with algorithms can lead to wrong operationalizations or misinterpretations; visualization because more often than not, results need to be communicated to a nondata audience (think about other departments or even citizenship); and, finally, domain knowledge because data science is not just doing analysis in a vacuum—before doing any analysis, one must to know the right question to answer, which means a data scientist doesn't just needs the skills to answer questions but also the ability to understand the needs of the organization. According to Hal Varian, Chief Economist at Google (Forbes, 2016), "The ability to take data—to be able to understand it, to process it, to extract value from it, to visualize it, to communicate it—that's going to be a hugely important skill in the next decades." However, finding the expertise for all four skills in one single person is not easy. But this is not a problem, because data science is a team sport.

2.1 Managing data science teams

Alex Pentland, the most cited computational scientist and director of the Human Dynamics group at MIT, wrote that "studies of primitive human groups reinforce the idea that social interactions are central to how humans harvest information and make decisions" (Pentland, 2015). Therefore, effectively applying a data science approach for managing smart cities is not only about the data you collect, store, and analyze but also about how people use the output of these analysis (including how decisions are made). While many of the information and publications about data science are centered on technology, methods, or fancy applications, we do believe that the focus should be on people, because every data science project is shaped by the people involved. However, how should these people be organized?

The mix of skills described in the previous subsection serves as the basis to decide how to organize a data science team and how to calibrate the breadth of positions that should reinforce each other. First of all, it is important to note that there are a variety of profiles depending on the expertise in each skill. Carl Anderson, Data Vice President at WW, created a taxonomy of data-related roles in his book "Creating a Data-Driven Organization" (Anderson, 2015) with the following categories: data analyst, data engineers, data scientists, statisticians, and data-visualization specialists; each one has a different mix of skills.

Data analysts have a broad role with experience in many skills and a deep understanding of at least one of them. They are commonly known as domain experts. Data engineers are specialized in collecting, cleaning, and storing data so that more analytical roles can focus on their core capacities and competitive advantages. Data scientists have statistical, programming, and business skills in a, somehow, equilibrated distribution. Statisticians focus on statistical modeling and designing methods for collecting data through surveys, experiments, etc. Data-visualization specialists are people with strong design skills.

After seeing the taxonomy or roles, one may be inclined to think that the best solution is to have a lot of employees in each role. However, it is advisable to follow Jeff Bezos' and his "two-pizza rule" (The Guardian, 2018). This rule states that teams should be small enough to be fed with two pizzas. Of course, the goal of the rule is not to reduce the catering bill but to gain efficiency and scalability. For example, here we have the team profile of Nordstrom's data lab in 2013 (Fig. 3.2).

Creating a data science team is somehow like playing Tetris: you need to fit every piece. By looking at the graph, you can easily spot the experts in statistics, programming, data visualization, business, or those people with more equilibrium in their skill composition. The main idea here is that you do not need a team of superstar programmers but the right equilibrium of skills to look at the same problem from different angles.

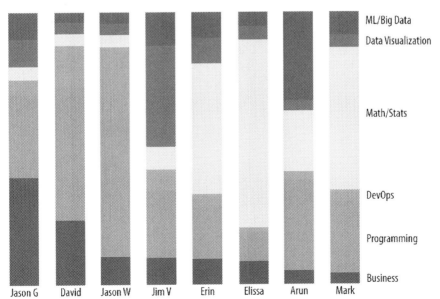

FIG. 3.2 Example of a Data Science team. *(Source: Creating a data-driven organization (https://www.oreilly.com/library/view/creating-a-data-driven/9781491916902/).)*

2.2 Managing data science departments and organizations

Should the data science team be centralized in a single unit or decentralized in different departments? Should we hire a data scientist for each department, or should we train our own employees in data science skills? Should data scientists be managed by the CIO or the city council, or should they be under guidance of other policy-oriented roles? These are important questions that smart city managers are thinking about. However, this type of question assumes enough transformational power inside the organization to make the necessary changes. Since it is not usually the case (unless the reader is a mayor of a city council with enough support and budget), we should focus on a different set of questions. Mathematician DJ Patil, former Chief Data Scientist of the United States Office of Science and Technology Policy, proposes the following questions (Patil & Mason, 2015):

- What are the short-term and long-term goals for data?
- Who are the supporters and who are the opponents?
- Where are conflicts likely to arise?
- What systems are needed to make the data scientists successful?
- What are the costs and time horizons required to implement those systems?

Therefore, the focus is not about what technology we should use but rather what are we going to do with our data? In fact, technological tools are almost irrelevant because disruption in the software industry is the norm. Mastering specific software can be useful in the short term but an obstacle in the mid-long term if we fail to adapt to new developments or create too many routines. In contrast, what really matters is organizational culture. It is well-known that "culture eats strategy for breakfast" (a phrase originated by Peter Drucker), so having an organization that is able to understand their problems, formulate the right questions, collect and analyze the necessary data, and, finally, implement the results, is far more important than the specific technology used in any of these steps. As Michael Flowers, former New York City Chief Analytics Officer (NYC Office of Data Analytics) states, "being data-driven is not primarily a challenge of technology; it is a challenge of direction and organizational leadership" (Goldstein & Lauren, 2013).

3 Managing data science projects to solve urban issues

Putting data science to work for smart cities supposes to manage such projects efficiently (Grimaldi, 2019; Grimaldi, Diaz Cely, & Arboleda, 2020; Grimaldi, Fernandez, & Carrasco, 2019). We propose a three-main-step process as guidance, which we encapsulate in a framework, the Urban Data Canvas Model, represented in Fig. 3.3:

- Problem statement:
- Developing the solution

Data Science technologies Chapter | 3 97

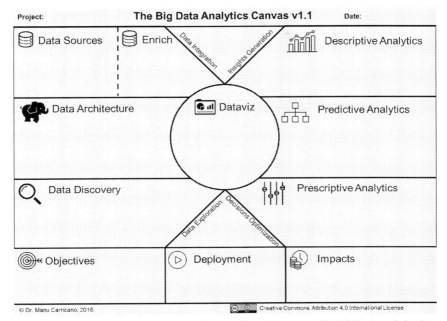

FIG. 3.3 The Big Data analytics canvas. *(Source: Manu Carricano, ESADE Business School.)*

- Data sources
- Data architecture
- Data exploration
- Insights generation
- Advanced models
• Governing the solution implementation

3.1 Problem statement

One of the main challenges is to clearly define the problem we need to resolve. A committee needs to be set and follow the next steps (Fig. 3.4).

3.2 Developing the solution

The canvas provides guidance on how to execute—sequentially—the different steps of the data-driven resolution of urban challenges:

- **Data Sources**
    In a city, the data can be mainly captured either by sensors or from citizens (Derqui & Grimaldi, 2020; Grimaldi & Fernandez, 2017). Sensors are devices connected through different technologies like Wifi, NFC, 2G or 3G (Derqui, Grimaldi, & Fernandez, 2020; Grimaldi & Fernandez, 2019). Their

- ✓ Write down the top 5 business problems you would like to solve.
- ✓ What data will be required to solve each of these business problems?
- ✓ Which 2 business problems demostrate the highest impact and feasibility? These are the ones should should focus on.
- ✓ What respective back-of-the-envelope calculation of the ROI for these 2 use cases?
- ✓ What machine-intelligence models might be tested on and applied to this data to solve your business problems?
- ✓ What are the change-management and operational processes required for the implementation of the machine-intelligence solutions?
- ✓ What are your short- and long-term implementation strategies?

FIG. 3.4 Applying Data Science workflows to business problems. *(Source: Manu Carricano, ESADE Business School.)*

connection to the existing Internet is usually called the Internet of Things (IoT), permits the collect of data and to transform them into information which helps to monitor and manage the urban services (Vojnovic, 2014). Besides, they represent business opportunities for companies or entrepreneurs who develop services for citizens or public authorities (Grimaldi & Fernandez, 2017; Grimaldi et al., 2019). They are important drivers to build smart cities and can address five type of urban needs as described hereunder: (Badalian, 2015; Gubbi, Buyya, Marusic, & Palaniswami, 2013; Jin, Gubbi, Marusic, & Palaniswami, 2014):

(1) Geolocalized traffic information permits to determine the fastest or shortest path and the corresponding time of duration to the desired destination. Besides, the algorithm takes into account the actual size of the traffic and the average speed of the vehicles. This real-time information can be used to alert Public Authority, Police, or Emergency and optimize the protection and the transport of wounded to hospitals.

(2) Combining information about atmospheric conditions (temperature, rain, humidity, pressure, wind speed) with water levels (at oceans, rivers, lakes, dams, and other reservoirs) allows Public authorities to develop preventive and prescriptive actions plan to mitigate the effects of flood, snow melting, and dam breakage and correctly ascertain the needs of water to citizens.

(3) Looking for car parking space is time and fuel consuming. Drivers spend time trying to find a parking slot (while they could be spending more efficiently this time in the marketplace or in leisure) at a slow speed (which increases fuel consumption and pollution).

(4) Pollution is especially risky for people at the two ends of the population spectrum: children and elderly. Therefore, providing real time environmental data allows to generate alerts when dangerous gases (like metals, carbon monoxide, sulfur dioxide, or ozone) exceed authorized thresholds in a specific area of the city.

(5) Security is another concern in many cities around the world. Installing cameras to monitor behavior can contribute to diminish or

disincentivize unwanted behaviors. However, this type of intervention comes with two associated costs: the need for a specialized analytics software to detect real time events like robbery, fightings, etc. and the need to balance the intervention with citizen privacy.

Sundmaeker, Guillemin, Friess, and Woelfflé (2010) define IoT as a technology that connects physical objects to the Internet and enables interaction capabilities between these objects and other systems. He named it as the third phase of the internet revolution, after the World Wide Web (www) in the 1990s and the mobile Internet in the 2000s; moreover he names IoT as the most disruptive of them. Manyika et al. (2014) estimate that there exist more than nine billion connected devices in 2014 and estimates 50 billion by 2025. This growth of connected devices creates endless possibilities in terms of how to apply the technology.

Citizens as sensors

Data can come also from citizens (Boulos & Al-Shorbaji, 2014). There are posts uploaded in social channels or instantaneous messages of communication. Data captured from citizens can be split also in two categories: with formal consent or without.

- **Data Architecture**

    Today, smart cities (and especially brown-field—see Chapter 1) usually inherit from many transactional systems designed to respond to the needs of specific municipal departments. This vision in silos (as we have already commented) has huge limitations. One of the main challenges resides in to map the existing information system and determines where the required data is located and how it can be intercorrelated to the rest of data of the model. Usually, the solution is to create a datalake, a repository that receives and integrates all the data coming from the municipal transactional systems. At that moment, the problem of consent of the data needs to be resolved: how can we justify that data collected for this purpose can be used for the purpose (maybe different) of the project that we are about to tackle? It could be difficult to seize, but the main issue is not that the data does not exist but is how to get access to it. Experts reveal only 5%–10% present in the transactional systems are really used, managed, and valued.

    If data are missing, a subproject can be defined that aims at organizing that collects: manually (for example, contacting the citizens) or developing an interface to an information system not integrated in the datalake environment. In this phase, different meetings with the specific owners of the data to resolve legal and technical issues are necessary. These meetings can include private and public entities through a PPP model.

- **Data Exploration**

    Data captured usually do not meet the necessary requirements of quality to be analyzed to define urban models (Spruit & Pietzka, 2015). Nevertheless, the urban data need an important level of accuracy to be used by technicians and politicians to manage changes of urban services; for example, take the decisions that will affect citizens' daily life. A long and time-consuming period of exploration and data cleaning is usually necessary. The main issue is to integrate all the data coming from different sources and formats. This phase aims at improving the unity of the data (same data are present in different ways in different information systems), the consistency of the data (inadequate data in the wrong format can be included in the resulting dataset), the accuracy of the data (values need to have enough precision to give the information we are expecting), correct frequency (how timely is the data?), correct level of aggregation, etc.

- **Insights Generation**

    In this phase, the data analysis and modeling must be divided into three levels:

    Personal data with previous consent to take actions at the individual/citizen level; the data modeling is an opportunity to identify gaps in the management of urban services (poor people who should have access to subsidies and don't ask for it, for example)

    Aggregated and anonymized data to follow, understand, and anticipate future trends

    Research and science purposes

4 Interview with Miami's CIO

4.1 The backbone of data-driven cities

"The hardest part of any data-related project is not technology per se but arranging the team and all the people infrastructure you need to succeed. For example, we did a training in Power BI because people had an appetite for it. However, there was no project to implement what they learned about dashboards. We noticed that data projects are like a life cycle; you need to have a complete roadmap in mind. Is not that you say: 'let's do a training on this' and next week you have dashboards everywhere. That's why we focused on training through our Innovation Academy; for example, teaching people how to apply design thinking tools. In one of these courses, we focused on metrics to account for different stages of existing processes. This allowed us to show our staff how, by using just a little data, you can improve things a lot. By only counting how much time it takes to go through each step of a process, they realized how things could be improved and in what step they should focus the improvements. In that sense, we took a very elementary approach back to the basics to create the spark to light a big fire, which ultimately was our goal. And the most important thing: it was not the data team who was looking at this data but everybody involved, from frontline staff to internal personnel. The appetite for the data-related project was incentivized through the whole organization. This is still an ongoing process and probably will ever be. You need people at every position to value the benefits of using data no matter how small their problem is."

4.2 The shinning projects of data-driven cities

"Once you have the backbone in place and the right culture has trickled down to the whole organization, it is time to start working on more sophisticated projects. This year we launched a partnership with Google that started with a 16-day project to design and set-up our future data warehouse. We were able to do it fast because the people infrastructure was already in place. Nobody was surprised that we did it because they were already convinced about the power of data. We also started another project with Mastercard to know how businesses are opening and closing in our city. This type of advanced project needs to be grounded in people who have an appetite for data."

4.3 The team

"As for the data team, we look for business analysts. In that sense, we need people that do not just understand data but the problems we are dealing with. Of course, we also have data scientists that deal with data-intensive projects and focus much more on visualization or front-end development than business analysts. Then you need an architect, especially if you have legacy systems. You need somebody who is capable of adapting these legacy systems into a common environment. If you want a solid team, I would say you need two or three people in each position. That's the core we need as a technology department to support all the other departments."

4.4 Linking data teams with the whole organization

"We have been working really close with the Strategic Planning team at the city council. This is important to make sure that data is a central part of the city strategy; to make sure that data is really entitled to the city strategic plan. Now the strategic plan is heavily informed by data. Moreover, we created the figure of 'data lead' that sits in each department working with their performance metrics and make sure that we get all the data we need."

4.5 DTFT: Do the fucking thing

"I have a paper on my desk that says 'DTFT: Do the fucking thing.' That's important because many departments have great minds discussing what to do, but at the end of the year almost nothing is done. To avoid this situation, I would recommend finding an external partner that is willing to help and that can inspire your staff. It's always about straightforwardness. Even if you are collaborating with a big company, you need to ask them for a small team with compromised people. For example, the Google project that we did was only 16 days on purpose, very compressed, and we allocated the time for it. It is not that you dedicate somebody 10% of the time to that project; it is more like a cluster with committed people meeting in the same room to solve a specific problem. Then it becomes real. In addition, acting fast shows you where your organizational gaps really are, something hard to detect just by thinking about it; many of the things we detected for improvement were small steps in the middle of procedures nobody ever thought about. You never know until you try it. If it's a fail, it's a fail, but at least you learn why you failed."

4.6 Do something useful

"When you observe resistance to collaboration, data sharing from other departments, or resistance because they do not see the value of what you're proposing, it is probably because there is some truth in that. The way to approach nontechnical people is solving problems for them. You're not using technology or data just because it is fancy. You need to solve people's problems. Which are the two or three most pressing problems in each department? Once you identify one, for example, business licensing, you go for it. You split the problem into smaller parts (for example, you split the process to get a business license step-by-step), and you start to identify barriers or improvements. Once you explain in a transparent way a process and how to improve it to a department manager, you become an asset for him. Collaborating with you is not an extra thing to do anymore; you become part of their team by solving problems. You have to be the first in breaking these organizational silos. You have to scan the organization looking for pain. Then you go and embed yourself in that pain. You need to not just analyze but live the process to understand that pain. Suddenly, you are not a pain anymore but a resource for the department. In the same way businesses have to put themselves in the shoes of their customers, we need to put ourselves in the shoes of department managers. In that sense, it is very important to know how to formulate problems. The problem cannot be 'I do not have this or that technology.' That's not the problem; that's a potential solution to your real problem. With these actions, we become the problem-solvers of the organization. And then you can do data-driven things, because that's part of the solution, but you need to start with the problem."

Data-driven tools for urban resilience

For the last few years, with several initiatives from research and multilateral organizations, the concept of resilience opened up a range of theoretical conversations that often focused on building long-term resilience strategies to cope with stressors derived from climate change or social inequalities. Different initiatives were aimed at equipping city managers with digital tools based on the operative side of the concept. Emergency and risk managers were also coping with incidents demanding resources to improve their capacity to deal with disasters or business continuity.

The results of this situation are that we can find ready-to-use value propositions in the market and, more importantly, also find creative teams available to adapt and launch methods, tools, and technologies to improve the resilience of our communities and organizations. The COVID-19 virus has not affected all of these assets. Before the pandemic, researchers, practitioners, and innovators were already trying to promote strategic, tactical, and operational tools for a resilience-thinking approach ready to be used by cities and businesses. However, adoption of these tools by the market was sometimes slow, and tech evangelization remained necessary. The COVID crisis could have changed this scenario and provided the opportunity to help with the global situation, boosting the use of data to build more resilient cities.

As data science is proliferating in all fields of expertise, urban resilience is no exception—new applications are being developed every day. In every cycle of the DRR, data management can add value to the mission to build resilient cities. The World Bank, UNDRR, GFDRR (GFDRR, 2018), UN (UNCTAD, 2019) are considering, ML data analytics and big data offer great support for emergency response and urban resilience. This multilateral organizations are supporting initiatives to tackle physical exposure and vulnerability, risk mapping and damage prediction, or postdisaster event mapping and damage assessment with open-source software and open data (Berrone, Ricart, & Carrasco-Farré, 2016; Carrasco-Farré & Sobrepere, 2015), but we can also find impact innovators and private SMEs participating in innovation ecosystems (European Commission, 2021) building new approaches based on data-driven tools. For example, we can find emerging specialized solutions in the market to build resilience by digitalizing resilience and business continuity plans to obtain the key data that will allow more advancing use of datasets to simulate scenarios with cascading effects predictions, using graph theory and ML techniques (Rezilio, 2021). Using these approaches, operational resilience will be improved in all phases of its cycle (preparation, response, recovery, and mitigation).

Never before have we had so many tools accessible to nonprogramming experts thanks to virtualization and cloud service offerings. Business continuity and disaster recovery principals can fuel the movement of data-driven cities to build resilience, integrating this myriad of innovative systems (proprietary, open-source or hybrid, public or private). Therefore, to drive toward the vision of creating more resilient value chains, urban services, or local communities, we will need the convergence of different skills and knowledge to ensure and sustain the adoption and operation of business continuity and resilience management frameworks supported by the sober use of technology (Grimaldi, 2020).

5 Indicators for urban retail

5.1 The importance of indicators

Most decisions made by many stakeholders and public administrations regarding performance criteria are usually based on individual perception or specific analysis at a given time. This lack of valid information means that decisions are not always right, leading to an inefficient allocation of private or public resources. In contrast, the best way to make decisions is to have a battery of data and indicators.

But what do we mean by indicators? Can they help us design the redefinition of a city? Do they serve as a tool to determine the best area for setting up a business? Do they allow you to see trends in the evolution of a municipality? All these questions can be answered using data. In fact, if there is a way to achieve the best possible result in these challenges, it is by collecting and analyzing indicators.

5.2 How to select indicators

An indicator is a number that, once measured, can be interpreted and compared to provide information on patterns or trends, which will ultimately allow us to make more accurate decisions. The system is applied to various fields of science when observing and analyzing processes. Sciences such as medicine, physics, meteorology, economics, and sociology are common users of different indicators.

The difficulty lies in determining what the relevant information is, what indicators will allow us to obtain the most accurate results, whether temporary monitoring can be applied, and, above all, the task of data collection. At this point, it is important to mention that data cannot be static and independent; you need to look for the relationship patterns that exist. In addition, if historical records are available, you can add a lot of value to the information by simply observing the evolution of the system, as well as the effect of different actions carried out over the period analyzed. On the other hand, having a historical record of indicators allows us to make retrospective studies (see the effect of the decisions made) and prospective ones (such as the simulation of possible future scenarios from the patterns found).

The possibilities of working with urban indicators are endless. From how many people drive on a given street to the time spent visiting a monument or retailer, through the prediction of the behavior of citizens or tourists. If we also have historical data, we can determine the times of maximum hourly, weekly, and monthly activity of a street. Applicability to issues such as what is the best location for retailers or when to open and close a business is obvious.

5.3 Retail streets and the principle of agglomeration

Retail streets, as well as shopping malls, are two of the clearest examples of the economic concept of agglomeration. It's really nothing more than the spatial concentration of retail spaces. Retail streets were born as a result of the location of stores without prior coordination, while shopping malls are their logical evolution. In shopping malls, it is the owner of the space who promotes the process of commercial agglomeration.

The success of retail streets and shopping centers is based precisely on the principle of agglomeration:

First, there is a willingness on the part of buyers to reduce the cost of travel to buy. This cost not only includes the actual price to be paid in money (gasoline expenses, public transportation, etc.) but also includes the cost in time.

If shops are located in a small space or a short distance away, the cost (both in money and time) of consumers is reduced. And it shrinks as this space gets smaller or the agglomeration bigger. That is, a buyer will prefer to travel to a commercial hub to do their shopping rather than visit a number of isolated shops. Therefore, businesses attract greater customer traffic when they are spatially concentrated than when they are dispersed.

Second, for consumers there is also another benefit of business agglomeration: the ability to compare products. The possibility of being able to compare similar products generates a better purchasing decision, increasing the benefits of buying in a retail street or a mall. Comparison is easy in a crowded commercial environment and, conversely, very expensive when businesses are spatially separated. In fact, having shops separated spatially can become so costly that it outweighs the relative benefit of product comparison, making it only economically viable on one retail street or a mall. This added benefit (that of comparison) will also generate more buyer traffic.

Third, it is also important to note that competition over the prices of similar products is more intense when retailers are spatially concentrated. This competition, which generates lower prices or higher quality products, is beneficial to the consumer.

Fourth, another factor of paramount importance is the complementarity of certain retail activities. For example, those shoppers who approach a shoe store in a mall will also tend to visit some clothing store and vice versa, so certain types of shops (e.g., shoe stores) benefit from the presence of other types of shops (e.g., clothing stores).

In short, it is vitally important to choose the location of a business taking into account the space agglomeration and neighboring businesses to generate complementarity. If we do it right, we will ensure good consumer traffic, so sales will depend on the competitiveness of a city retail sector. In addition, this economic healthiness promoted by retail activities will also generate taxes to public authorities.

5.4 Retail location

"The three key elements to a successful business are location, location, and location." This phrase, attributed to McDonald's founder Ray Krok, perfectly illustrates the importance of choosing a good location for a retailer. In fact, it is not enough to have the most competitive prices in the city, a prestigious brand, or a unique product. If the location is not right, the failure of the project is assured. When things go wrong, we can improve the product, renovate the establishment, or redefine the marketing strategy. But having to change location again has very high economic and logistical costs. It is therefore advisable to make the decision in a slow, responsible, and data-driven approach. However, what factors need to be considered to locate a business?

There is no single answer to this question as it will depend on the type of business and the contextual factors of each city. In any case, some of the location criteria that determine the success or failure of a retail project are its urban centrality, the socioeconomic characteristics of the neighborhood and its population, an analysis of competitors, transportation options, among others.

That is why it is necessary to have the most accurate and up-to-date knowledge of the city: retail streets, urban projects, socioeconomic data, land price, legislation, typology of existing commercial establishments in the area, etc.

5.5 How to revitalize empty premises?

One of the main problems facing city councils is the high presence of empty commercial premises in the urban space. In recent years, the situation of economic crisis and the COVID pandemic has led to the closure of many businesses. Likewise, the completion of real estate operations initiated during the boom period has introduced new commercial premises that are difficult to rent due to their peripheral location. Apart from the economic damage caused to the owners of these retail spaces, the proliferation of empty premises generates a situation of commercial discontinuity and a risk of increasing desertification of the streets and main thoroughfares. Therefore, what data-related steps should a city council follow to revitalize empty premises?

In general, these strategies must necessarily be based on a thorough knowledge of the urban environment in which the empty premises are located. For example, we cannot adopt the same policies of dynamization and promotion of the empty premises in a central street than in a retail space in the outskirts of the city. In particular, economic development departments in a city council should follow three phases:

> Phase 1: Prepare a census of empty premises and economic activities. To begin with, it is necessary to know how many empty premises we have and where they are located. If possible, it is important collect it at the cadastral parcel or with specific coordinates. By doing so, we can then aggregate the information at different administrative levels.
>
> But if we only counted the empty premises, we would lose very useful information for their dynamization. For this reason, we need to know what other retail spaces are active using a classification of activities.
>
> Phase 2: Prepare a diagnosis of empty premises based on indicators. From the census of empty premises and economic activities, we could generate indicators that allow comparison with other municipalities and disaggregation at the district, neighborhood, and retail street. In this way we can offer an objective diagnosis of the situation of empty premises at all territorial

scales and their evolution over time. The first two indicators we use refer directly to empty premises:
The Retail Occupancy Index (ROI) has a direct relationship with the health of the retail sector, although it may also be linked to the urban model (use of street-level spaces for other uses such as parking or housing) or to the owner's expectations. In general, a healthy occupation rate is above the 80% occupancy threshold, below which it is considered that the situation is beginning to be problematic as there is a risk of increasing retail desertification. Before, we explicitly mentioned the need to collect all this information at the coordinates (latitude and longitude) level because it may be the case that some specific streets are facing problems of occupation while a parallel street does not. Therefore, having disaggregated data for being able to make accurate interventions is key.
Shops that generate attraction (equipment for the person and home and culture and leisure) with respect to the total of occupied premises. Thus, for example, in neighborhoods with high density and commercial attraction, it is necessary to propose new specialized and innovative activities and avoid the main retail streets if they are to achieve affordable prices. On the other hand, in neighborhoods with low density and low commercial attraction, it is necessary to focus on the main retail streets and look for business opportunities in everyday sectors that cover specific and localized needs.
Phase 3: Define measures to revitalize empty premises. Based on the information provided by the indicators, we can design the best type of strategy to revitalize empty premises in the area under study. If the city or neighborhood we are in enjoys good retail health, the measures to revitalize empty premises can be relatively simple and will probably suffice in retail promotion or urban microsurgery. If, on the other hand, we have detected serious problems, more drastic measures will be needed that involve substantial urban changes, agreements with real estate agents or incentives for citizens interested in developing an activity. Specifically, we can distinguish three types of measures that can help revitalize the empty retail spaces like improving the public space (wider sidewalks or pedestrianization, improve the lighting system, etc.) or reaching agreements with real estate owners to promote the occupation of retail spaces. Although these previous interventions will also benefit from a data-driven approach, another option stands out as a measure that can highly benefit from data availability: a recommender system for entrepreneurs.

Many entrepreneurs and citizens usually ask their city councils for information about how and where to open a new business. In these cases, city councils can offer location information to identify business opportunities through publishing layers of data like population density, public transportation, or retail location studies. Another possibility is for the city council to contact the real estate owners that are less motivated to rent their premises (in some cases due to previous bad experiences) and offer them a feasibility study to find out what type of activity would be possible taking into account the urban and environmental regulations, the characteristics of the premises, and the type of business in the area. Based on this study, an indicative budget can be drawn up for the cost of the reform. From there, the city council could put the owner in contact with citizens who want to carry out an activity suitable for the premises.

In addition, a very useful tool is to publish information on empty premises for sale and rent on web platforms so that all those people or franchises that are interested can access the entire offer. To offer additional information that is very useful for those who want to start an activity, the following aspects should be included: search options by map, by price, or by area, in addition to mapping of the urban planning regulations in relation to the uses of the ground floors. Finally, it is also important to offer data about the location of the retail activities located around the empty premises.

In short, it is only from an exhaustive knowledge of the retail reality that public administration can take actions for economic dynamization.

5.6 Indicators to measure the health of urban retail

While the technological advances have provided us with complicated techniques and algorithms, the use of statistical indicators to guide the decision-making of private and public agents linked to the retail sector do not necessarily need to be rocket science.

What is the best location for a business? What business clusters work best? Do we have a problem of empty premises in our neighborhood? Does my city attract or expel consumers? Should the use of the ground floors be regulated to favor retail activities?

All these questions asked by private and public agents linked to the retail sector do not have an easy answer. Most of them make decisions on the location of new businesses or on commercial dynamization based on subjective parameters such as their experience, their knowledge of the environment, or the opinion of real estate agents. However, to choose the best option it is essential to look for objective parameters.

For example, EIXOS Economic Observatory, a Catalan company, has a geospatial information system with almost 1,000,000 retail premises in their database of cities around the world. The data-capturing method is through field work with mobile devices and periodic updating. The EIXOS database makes it possible to distinguish, in addition to empty premises, between 72 commercial subsectors that have been grouped into 8 large sectors (home apparel, personal equipment, hotels and restaurants, commercial services, culture and leisure, daily food, private transport, and other sectors).

Graph 1 Commercial layers in the center of Madrid captured by EIXOS.

From all this information, indicators can be generated that allow city managers and entrepreneurs to evaluate the health of the retail sector.

5.6.1 Commercial occupation

The Occupancy Rate calculates the number of occupied premises in relation to the total number of premises with commercial use in a given area. It is evident that high occupancy is directly related to good retail health, although it can also be linked, for example, to an urban model that prioritizes commercial use in the main streets and encourages other uses in the rest of the city (parking, housing, etc.). In any case, the studies carried out by EIXOS Economic Observatory have been able to establish a threshold of 80% occupancy, below which a street runs the risk of suffering from growing commercial desertification that leads establishments to gradually close their points of sale.

Thus, for practical purposes, the best option is to locate the points of sale in streets where the commercial occupancy exceeds 80%. However, the possibility of making a risky bet—streets with low occupancy and, consequently, with low rental prices—should not be ruled out if there is some external factor that could reverse the situation: urban improvements, new equipment, fashionable neighborhoods, etc.

The revitalization of streets with a low commercial occupancy is an arduous task that has to be undertaken in collaboration with the public administration, among others, of the real estate agents and neighborhood associations. The most common actions are the improvement of the public space—pedestrianization, expansion of sidewalks, lighting, signage—and the online publication of the offer of available premises or the promotion of the relocation of activities toward empty premises. Local administration can also take a more active role through mediation between owners and entrepreneurs. Another option is to carry out feasibility studies to find out what type of activity could work in an empty place (according to regulations, characteristics of the place, competition, and characteristics of the neighborhood) and offer this study to those who want to establish a business.

References

Anderson, C. (2015). *Creating a data-driven organization: Practical advice from the trenches.* O'Reilly.

Badalian, R. (2015). IoT: The gateway to sensor data analytics. *Advancing Microelectronics, 42*(3).

Berrone, P., Ricart, J. E., & Carrasco-Farré, C. (2016). The open kimono: Toward a general framework for open data initiatives in cities. *California Management Review, 59*(1). https://doi.org/10.1177/0008125616683703.

Boulos, M. N. K., & Al-Shorbaji, N. M. (2014). On the Internet of Things, smart cities and the WHO Healthy Cities. *International Journal of Health Geographics.*

Carrasco-Farré, C., & Sobrepere, X. (2015). Open government data: An assessment of the Spanish municipal situation. *Social Science Computer Review, 33*(5). https://doi.org/10.1177/0894439314560678.

Davenport, T. H., & Patil, D. J. (2012). Data scientist: The sexiest job of the 21st century. *Harvard Business Review.* In press.

Derqui, B., & Grimaldi, D. (2020). Data on the sustainability profile and food waste management in primary and secondary schools: The case of the Catalonia region in Spain. *Data in Brief*, 28. https://doi.org/10.1016/j.dib.2019.104825. In press.

Derqui, B., Grimaldi, D., & Fernandez, V. (2020). Building and managing sustainable schools: The case of food waste. *Journal of Cleaner Production*, 243, 118533. https://doi.org/10.1016/j.jclepro.2019.118533. In press.

European Commission. (2021). *Horizon Europe programme (HORIZON)—Work programme 2021–2022*.

Forbes. (2016). (Accessed 16 June 2021).

GFDRR. (2018). *Machine learning for disaster risk management*. Washington, DC: GFDRR.

Goldstein, B., & Lauren, D. (2013). *Beyond transparency: Open data and the future of civic innovation*. Code for America Press.

Grimaldi, D. (2019). Can we analyse political discourse using Twitter? Evidence from Spanish 2019 presidential election. *Social Network Analysis and Mining*, 49. https://doi.org/10.1007/s13278-019-0594-6. In press.

Grimaldi, D. (2020). Exploring challenges and solutions to improve urban resilience. *International Journal of Environmental Sciences & Natural Resources*, 26(2), 53–54. https://doi.org/10.19080/IJESNR.2020.26.556182.

Grimaldi, D., & Fernandez, V. (2017). The road to school. The Barcelona case. *Cities*, 65, 24–31. https://doi.org/10.1016/j.cities.2017.01.013. In press.

Grimaldi, D., & Fernandez, V. (2019). Performance of an internet of things project in the public sector: The case of Nice smart city. *The Journal of High Technology Management Research*, 30, 27–39. https://doi.org/10.1016/j.hitech.2018.12.003.

Grimaldi, D., Fernandez, V., & Carrasco, C. (2019). Heuristic for the localization of new shops based on business and social criteria. *Technological Forecasting and Social Change*, 142, 249–257. https://doi.org/10.1016/j.techfore.2018.07.034.

Grimaldi, D., Diaz Cely, J., & Arboleda, H. (2020). Inferring the votes in a new political landscape: The case of the 2019 Spanish Presidential elections. *Journal of Big Data*, 58(7). https://doi.org/10.1186/s40537-020-00334-5. In press.

Gubbi, J., Buyya, R., Marusic, S., & Palaniswami, M. (2013). Internet of things (IoT): A vision, architectural elements, and future directions. *Future Generation Computer Systems*, 29(3).

Jin, J., Gubbi, J., Marusic, S., & Palaniswami, M. (2014). An information framework for creating a smart city through internet of things. *IEEE Internet of Things Journal*, 1(2).

Manyika, J., Chui, M., Bisson, P., Woetzel, J., Dobbs, R., Bughin, J., & Aharon, D. (2014). The internet of things: Mapping the Value beyond the Hype. *McKinsey*.

Patil, D. J., & Mason, H. (2015). *Data driven: Creating a data culture*. O'Reilly.

Pentland, A. (2015). *Social physics: How social networks can make us smarter*. Penguin.

Provost, F., & Fawcett, T. (2013). *Data Science for Business: What you need to know about data mining and data-analytic thinking*. O'Reilly Media, Inc.

Rezilio. (2021). rezilio.com.

Spruit, M., & Pietzka, K. (2015). MD3M: The master data management maturity model. *Computers in Human Behavior*.

Sundmaeker, H., Guillemin, P., Friess, P., & Woelfflé, S. (2010). Vision and challenges for realising the Internet of Things. *Cluster of European research projects on the internet of things, European Commision*, 3(3).

(2018). The Guardian. (Accessed 16 June 2021).

UNCTAD. (4 March 2019). *The role of science, technology, and innovation in building resilient communities, including through the contribution of citizen science*. Report of the Secretary-General.

Vojnovic, I. (2014). Urban sustainability: Research, politics, policy and practice. *Cities*.

Chapter 4

Roadmap to develop a data-driven city

Didier Grimaldi[a], Jose M. Sallan[b], Josep Miquel Piqué Huerta[c], Jesús Soler Puebla[d], Kristi Shalla[e], and Carlos Carrasco-Farré[f]

[a]Ramon Llull University, La Salle Faculty, Barcelona, Spain, [b]Universitat Politècnica de Catalunya, BarcelonaTech, Barcelona, Spain, [c]Technova, Ramon Llull University, La Salle Faculty, Barcelona, Spain, [d]Virtual Abogados, Barcelona, Spain, [e]Smart City Consultant, Washington, DC, United States, [f]Ramon Llull University—ESADE Business School, Barcelona, Spain

1 The data-driven strategy decision

1.1 The smart city approach

Cities play a relevant role in economic and social development. According to data from the United Nations (United Nations, Department of Economic and Social Affairs, Population Division (2019), 2018), 55% of the global human population lives in cities, amounting to 4.2 billion people. From the same source, we learn that this fraction amounts to 78.5% in more developed countries. On the other hand, cities are estimated to consume 2% of land, generate around 70% of global GDP, and use 60% of global energy. As much of the growth of urban population is coming from less developed cities, it is safe to predict that the weight of cities in the global social landscape will increase in the coming years (Madlener & Sunak, 2011).

The smart city concept was born to provide tools to increase cities' sustainability and ability to meet the needs of its inhabitants (Albino, Berardi, & Dangelico, 2015). Technologies of information and communication (ICT) play a relevant role in the field of smart cities. The ICT approach to smart cities can be summarized in the definition of the smart city as an "instrumented, interconnected, and intelligent city" (Harrison et al., 2010). The "instrumented" term refers to extensive use of technology such as Internet of Things (IoT) to retrieve data from the city; "interconnected" means that those data are consolidated in large repositories; and "intelligent" denotes the use of those data in analytics and modeling tools to inform strategic and operational decisions and to provide services to citizens. This approach to smart cities has been criticized as too close to the interests of IT corporations and considers citizens as their captive clients (Grimaldi & Fernandez, 2017; Grimaldi, Fernandez, & Carrasco, 2018).

A response to this criticism is to build a smart city with a new transformation approach that uses insights from urban technology (Tran Thi Hoang, Dupont, & Camargo, 2019), innovation ecosystems (Zygiaris, 2013), entrepreneurship (Kummitha, 2019), and economic geography (Bunnell & Coe, 2001; Komninos, Pallot, & Schaffers, 2013). This approach will be developed in this chapter.

1.2 The transformation to a data-driven city

Making good decisions depends on data quality (Derqui & Grimaldi, 2020; Grimaldi, Diaz, Arboleda, & Fernandez, 2019; Grimaldi, Fernandez, & Carrasco, 2019). In the context of cities, this assertion is valid in multiple contexts: city hall members need high-quality data to make decisions (Grimaldi, 2019); entrepreneurs can take advantage of high-quality data about city life to make strategic decisions; data availability can make city systems more effective, thus enhancing sustainability; and citizens' everyday life can be improved with city data, sometimes through products built by entrepreneurs or city hall. To achieve those benefits, present-day cities must engage in transformation into a data-driven smart city. We believe that being data-driven leads to a positive effect on the triple bottom line: profit (economic development), planet (sustainability), and people (increase of citizens' well-being).

One of the main benefits of the data-driven concept is that politicians and urban managers can make more informed decisions. Decisionmakers can use dashboards (Grimaldi, 2019) and machine learning algorithms as inputs in the decision-making process. Those tools help to make better decisions than when based on intuition and anecdotal evidence alone. But data-driven decision processes are not exempt from drawbacks. The belief that algorithm automation brings efficient, neutral decisions leads to technocratic governance (Janssen & Kuk, 2016). This belief is far from being true, as we have evidence that algorithms can introduce unintentional biases, reinforce previous discrimination, or discard relevant information. Kashin, King, and Soneji (2015) report systematic bias in U.S. Social Security Administration forecasts, introduced by the econometric models used to perform those forecasts. Algorithms used to calculate risks of reoffending criminals are fed with criminal records of previous offences, which can be biased by previous decisions based on discriminatory beliefs. Decisionmakers must be aware of these potential biases and keep in mind that the outcomes of decisions based on automated algorithms are as good as the data they are fed and the human beings who govern the decision-making process. The ethical implication coming from algorithm bias can be overcome by techniques like algorithmic effect assessment (Reisman, Schultz, Crawford, & Whittaker, 2018), so that the benefits of a data-driven approach can overcome the costs. We will discuss the ethical implications of algorithms and machine learning concerning urban strategy and data governance for smart cities at the end of this chapter.

In the following section, we provide a roadmap to develop data-driven smart cities, defining the steps that go from the inception of the idea of smart city to maturity. In Appendix I, we provide a questionnaire that acts as a self-assessment tool to help urban managers recognize the stage of development they are in and suggest the next steps to take to enhance city transformation.

2 Roadmap for developing data-driven smart cities

Smart cities need urban, economic, social, and governance transformation. Technology (sensors, communication, storage, visualization, robots, 3D printing, drones, etc.) will create value if we understand who needs the data and for what kind of decisions and actions: in the public dimension, for better management of the infrastructure and services in the city; in the private dimension for providing products and services personalized at the right time and place; in the academic dimension for learning, researching, and proposing what's next; and in the societal dimension for making their own decisions, making their activities, and sharing their experiences. In this chapter, we shed light on the process to build a Data-Driven Smart City as the last stage of the Smart City Transformation in the Urban, Economic, Social and Governance dimension, with the alignment of the actors (government, industry, academia, society). This model follows the work developed by Josep Pique (IASP President 2016–18) and Luis Sanz (IASP Director General 1996–2019), which was presented at IASP World Conference on Science and Technology Parks in Recife in 2013 and Beijing in 2015, and applied among others at 22@Barcelona in Spain (European Capital of Innovation 2014–16) and Ruta N—Medellín in Colombia (Most Innovative City of the World 2013—WSJ). In the next chapter, we analyze the legal and ethical issues related to a data-driven smart city implementation.

2.1 Smart cities need to include urban, economic, and social development

Smart cities need development in urban, economic, social, and governance dimensions. We can summarize the lessons obtained from the Barcelona case:

- **Holistic approach**: Smart cities need an integral approach, including (1) the infrastructure and urban dimension, (2) businesses and economic dimension, (3) talent and social dimension, and (4) governance dimension.
- **Urban transformation—Hard factors**: Each smart city needs (1) an urban plan; (2) a legal framework for land, public services, and data; (3) an infrastructure plan (water, energy, mobility, waste, information technology); and (4) a sustainability plan.

- **Economic transformation—Soft factors and companies**: Smart cities need smart specializations. This implies selecting (1) what sectors (clusters) to be developed, (2) what agenda of technologies is needed for the value chains of innovation, (3) how to attract and promote that startups and companies are using the city as a lab and showroom for growing internationally, and (4) what kind of pilots (fab labs) can be developed (living lab).
- **Social transformation—Talent**: Citizens are the key asset of the knowledge-based economy and society. Smart cities must provide an e-place for smart citizens and develop a strategy for (1) adoption of technologies for living in the city, (2) education (talent creation and development), (3) health and inclusion, and (4) security and cybersecurity.
- **Governance**: Smart cities are a continuous process of development; for this reason, they need governance with (1) hybrid organizations (public private partnership platforms) to (2) share the vision to achieve in the smart city, and to (3) add actions to be developed in all the dimensions of the project (Fig. 4.1).

2.2 The lifecycle of a smart city from inception to maturity

Politicians can decide to start the process of a data-driven transformation that follows four different phases: inception, launching, growing, and maturity. This lifecycle model is similar to process innovation.

The case of Barcelona provides evidence that, in each phase, each agent works in a different way, and all agents are necessary to fulfill all the phases. A co-evolution process is therefore developed, interacting government, universities, and industry. All agents need the others to evolve, and hybrid

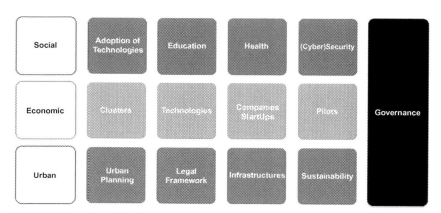

FIG. 4.1 Dimensions of a data-driven smart city.

organizations as clusters are coordinating expectations and actions. The main roles that should be performed at each stage are summarized as follows.

2.2.1 Inception

Clear public leadership and the involvement of academia, industry, and society are key factors to generate the vision and trust in the project of a smart city. Without clear vision about the type of smart city, it will be difficult to commit the agents and coordinate the actions.

This phase consists of defining the vision that will make the whole city learn about the benefits and challenges related to this transformation. The vision will be defined involving the quadruple helix agents, co-creating with them to share and commit.

2.2.2 Launching

Smart cities will need basic infrastructure to start, as well as the first projects and users. Also, anchor companies and institutions will be necessary for stimulating projects and others to come. The smart city will need full-time managers for promoting the projects and orchestrating the top-down and bottom-up data-driven strategies and actions.

This phase consists of realizing the pilots and analyzing the findings for future phases. The project team is ad-hoc. The resources are assigned at the beginning of the project and released once the project is finished. They come from the existing city hall organization from different departments depending on the nature of the project. They usually have support from an IT department and other external providers. At the end of this phase, we may be able to get information on the outcomes of the project, i.e., if the objectives set at the beginning were met and if the benefits expected have been achieved. The pilot also permits us to understand how the organization is adapted to this new challenge of the data science. It will conclude with recommendations, constraints, limits, and conditions to transform the organization to be data-driven.

2.2.3 Growing

The infrastructure will be growing as the backbone of the smart city. A cluster strategy should be developed for promoting smart city industry. The creation of startups will be one of the sources of growing and innovation. Synergies among the actors about data-driven strategies and solutions should be developed. In the social dimension, more smart citizens will be educated as users of the smart city (competencies, skills, and tools).

This phase consists of multiple projects to better use the power of the data. The team is mixed; part of them comes from existing organizations and another part from a specific structure dedicated to the project.

2.2.4 Maturity

The city has a twin city in the cloud. The economy is data-driven-oriented. The smart communities work in the cloud and live (wherever) in the city. New waves of projects are included, and the city is a resilient and innovative city.

This phase consists of generalizing and creating a data-driven organization. We propose the following city hall organization for a data-driven strategy (Fig. 4.1). We recommend the creation of a data-driven decision center that directly reports to the city hall/mayor for high visibility. Each department has a CDO figure who collects the needs and works with the data-driven decision center. This center can't be the IT department, which is usually very deep down in the organization. The data-driven decision center encompasses business analysts, data scientists, and IT specialists.

Each agent of the triple helix has its internal agenda: universities play a long-term vision, government has the election timeline in its agenda, and industry pays salaries every month and shows the results on an annual basis. Aligning agendas at short-, middle-, and long-term visions is a key issue in the governance performance to evolve the ecosystem in a synergic way (Fig. 4.2).

2.3 Quadruple helix agents develop different functions in the development of smart cities

Smart cities need urban, economic, and social transformation. The role of each agent of the quadruple helix model (government, universities, industry, and society) is different depending on the dimension of the transformation:

1. **Government**, at the local, regional (state), and national (federal) levels plays a key role in the transformation. In the urban dimension, it defines the uses of the land, the infrastructure plan, green spaces, and the regulation

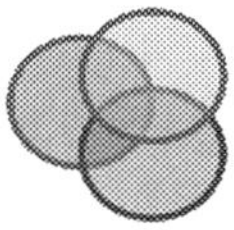

	Definition	Launching	Growth	Maturity
	Key: Co-creating the Vision	Key: Smart City Full Time Managers	Key: Clustering	Key: Twin City
SOCIAL	Involvement of the society	Users	Smart Citizens	Smart Communities
ECONOMIC	Involvement of Key Institutions: Universities, Government and Associations of Companies	First Projects Anchor companies and institutions	Cluster of Smart City Industry Start Ups Corporations	Data Driving Economy
URBAN	Planning	Infrastructures	Backbone of the Smart City	Resilient City

FIG. 4.2 Dimensions for developing a data-driven smart city.

of the data. In the economic dimension, it invests in research and technology, promotes attraction of companies and the creation of new startups, promotes clusters, and creates conditions for pilots. In the social dimension, it promotes the awareness and adoption of technologies, education, health, and security, and the adoption of data-driven strategies and solutions.

2. **University** is the source of talent and technology. The university is a key tool affecting all the dimensions. In the urban dimension, they can apply the research in smart city solutions as a living lab. In the economic dimension, they provide science, technology, fab labs, and entrepreneurs to the ecosystem. In the social dimension, they provide fresh young talent to the smart city (with students as early users).

3. **Industry** represents all the companies—of different sizes and sectors—in the smart city. In the urban dimension, on one hand, through real estate, they develop and build smart buildings, and utilities companies provide key infrastructure. In the economic transformation dimension, large corporations, SMEs, and new startups are clustered with universities and institutions, creating products and services for smart cities. Last, in the social dimension, industry provides professionals as smart workers.

4. **Society** represents all the citizens. They are the goal of the smart city. They are users and testers of the data-driven smart city solutions, but they are also the demanders of new needs. They e-work and e-live in the city. They provide data (in an active and passive way) and they are the users of data for making their own decisions. If there is an appropriate platform and environment, they can identify challenges and co-create and co-design solutions (Fig. 4.3).

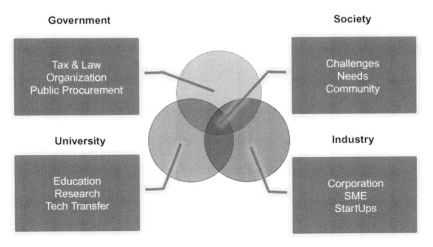

FIG. 4.3 Quadruple helix in data-driven smart city.

118 Implementing data-driven strategies in smart cities

2.4 Effective roadmap

Fig. 4.4 shows the roadmap for developing data-driven smart cities.

2.4.1 Mapping the assets, agents, and activities of the city

The mapping of the assets, agents, and activities of the city is the starting point to understand the capabilities linked to the urban, economic, social, and governance dimensions:

- Map all the assets, agents, and activities linked with the data-driven smart city
- Categorize all the agents (quadruple helix model)
- Analyze the assets and activities in terms of:
    - Urban dimension: urban planning, infrastructure, legal framework, sustainability plan
    - Economic development: research and tech centers, clusters, labs, startups, and corporations
    - Social development: adoption of technologies, education programs, health system, security

2.4.2 Defining the vision of the data-driven smart city

The creation of a vision takes advantage of the internal strengths and captures the opportunities. To engage the agents with the vision, it's important to involve the agents in the co-creation of the vision.

- Understanding the strengths and weaknesses of the city

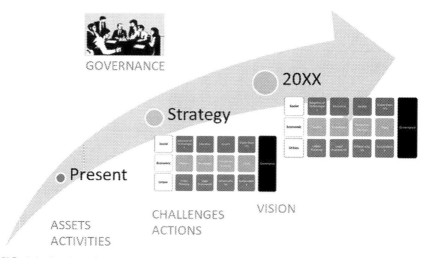

FIG. 4.4 Roadmap for developing data-driven smart cities.

- Recognizing the opportunities and threats of the city
- Benchmark with top data-driven smart cities
- Co-creating the vision of the data-driven smart city, taking advantage of the opportunities and strengths and reducing the weaknesses and threats

2.4.3 From data-driven smart city vision to strategic challenges

Knowing the starting point and sharing the vision, at this point it will be important to understand, evaluate, and prioritize what challenges we need to solve to build the data-driven smart city model, deciding the best strategy in all the dimensions. It will be necessary to list the challenges in the framework of the data-driven smart city vision and model:

- Urban dimension
- Economic dimension
- Social dimension
- Governance dimension

2.4.4 Identifying of the key strategic actions for delivering the data-driven smart city

With a clear understanding of the challenges, we will need to identify actions, inspired by how other data-driven smart cities of the world solved those challenges.

- Identifying actions needed for every challenge
- Design the pull of actions
- Implement the pull of actions
- Monitor and evaluate the pull of actions

2.4.5 Governance and management

A data-driven smart city needs regular involvement of the agents and management to manage the assets and activities of the smart city, interacting with the private/public sector at local/regional, national, and international levels:

- Selecting the quadruple helix agents
- Involving the quadruple helix agents in the governance bodies
- Designing the government and governance bodies
- Launching the government and governance bodies

2.4.6 The pact for data-driven smart city

To involve and celebrate the articulation of the data-driven smart city, we propose to create a pact for the data-driven smart city with the participation and representation of the quadruple helix agents.

- Designing the model of pact for the data-driven smart city
- Writing the proposal of pact for the data-driven smart city

- Involving the agents in the pact for the data-driven smart city
- Launching the pact for the data-driven smart city and the brand

2.4.7 Global alliance

To exchange experiences and promote the performance of the data-driven smart city, we propose to create a global alliance with at least the top five cities of the world.

- Mapping the cities linked with the same dimension and specialization
- Selecting the best data-driven smart cities as partners
- Involving the data-driven smart cities of the world as a global alliance
- Signing the global alliance with the data-driven smart cities
- Launching the global alliance

2.4.8 Symposiums and awards

We need to show and celebrate the advance of the project every year, both locally and globally. The participation in international events, the celebration annually of the international symposium of smart cities, or the submission of awards and recognitions will help to position the city both nationally and internationally.

- Organizing an international symposium in the city
- Participation in international symposiums
- Participation in awards and recognitions

2.5 Smart index

There is a broad consensus on the importance of cities' performance evaluation through a variety of metrics or datasets. It helps not only to improve the quality of their public services but also to understand the strengths and challenges of the city to create public policies more tailored to their particular situation. Consequently, data-driven smart cities' strategy should have appropriate and useful indicators to track the performance of the city in a transparent, reliable, and objective way.

The Smart City Index is a tool aimed at measuring the performance of smart cities through a standardized and replicable methodology to guarantee the quality, objectivity, and relevance of its indicators. It is made up of a total of 110 indicators grouped into 17 categories and 4 dimensions. This Index has been developed by Idencity Consulting in partnership with corporations and public administration.

Its approach is useful to create a baseline assessment to identify those dimensions in which the city needs to make bigger efforts to improve its level of intelligent development. In fact, each indicator is measured from a

Roadmap to develop a data-driven city **Chapter | 4** 121

perspective that understands that smart cities go through different moments of development in line with the lifecycle of smart cities.

2.5.1 Sustainability with smart infrastructures and mobility

A smart city uses technology to respond to the demands of institutions, companies, and citizens in a sustainable way. In this sense, a smart city offers quality services, respects the environment as much as possible, uses natural resources wisely, and correctly manages waste. Technology in this sense offers new possibilities for better management.

The Smart Index allows leaders of the public and private sectors, as well as the inhabitants of the cities themselves, to take advantage of the opportunities offered by the so-called "Fourth Industrial Revolution" to benefit the environment.

A more aware citizenship, companies, and public administration will contribute by carrying out joint actions that help reduce levels of air pollution, increase the volume of recycled waste, and help boost investment and innovation in favor of the environment.

A smart city also requires more recharging points for electric vehicles, more fiber optics, greater coverage and integration of new technologies in its mobility services, public transport apps, smart parking, and bicycle loans. These technology renovations are a constant fact, and a smart city must know how to adapt to evolution and permanent changes in the physical and digital environment. The Smart Index already includes mobility services and urban infrastructure.

The Smart Index includes five categories covering sustainability, smart infrastructures, and mobility dimension (Fig. 4.5).

2.5.2 Smart economy

A smart economy applies and develops new technologies and leverages knowledge and innovation to encourage growth and prosperity. Universities and companies have a leading role, as they encourage other agents (citizens, public administrations, etc.) to adopt technology in their day-to-day activities. Innovation, digital skills development, training, and talent provide new possibilities for the development of cities.

With this Index, we observe companies electronically interacting with the public administration and the technological development within companies.

Waste Management   Environment Protection   Mobility   Infrastructure   Connectivity

FIG. 4.5 Sustainability, smart infrastructures, and mobility dimension.

The Smart Index reveals in this dimension the penetration in corporations of cloud computing and the use of the Internet (web pages, social networks, and automatic information processing applications).

In the smart economy dimension, the Smart Index identifies R&D opportunities in the high technology sector as well as in the promoting entrepreneurship within the innovation ecosystem.

The Smart Index includes four categories in the smart economy dimension (Fig. 4.6).

2.5.3 Smart society

A smart society is one that is structured and its potential basis is on the use of ICT. Its main objective is the development and improvement of the quality of life conditions of the people who make it up, adopting technology in an inclusive, democratizing, and safe way.

Inside of a smart society, the new ICT has the potential to improve the quality of life of the citizens in multiple fields: education, work, shopping, etc. That is why that the integration of new technologies must be done in an inclusive way that is democratizing and safe.

The results of the Smart Index in this dimension show us the use of technology by the citizens as card payments, use of electronic banking services, working in computerized jobs, and living in homes where technology and cybersecurity are fully installed.

Deepening in this dimension, the Smart Index also evaluates the progress in the educational environment like more training in new technologies from an early age and promotion of the vocation of the students toward university careers related to the technology of information.

The Smart Index includes four categories in the smart society dimension (Fig. 4.7).

2.5.4 Smart government

A city in the information age is leveraged in the use of ICT to involve all urban agents, especially citizens, in the decision-making processes of governments and public institutions. The application of technologies and innovation helps improve the processes by which decisions are implemented.

Digitization of Business   Digital interaction Business-Government   Performance High Tech Sector   Ecosystem of Innovation

FIG. 4.6 Smart economy dimension.

Technology Adoption   Education   Equality and inclusion   Cybersecurity

FIG. 4.7 Smart society dimension.

The Smart Index shows how cities are adopting a fully intelligent vision and strategy, and the progress along this path. In general terms, it is necessary that all cities integrate smart city strategic plans that are adapted to their specific reality of size, priorities, and possibilities.

This dimension evaluates the involvement of citizens by participation processes through the Internet, the compliance with transparency and accountability, and the communication by the Internet of the administration with the inhabitants of its cities.

The Smart Index includes four categories in the smart government dimension (Fig. 4.8).

3 Legal, security, and ethical considerations for a data-driven smart city

Before continuing with the study of smart cities, it is convenient to stop on the legal implications of data processing in the big data environment.

3.1 Legitimation for the use of big data

Personal data has become a great fundamental element, a commodity of the 21st century, essential for any type of business and especially necessary for research of all kinds, statistical, medical, or commercial. This importance as a commodity cannot make us lose sight of the sole owner of personal data who is, precisely, the natural person, and it is only them who may authorize or compromise on how their data are to be used, for what purposes, and who can use it.

Denying this ability to a person can lead to violations of privacy, discrimination of all kinds, by any of the personality traits, and damage to the rights and

Smart Vision and Strategy   e-Government   Citizen participation   Transparency and accountability

FIG. 4.8 Smart government dimension.

freedoms of the subjects concerned. To avoid consequences of the use (and not necessarily misuse) of personal data in a big data environment, it is necessary to consider when it is possible to process this data on a large scale, what problems can the use of data cause, and solutions that have been raised by different regulators for different scenarios of usage, mainly focused on the doctrines dependent on the General Data Protection Regulation (GDPR) in the European Union and those raised through the Health Insurance Portability and Accountability Act (HIPAA) standard in the United States. (The Privacy Act of 1974 can only be used for the maintenance of information by the federal government and not between individuals and data controllers.)

We should also clarify that big data procedures should usually use only anonymized (de-identified) or pseudonymized data, which is personal data to which encryption procedures have been applied, exclusively for their studying or processing, but through which applying a new algorithm or procedure can be re-decrypted.

The European GDPR determines that it applies only to "personal data", understanding that "personal data" refers to information relating to an identified or identifiable natural person; an identifiable natural person is one who can be identified, directly or indirectly, in particular through a reference of an identifier such as a name, identification number, location data, an online identifier, or to one or more factors specific to the physical, physiological, genetic, mental, economic, cultural, or social identity of that natural person (Art. 4 GDPR). Therefore, when data cannot be assigned to a natural person, either because it is disconnected from the name or some identification of its owner, or because it is encrypted following a secure procedure, it will not be considered "personal data", and its treatment and use should not be subject to the legal norms that limit its use and treatment.

Finally, it is important to determine which personal information can identify a person, since not only can an individual be identified by name or identity card (in those countries where it exists), but it is possible to identify a person through more than one data. The following types of data allow for one person's unique identification and should be considered as personal data:

- Telephone numbers
- Fax numbers
- Email addresses
- Social security numbers
- Medical record numbers
- Health plan beneficiary numbers
- Account numbers
- Certificate/license numbers
- Vehicle identifiers and serial numbers, including license plate numbers
- Device identifiers and serial numbers
- Web Universal Resource Locators (URLs)

- Internet protocol (IP) address numbers
- Biometric identifiers, including finger and voice prints
- Full face photographic images and any comparable images

When we want to use any of these identifiers, we must apply the legitimation basis, to which we will refer later, unless we resort to de-identification or encryption, turning this information into a hash.

3.2 Legitimation basis

The justification for data processing can be done according to two different approaches, polarized in the European Data Protection Standard (GDPR) and the U.S. HIPAA standard. In the first, consent, among other basis of legitimacy, always emanates from individuals, regardless of who the data processor is, while in the HIPAA standard, certain organizations (healthcare clearinghouses, employer-sponsored health plans, health insurers, and medical services, generally) are authorized.

The key difference between GDPR and HIPAA resides on what they focus on. GDPR focuses on protecting EU citizens' personal identifiable information. Therefore, any organization that handles an EU patient's information can be subject to GDPR regulations. In contrast, HIPAA is focused on organizations—covered entities and business associates–that handle protected health information within the United States. In addition to this fundamental difference, GDPR has a much broader scope of coverage than HIPAA.

3.2.1 European model (ART. 6 GDPR)

The European GDPR, in application since May 2018, states that data processing is only possible when there is a legal basis authorizing it.

Art. 6 GDPR. *Processing shall be lawful only if and to the extent that at least one of the following applies:*

- The data subject has given consent to the processing of his or her personal data for one or more specific purposes
- Processing is necessary for the performance of a contract
- Processing is necessary for compliance with a legal obligation
- Processing is necessary to protect the vital interests of the data subject
- Processing is necessary for the public interest
- Processing is necessary for the purposes of the legitimate interests pursued by the controller

While any of these six bases could be used to process data in bulk, both the legitimate interest and the execution of a contract are very difficult to apply to mass data processing, provided that we do not apply high security measures or very detailed contractual clauses. Therefore, we can rule out these two legal bases. The doctrine and supervisory authorities in Europe have devoted most efforts to determine under what conditions consent should be given to constitute a valid legal basis for processing data in a big data environment, mainly the former Article 29 Working Group (WP29), currently called the Data Protection Commission Board (DPCB) (https://ec.europa.eu/newsroom/article29/document.cfm?action-display&doc_id-51030). The conclusion they have reached is that consent, to be valid, must be unequivocal, free, specific, and informed and must be determined as a legal basis before starting the treatment, because once the consent has been used, it cannot use another alternative legal basis.

As indicated in wp259 rev.01: "*the controller cannot swap from consent to other lawful bases. For example, it is not allowed to retrospectively utilise the legitimate interest basis in order to justify processing, where problems have been encountered with the validity of consent. Because of the requirement to disclose the lawful basis which the controller is relying upon at the time of collection of personal data, controllers must have decided in advance of collection what the applicable lawful basis is.*"

Therefore, consent has to be free (i.e., it is not mandatory to make the decision to contract a product or provide a service); unequivocal (i.e., there must be no doubts that it has been provided and that evidence can be provided); specific (i.e., for one or more purposes determined at the time of consent); and informed (i.e., the data subject has been offered all the information necessary to be able to give consent freely and with knowledge of whom, for what, how, and for how long the personal data will be used). In fact, the legal basis of consent is the most complex of all, since, in case any of the previous characteristics are missing or not completed, the consent has not been validly provided and, therefore, the subsequent data processing will not be adjusted to the law. This effect is especially important in environments where a large volume of data is used, because incorporating data obtained in an incorrect way can contaminate the entire database that it is used with, forcing you to label all sources of provenance of the information in the data recollection phase, to isolate the data obtained illicitly. In this situation, the work of a data protection officer (DPO), as an additional security measure, can be essential when it comes to preventing illegal data incorporations or presenting the necessary legal reports that validate the legitimate use of personal data. The rest of the legal basis offer fewer friction points in high-volume data processing. Authorization by a law, public interest, and the interest to preserve life are part of the same principle of protection of the person at a collective level, protection that is always given by the states, through a rule that enables treatment, and the need to perform such treatment to offer a service to the community (public interest), or to protect the lives of citizens too. This protection of the processing in favor of the collective does not exempt from the fact that, at the time of the collection of the data, the other requirements of Article 13 and 14 GDPR are met, which instruct that the data subject is offered timely information about what will be done with its data, as we will explain in the following section, dedicated exclusively to the principle of information.

3.2.2 U.S. model (HIPAA)

In the U.S. model, to process health data exclusively, the holders of the information must give their written consent to process the data in all medical treatment procedures they will receive. The HIPAA standard differentiates between consent (to receive the processing or make a payment) and authorization (any other data processing not included in the previous discussion).

Under the HIPAA privacy rule, you must obtain patient authorization to use patients' protected health information (PHI) for reasons other than routine treatment, payment, or healthcare operations, including: to disclose PHI about a patient to a third party (i.e., a life insurance underwriter); to market products or services except if the marketing communication is face-to-face with the patient or it involves the provision of services of nominal value; to raise funds for any entity other than your practice; to conduct research, unless your practice has signed a waiver approved by the Institutional Review Board for the use and disclosure of PHI or has de-identified PHI; or to disclose psychotherapy notes, unless disclosure is required for law enforcement purposes or legal mandates, oversight of the provider who created the notes, use by a coroner or medical examiner, or avoidance of a serious and imminent threat to health or safety.

3.3 Information principle

For any of the two models of consent to be valid, all the information necessary for the individual to give valid consent (free, unequivocal, specific, and informed) must be incorporated. The only guide that has been legislated on how this consent should be given is found in the European GDPR legislation, specifically in Article 13 thereof:

Where personal data relating to a data subject is collected from the data subject, the controller shall, at the time when personal data is obtained, provide the data subject with all of the following information:

> the identity and the contact details of the controller and, where applicable, of the controller's representative; the contact details of the DPO, where applicable; the purposes of the processing for which the personal data is intended as well as the legal basis for the processing; where the processing is based on point (f) of Article 6(1), the legitimate interests pursued by the controller or by a third party; the recipients or categories of recipients of the personal data, if any; where applicable, the fact that the controller intends to transfer personal data to a third country or international organization and the existence or absence of an adequacy decision by the Commission, or in the case of transfers referred to in Article 46 or 47, or the second subparagraph of

Article 49(1), reference to the appropriate or suitable safeguards and the means by which to obtain a copy of them or where they have been made available.

In addition to the information referred to in paragraph 1, the controller shall, at the time when personal data is obtained, provide the data subject with the following further information necessary to ensure fair and transparent processing:

- the period for which the personal data will be stored, or if that is not possible, the criteria used to determine that period
- the existence of the right to request from the controller access to and rectification or erasure of personal data or restriction of processing concerning the data subject or to object to processing as well as the right to data portability
- where the processing is based on point (a) of Article 6(1) or point (a) of Article 9(2), the existence of the right to withdraw consent at any time, without affecting the lawfulness of processing based on consent before its withdrawal
- the right to lodge a complaint with a supervisory authority
- whether the provision of personal data is a statutory or contractual requirement, or a requirement necessary to enter into a contract, as well as whether the data subject is obliged to provide the personal data and of the possible consequences of failure to provide such data
- the existence of automated decision-making, including profiling, referred to in Article 22(1) and (4) and, at least in those cases, meaningful information about the logic involved, as well as the significance and the envisaged consequences of such processing for the data subject.

All this information must be provided to the person at the time of giving consent, because otherwise the consent will not be valid and the data obtained may not be processed or incorporated into the rest of the information we use in big data. The European system is a very guaranteeing system for the rights and freedoms of the individual (data subject) since it starts from the idea that the person is the sole owner of the information, and all the necessary guarantees must be given so that their rights and freedoms are not diminished. The use, under the European standard, of any of the other legitimate basis, such as vital interest or public interest (especially in cases of epidemiological emergencies or research studies), does not prevent us from having to provide all the information about the data controller and destination. Article 89 of the GDPR enables the use of information for scientific studies but at no time circumvents the obligation to report, although it leaves a window open for the processing of information: the anonymization of information (de-identifier), meaning that this information cannot be linked to any identified or identifiable person.

3.4 Main problems

The main problems are:

3.4.1 Consent given without all the guarantees

In European law, for consent to be valid, it must be free, specific, and informed. With the current state of the art and its future evolution, it is practically impossible to predict future uses and purposes of certain data for which consent has been given today (Burke, Beskow, & Trinidad, 2018).

3.4.2 Entities that use data from sources that are not covered by HIPAA standards (governmental or private entities not subject to HIPAA standard)

These entities will not be diligent enough in the processing of data, since they do not have a standard that obliges them. Their de-identification practices are not audited nor have the consent validly obtained. The same problem can be found in other types of data about students, or voters, in which it is not possible to control whether the anonymization has been correct, by recording in many cases an aggregation of data that allows re-identification through added partial data. Re-identification of medical data that had been completely anonymized (de-identified) could be done by adding other data from open data, such as voter registration, electricity consumption, or student census. There is complexity in the anonymization of genome data since, with only 30% of the genome, a person can be re-identified by the peculiarities of its genetic sequence (especially in small population groups) (Gymrek, McGuire, Golan, Halperin, & Erlich, 2013).

3.5 Solutions

The main solutions have different approaches:

3.5.1 Technological approach

Encryption technology provides better solutions to avoid the legal basis that would prevent data processing in big data environments by not having all the necessary requirements to reach the principle of consent or information. Applying encryption protocols, with encryption monitoring and data testing, allows information to not be assigned to an identified or identifiable person.

3.5.2 Regulatory approach

A norm that regulates the form of anonymization and a consent regime (HIPAA and GDPR), in addition to a regime of sanctions and immobilization of files, it would have to be determined whether the principle of soft-law or hard-law is appropriate. In soft-law, we are left regulated the premises of anonymization and treatment and leave the application to the controllers, under compliance criteria and binding corporate rules. Under a hard-law criterion, minimum forms of anonymization are imposed and a system of immobilization and sanction are established in the event of noncompliance.

3.5.3 Compliance approach or binding corporate rules

There are self-imposed rules in the processes of collection, mining, or decision-making, which allow a compliance officer to complete the gaps that may have occurred in the provision of consent (new purposes derived, new research needs, aggregation of data by vital or public interest in the case of pandemics).

None of the three approaches alone should be a solution, since a hybrid soft-law, compliance, and technology system can optimize the results in the task of controlling that, in a big data process, the rights and freedoms of data subjects are not being violated.

A hybrid approach, based more on obtaining guarantees and monitoring by third parties, can be a right path. On this matter, both in Europe and in HIPAA standards, we find a similar figure. In systems dependent or similar to the European GDPR, there is the figure of the DPO, which is an independent office that oversees the application of the standard in companies, presents reports on regulatory compliance, and coordinates the processing activity and supervision of control authorities.

In HIPAA, entities controlled by the standard must have a compliance officer, with not-so-detailed functions, but ultimately similar, although it is not endowed with the independence presented by the regulated charge since the GDPR rules. Hybrid standards, self-regulation, and supervision of an independent third party (DPO) must be the way to exploit all the possibilities of big data without jeopardizing the rights and freedoms of individuals.

4 Value model in a data-driven smart city

A data-driven smart city cannot be developed by a single organization; as we have seen in Section 3, the urban, social, and economic transformation that the smart city project aims at requires the participation of all quadruple helix actors: government, university, industry, and society. In successful data-driven smart city projects, these actors are embedded in a *smart city ecosystem*. This ecosystem can be defined analogously to Adner and Kapoor's (2016) business ecosystem as "the alignment structure of the multilateral set of partners that need to interact for a focal value proposition to materialize". The difference between a business and smart city ecosystem is that, in the former, the recipients of value are shareholders, and in the later, citizens and organizations located in the city.

To be successful, the city ecosystem requires a *smart city ecosystem strategy*. Following again Adner (2016), this strategy is defined by how the focal organization "approaches the alignment of partners and secures its role". In this context, the focal organization is clearly the city hall, which is responsible to drive policies to implement the data-driven smart city project. Nonfocal actors can be placed into upstream or downstream positions in the flow of activities. *Upstream actors* collaborate with the city hall in activities of data acquisition and assurance of data quality and maturity.

The city hall, as the focal actor responsible of the smart city government, is the recipient of the data retrieved from the city, and usually has a long-term relationship with upstream actors. *Downstream actors* use the data retrieved from the city to offer value-added services. In the Nice case study (see Section 5), downstream actors are the developers of the Nice City Pass app, and in the Seoul case (see Section 6), the downstream actor is the Korean Railroad Research Institute (KRRI), the developer of the Integrated Public Transport Operation System (TRIPS). The relationships between downstream suppliers and the city hall are more heterogeneous than with upstream suppliers, as data exploitation activities are more diverse than data acquisition. The city hall can engage in long-term relationships with downstream actors, as in the Seoul case, or simply make available data through open data portal to any startup interested in developing a business venture using those data. Upstream and downstream actors can be university or industry agents: in the case of Seoul, it is a research institute (the KRRI) and in the case of Nice, a startup (InQBarna). A key difference between business and smart city ecosystems is that the latters need to deliver value to a more diverse set of stakeholders, with interests going beyond monetary profit.

The triple bottom line (Grimaldi & Fernandez, 2019) is a useful tool to describe the diverse sources of value that a data-driven smart city project needs to deliver. In Chapter 1, we referred to this triple bottom line framework to address and measure sustainability, one of the challenges cities are facing today. First, the project must deliver value to *people*: it must make a citizen's life easier and facilitate social equity and the inclusion of disadvantaged groups. It must also deliver economic value or *profits* for the city. According to the quadruple helix theory, data-driven smart city projects can generate positive spillovers as they attract world-class firms and top leading universities. Finally, data-driven smart cities must be able to make city activities more sustainable, thus obtaining benefits for the planet.

In Fig. 4.9, we summarize the value model for the data-driven smart city.

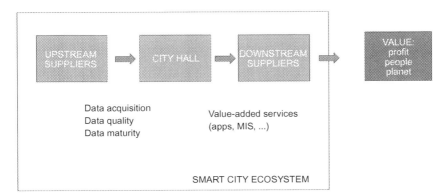

FIG. 4.9 The smart city ecosystem.

5 Case study of Nice (France)

Nice is the second largest city in the French Mediterranean coast after Marseille and the capital of the Alpes-Maritimes department. Including its metropolitan area, Nice has around one million inhabitants, which makes it the seventh most populated area in France. In 2010, Nice city council and Nice metropolitan area authorities launched the *Connected Boulevard* project, a pioneering initiative aiming to implement smart city and IoT technologies. This project made Nice take fourth place in the Juniper Smart City Ranking, after Barcelona, New York, and London. In 2019, Nice is the 13th smart city of the world according to Juniper Research and the only French city in the ranking. The *Connected Boulevard* project consisted of installing sensors and other IoT devices throughout the city downtown, starting from the Boulevard Victor Hugo, the main street of Nice. The aim of the project was to gather, store, and offer data on key aspects of city life like parking, traffic, and waste disposal. The infrastructure was built on three layers:

- A first layer of sensors and networked IoT devices that capture information from the city in real time.
- A second layer of distributed points of data capture and storage that ensure readiness and scalability.
- A third layer of central data collection and storage, available to application programming interfaces (API) that can feed mobile or computer apps.

Nice city hall built this infrastructure through a network of external upstream suppliers:

- Mentis Services acted as project leader
- Cisco System provided the network hardware
- Urbiotica provided the sensors
- Prismtech provided the platform and tools for IoT

The Connected Boulevard infrastructure began to offer data in June 2011. Those data was expected to be used by downstream suppliers to offer services to citizens. So upstream suppliers built and maintained the structure that collects, stores, and makes data from the city available from APIs.

5.1 The Nice City Pass app

The *Nice City Pass* app was developed by the Barcelona-based startup InQBarna to integrate information from all means of transportation in Nice downtown: bikes, buses, trams, electric vehicles, etc. The app integrates data from sensors installed in Nice downtown with complementary services like Meteosim for weather forecasts or Mappy for geographical information. *Nice City Pass* is an example of how services in the data-driven city are constructed as an integration of a network of upstream and downstream suppliers. Upstream suppliers curate data from the city, and downstream suppliers use those data to offer value-added services to citizens, frequently integrating city data with data from complementary services. The app was deployed in June of 2014, just at the beginning of an expansion of sensors in parking lots (Fig. 4.10).

One of the features of the *Nice City Pass* app is the possibility of knowing the paid parking places available in Nice downtown in real time, so that drivers reaching Nice downtown can park more effectively. To evaluate the effect of the app on the paid parking service, we have used rotation count data from June 2013 to February 2015. Then, we computed the rotation index as the average rotation count in each spot for each day. That count can be considered as a metric for acceptance of the paid parking service. The results are shown in Fig. 4.11.

In Fig. 4.11, we can observe that the acceptance of the paid parking service was diminishing since it began to be measured in 2013, although the number of sensors was increasing, as seen in Fig. 4.1. Rotation index reached a minimum of 1.742 on August 17, 2014. The introduction of the app in June 2014 led to an increase of the rotation index, reaching a maximum level of 6.052 on February 25, 2015. The implementation of the *Nice City Pass* app leads to a higher rotation of the paid parking services and a revenue increase from this service to the city hall.

5.2 Benefits of the *Nice City Pass* app

The implementation of a system of signaling free parking spots in Nice downtown can have immediate beneficial effects on traffic management, as it can reduce traffic cruising, i.e., the traffic generated by vehicles in motion because drivers are looking for a place to park. This traffic can account for up to 30% of

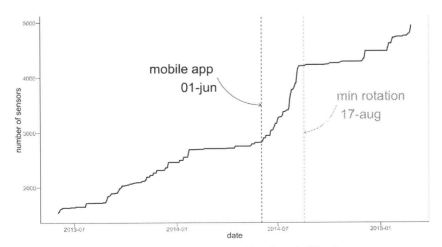

FIG. 4.10 Evolution of sensors installed in paid parking places in Nice downtown.

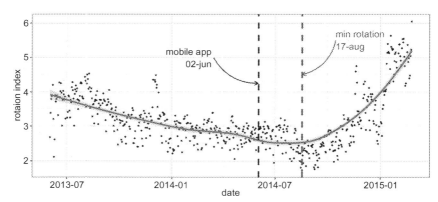

FIG. 4.11 Rotation index of parking sensors in paid parking places in Nice downtown.

total traffic in downtown cities, so a significant reduction of that traffic can yield a reduction of undesirable consequences of traffic, like pollution or accidents. The number of accidents can be significantly affected by traffic cruising, as drivers looking for a parking place can be more distracted and also more prone to negative emotions, two well-known antecedents of city accidents (Grimaldi & Fernandez, 2019).

To evaluate the influence of the implementation of the app on city accidents, we retrieved information of the hourly number of accidents in downtown Nice from the French government open data portal (https://www.data.gouv.fr) for the period 2010–14. We matched that accident data with the number of active sensors in each hour for that period. We have seen previously that the *Nice City Pass* app increased sensor activity (see Figs. 4.1 and 4.2), so we can assess app use with the number of active sensors at each hour. To account for differences in traffic intensity within each day, we have separated data for each day into two ranges: from 06:00 to 18:00, the peak traffic hours in France, and the rest of the day. We have collapsed hourly data into these two ranges, so we have two observations for each day: one for peak hours, and other for hours of lower traffic intensity. The dummy variable, daylight, is equal to one for peak hours, and zero for hours of lower traffic. We have also accounted for within-week differences in traffic, defining a Sunday dummy variable equal to one for Sundays. The sensors' variable is equal to the number of active sensors for each day and hourly range. The resulting dataset has $N = 3652$ observations.

The dependent variable is the number of accidents in downtown Nice; accidents_metro is a count variable, so we have used a negative binomial linear regression to examine the influence of the variables described earlier with the number of accidents. We have also adopted a hierarchical regression model, examining the effect of daylight and Sunday control variables in the first model, and adding the sensors' explanatory variable in the second model.

	Dependent variable	
	accidents_metro	
	(1)	(2)
Daylight1	1.248*** (0.027)	1.250*** (0.027)
Sunday	−0.559*** (0.040)	−0.561*** (0.040)
Sensors	−0.0001*** (0.00001)	
Constant	0.162*** (0.023)	0.214*** (0.025)
Observations	3652	3652
Log likelihood	−6461.824	−6441.294
theta	14.139***(2.145)	15.264***(2.457)
Akaike Inf. Crit.	12,929.650	12,890.590

Note: *$P<.1$; **$P<.05$; ***$P<.01$.

The table shows the results of the negative binomial, hierarchical regression model with number of accidents in Nice downtown as dependent variable. We observe that the number of accidents tends to be higher in peak hours and lower on Sundays. When we introduce the number of sensors, the coefficients of the control variables are not affected, while we observe a negative small, but significant effect of number of sensors on accidents, indicating that the number of active sensors reduces the total number of accidents.

To evaluate model consistency, we have run a similar model with the number of accidents in Nice suburbs (accidents_suburban variable). In that model, we observe that the number of accidents is higher in peak hours but is not affected by weekday or by the number of sensors in Nice downtown. This last result was to be expected as sensors are installed in locations different from where accidents are counted but helpsto assess the consistency of the first model.

	Dependent variable	
	accidents_suburban	
	(1)	(2)
Daylight1	1.146*** (0.079)	1.147*** (0.079)
Sunday	0.043 (0.097)	0.042 (0.097)
Sensors	−0.00003 (0.00002)	
Constant	−2.100*** (0.070)	−2.074*** (0.074)
Observations	3652	3652
Log likelihood	−2197.817	−2197.240
Theta	3.030*** (0.956)	3.035*** (0.958)
Akaike Inf. Crit.	4401.635	4402.481

Note: *$P<.1$; **$P<.05$; ***$P<.01$.

Another effect of reduction of traffic control can be reduction of pollution, thus obtaining an environmental beneficial effect. To evaluate this environmental effect, we retrieved information about air quality from Air PACA (Provence-Alpes-Côte d'Azur), a nonprofit association that shares data on air quality on the region of the south of France. Unfortunately, at the moment that data were retrieved, there were no sensors evaluating pollution in Nice downtown, thus we cannot measure the effect of pollution directly. Our approach has been retrieving data from the level of NO_2 pollutant and number of accidents from a point existent in data.gouv.fr and Air PACA, and as close as possible from Nice. The selected point was on the Highway M6098, at the entrance of Nice. Data from years 2012, 2013, and 2014 on accidents and air quality was retrieved, counting now with 1775 observations. We defined the same control variables daylight and Sunday as in the previous analysis and performed a Poisson regression analysis now using the level of pollution NO_2 as a predictor.

	Dependent variable	
	Accidents	
	(1)	(2)
Daylight1	0.871*** (0.033)	0.878*** (0.033)
Sunday	−0.419*** (0.047)	−0.387*** (0.048)
NO_2	0.002*** (0.001)	
Constant	0.561*** (0.029)	0.449*** (0.046)
Observations	1775	1775
Log likelihood	−3213.287	−3208.118
Akaike Inf. Crit.	6432.573	6424.236

Note: *$P<.1$; **$P<.05$; ***$P<.01$.

Results of the Poisson regression analysis show that control variables have an effect on the number of accidents on the highway similar to Nice downtown: more accidents on peak hours and fewer accidents on Sunday. Now we observe that NO_2 increases the number of accidents. As there is no clear causal relationship relating NO_2 concentration and number of accidents, we have come to the conclusion that there is a positive relationship between level of NO_2 and traffic volume. Therefore, we can conclude that an action leading to a reduction of accidents in Nice downtown reducing traffic volume, like the implementation of *Nice City Pass* app, should also lead to a reduction of pollution.

5.3 Value model

The *Connected Boulevard* project has placed Nice, an important city of the French Mediterranean coast, in the landscape of urban areas implementing strategies related with the data-driven city. Nice city hall has built a network of upstream suppliers providing an infrastructure that allows gathering data from the city systematically. These upstream suppliers provide network hardware (Cisco Systems), the software platform (PrismTech), and sensors (Urbiotica). InQBarna, a Barcelona-based startup, used this infrastructure to develop the

Nice City Pass app. This app allows Nice citizens to obtain real-time information on means of transportation in the city. One of the features of this app is to provide information on free paid parking spaces in Nice downtown.

We have used data gathered during the project implementation about sensor rotation index, number of accidents, and level of pollution to examine the benefits of the project from a triple bottom line perspective. The app makes the process of parking more efficient and reduces traffic cruising in the city downtown. This delivers benefits for *people*, as it helps to save time for Nice citizens and reduces the number of accidents. The reduction of traffic cruising also helps to reduce pollution, helping to make Nice a more sustainable city and making a positive effect to the *planet*. Finally, as some of the economic spillovers of traffic cruising are returned through an increase of revenues from parking spots, the project also contributes to monetary profit to the city hall and app developers.

5.4 Nice in the third stage in the roadmap

The Connected Boulevard project places Nice between the launching and growing development stages of the data-driven city (see Table 4.1). Nice has implemented a strategic plan to achieve the status of a data-driven city, a practice of the growing stage, although the city hall has not developed an organizational unit to develop data-driven city projects, which sets Nice in the launching stage regarding that aspect. Regarding technology, the project uses mobile apps and IoT, technologies of the growing phase. Data maturity and data quality practices in Nice are on the growing phase, as they are supporting at least a mobile app, although there is little evidence of exploitation of data across projects and apps. The most involved stakeholders are the industry, integrated in a network of upstream and downstream suppliers, with Nice city hall in the center coordinating and promoting the project. There is no evidence of participation of universities in Nice data-driven projects, while the extensive use of mobile apps and press coverage of data-driven initiatives shows that Nice citizens are users of data-driven city projects.

TABLE 4.1 Stages of data-driven city development of Nice.

	Organization	Technology	Data management	Stakeholders
Inception				Universities
Launching	Structure	Mobile apps	Exploitation	
Growing	Strategy	IoT	Maturity, quality	Industry, society
Maturity				

The following steps of the development of Nice as a data-driven city require that Nice develops a stronger structure of data-driven activities with in-house capabilities for data exploitation. This would position Nice city hall in a more favorable position to adopt more cutting-edge technologies, like chatbots and the development of a twin city in the cloud. Nice city hall may engage in joint initiatives with universities and research centers to facilitate technology adoption and data exploitation.

6 Case study of Seoul

In the past, a number of varied strategies were undertaken in major cities to transport residents and nonresidents efficiently. These strategies met with varying degrees of success due to the inability of transport authorities to do more than make educated guesses as to where, when, and how people would move around their city. All of this changed with the onset of smart devices and the data they produce. Now the issue for most transport authorities is not only how to use the abundance of data they receive for the optimization of transport systems but also to achieve greater triple helix integration between the government, industry, and university sectors.

Seoul, South Korea, is a dense metropolis and has one of the highest levels of public transportation ridership in the world with a mode share of 63%. It is also an area of the world with high levels of citizen participation, so there is pressure on the government of Seoul to create a plan that efficiently moves people around the city. In 2004, the city initiated public transport reform by reorganizing routes and unifying the payment system with the implementation of a smart card for all public transport.

Previously there had been a great deal of fragmentation in this sector due to a mix of many different operators, both public and private. The country had gone through 30 years of rapid economic development with high levels of urbanization, and Seoul's transport network had not kept up with the needs and changes in the city's structure. In the 1980s, there was an extensive amount of public infrastructure building to prepare the city for the 1988 Olympics, but this only added to the stress put on the public transport network brought on by economic changes. As the country grew and developed, many people moved to Seoul and the city quadrupled in size between 1960 and 2002. Additionally the city bus system was privately operated and, with increased competition from the expanded metro network built in the 1980s, became increasingly unreliable and inefficient.

The 2002 mayoral election in Seoul centered on public transport reform. For this reason, Mayor Lee Myung-Bak set a priority of restructuring the fare policy as well as the transportation network soon after taking office. This restructuring revolutionized the public transport sector in South Korea and became a global reference in efficiency.

In 2004, Seoul introduced an Integrated Smart Card for all public transportation that accomplished the two overriding goals of the reform: it unified the system by converting it to a fare-based, multimodal system and it moved the bus transport network from private to semipublic ownership. By accomplishing these two goals, the municipal city government was able to create a far more efficient transport network that incentivized use of the public transport system, which in turn decreased average travel times and saved users $530 U.S. on average annually (Audouin, Razaghi & Finger). It also enabled the city government to obtain an overview of the public transport system in Seoul from the user data from the smart card system. The result was a wealth of data that allowed authorities to map passenger movements around the city on the extensive public transportation network including a metropolitan subway system consisting of 15 lines and 500 stations and a bus network consisting of 600 lines and over 10,000 stops.

The implementation of the smart card required a common payment system referred to as the Automated Fare Collection system (AFC) that has unified the payment data for all urban transport throughout the city and that enables the city government to observe passenger movements and also manage mobility and mobility-related services of citizens more efficiently.

6.1 Data strategy: Smart public transport planning system

As early implementers of the smart card, transport stakeholders were able to see the value of the AFC data for transport optimization from the user's point of view, but there was little in the way of data strategy. Much like in the rest of the world, transport authorities in Korea had been relying on survey-based models for transport network changes and planning. Survey-based analysis is relatively expensive as it requires an extra work force to administer the survey and it also has a limited level of accuracy because sample sizes are relatively small. Furthermore, most public transport surveys are limited in scope and cover one segment of the rider's journey. Surveys cover one point at one moment in time; they cannot map out the entire trip of survey participants.

When the Tmoney Smart Card was implemented in Seoul in 2004, the idea was to create a unified system that charged users by distance traveled. This new system allowed users to pay transport operators through one unified platform; they tag in at the beginning of their journey and out at the end of their journey so that the fare can be accurately calculated for each individual ride. In this system, users also must tag in if they change types of public transport. For example, if a rider takes a bus to the metro and then they take one metro line five stops then change to another line for another three stops, the user is tagging in when they get on the bus then out when they exit bus and back in again when they enter the metro and then again when they exit the metro. The system recognizes transfer by tagging time between exiting the bus and boarding the next transport, which is within 30 min. That is, if you spend more than 30 min between two modes of transport, it counts as a new ride not a transfer.

6.2 Data capture: Automated fare collection system

The objective of the change in system was to make travel more streamlined for users (Fig. 4.12).

Fig. 4.12 illustrates how fares are transacted through the TMoney card and filtered through an AFC company, which then debits the fares from user's credit cards and pays the transport operators for the service. The process is more complicated on the backside with the creation of the AFC company to manage the process, but the user experience is considerably simpler with only one transport card/app to keep track of.

Initially the streamlining of transport from a user perspective was a political decision; the reform was created to make travel in the city of Seoul easier for users and to curb pollution levels. The reform took place before the world started to realize the power of data, and there was not an explicit data strategy in this case. Nonetheless, with this increased ease-of-use for users came a wealth of real and complete user data that was at first not taken advantage of. Later, researchers and city planners came to realize that this data showed not only each user's trip chain, but it showed their trip chain every day.

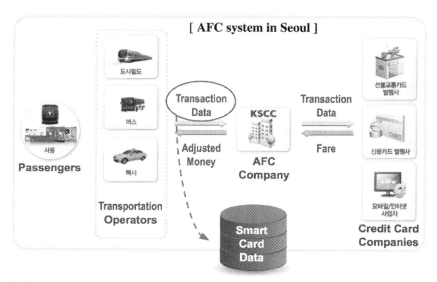

FIG. 4.12 How the Automated Fare Collection System collects and distributes fares in Seoul (Source: Korean Smart Card Co., adjusted by KRRI). *(From Korean Smart Card Co., adjusted by KRRI. AFC System in Seoul, https://seoulsolution.kr/sites/default/files/images/image00004(1).bmp.)*

This enabled transport analysts to accumulate data over time and tell with a high level of accuracy how many people passed through each station at any given time of day and which routes people tended to take as they moved about the city. If they could find a way to use this data, it would enable the streamlining of transport efficiency even further by adjusting the frequency of trains to the number of passengers actually riding at those times. This "smart" solution for citizens collected massive amounts of real public transport travel data that could eventually be used to optimize Seoul's system for much less cost and with much higher accuracy than the old survey-based analysis.

With the idea of taking advantage of the cache of data collected by the AFC System of Seoul's Tmoney smart card, The Korea Railroad Research Institute (KRRI) developed a tool (the Travel Record-based Integrated Public Transport Operation System [TRIPS]) that uses trip chain data from the smart card transportation data to map passenger behavior. Seoul had developed a similar system for its own exclusive use, but KRRI developed TRIPS for all other local governments and operators in Korea. To assist with this process, KRRI assisted The Ministry Of Land, Infrastructure, and Transport the amend the law to enable AFC managing companies to collect of smart card data in a standard format all over the country. The amendment to the law allows public organizations to use the collected smart card data without cost.

TRIPS takes smart card data from users and combines it with bus stop and route information as well as Internet map data to build trip chains for users. Because the smart card data has individual IDs (the IDs are like serial numbers for the cards and users' identities are masked), trip chains can be created and compared on an ongoing basis to map out long-term passenger behavior.

6.3 Data cleaning: Assessing available data

With the realization what the smart card data could do for transport planning, the first use of this data-based tool was to determine what data was available and assess the quality of the data. Because smart card utilization in Seoul is so high at 95%, trip chain data is extremely complete and reliable. With the TRIPS tool, operators could get a clear picture of how and when passengers were using public transportation to move around the city. This enabled transport authorities to do analysis for the current status of the system and identify service issues.

Under the new system implemented in 2004, transport operators in Seoul had a very complete set of data on traveler behavior and, coupled with additional data such as public transport routes and running times, were able to clearly map out the interactive and dynamic "big picture" of the urban transport situation in Seoul. They were able to assess passenger travel time, speed, mode share, number of transfers, number of boarding and alighting passengers at each station, transfer patterns, station influence area, etc.

6.4 Data analysis: The evolution of the TRIPS tool

The first task for the researchers was to analyze the data and assess all datasets individually and, as a whole, enabling transport authorities to not only be more reactive and proactive but also enabling them to assess priorities as well as cause-and-effect relationships so as to minimize effect of transport issues and keep the system running smoothly. This happened through the use of the TRIPS tool. Fig. 4.13 is an example of the TRIPS tool capabilities, showing a real-time snapshot of all 600 bus routes in Seoul that is color-coded for levels of congestion.

Further analysis of the system data served to assess demand for public transportation. Previous to the TRIPS analysis, authorities were only able to focus their analysis on the main mode of travel for each trip, but with the implementation of the TRIPS tool, authorities were able to get a relatively complete picture of how and when citizens move around the city. They were also able to get greater insight into how people travel. In a large city like Seoul with such a sophisticated transport network, there are many possible routes in public transportation to get from point A to point B. Up until the data became available and the TRIPS tool was created, transport authorities could only hypothesize about which routes were most popular.

Complete trip chain data has a big effect on transport planning because it allows planners to analyze not only primary but secondary effects of changes to the network. For example, a rider may take a bus two stops to the metro and then take the metro another seven stops to their job every morning. Under the old system, only the primary transport by metro would be assessed for

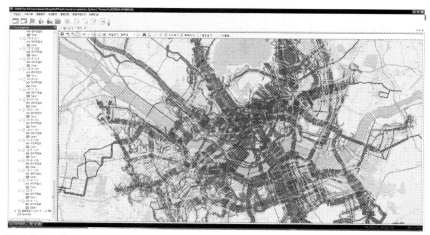

FIG. 4.13 Screen capture of TRIPS showing all bus routes in Seoul. *(From Min, J. (c. 2017). Data driven public transport operation by TRIPS. https://www.slideshare.net/ssuser6a129b/data-driven-publictransportationoperationbytripsjaehongmin.)*

planning. The secondary transport by bus would not have been visible on the user's trip data, but changes to those bus routes might have had a profound effect on the user's morning commute. The complete data chain from the TRIPS tools allows travel planners to assess the demand on each route for these short trips that connect users with their main form of transportation and include them as part of the equation when considering adjustments to the route.

With TRIPS, transport authorities are able to extract utility from smart card data to asses traffic demand and create plans not only for optimizing frequency in the current transport network but also as a touch point for future updates to the network.

"The development of TRIPS has had two main effects on transport efficiency," explains KRRI Principal Researcher Dr. Kyoungtae Kim. "The first is to standardize and collect transportation smart card data with MOLIT (Ministry of Land, Infrastructure, and Transport) so that it can be used for public purposes. No matter how good the data is, it is useless if it is difficult to access. The second is the development of a predictive algorithm to estimate the alighting location. Through this, more than 90% of the alighting information is accurately created, which greatly helps local governments that have been unable to even figure out whether they are doing well in their bus subsidy allocations."

The smart card data can also be used to focus on long-term planning. As a developed and proactive city government, Seoul is now using the data tool to optimize its public transport system. As described before, the tool has enabled Korean transport authorities to improve user experience through a complete analysis of the current situation and an assessment of the overall demand. This has enabled the system to be more resilient by minimizing service issues and resolving them quickly. It has also enabled authorities to understand their users better by mapping out and studying their behavior.

6.5 Data modeling: A proactive city government tool

While analysis and assessment of the current situation has undoubtedly improved the efficiency and performance of the Seoul public transport system, transport authorities and researchers have been able to take their data policies to maturity with the TRIPS tool and build models to work toward system optimization. Transport planners in Seoul are now able to use the results of the data-based analysis to develop optimal train scheduling through congestion analysis and model the effects of possible infrastructure changes on the transport system.

For example, the circular line in Seoul runs 48.8 km and has 43 stations. The scheduled train frequency of this line during rush hour is 2.5 min and the degree of congestion for this line can be as high as 220%! With such a high degree of congestion and tight rush hour schedule, it is clear that delays can easily occur. The transport modeling capacity of the TRIPS tool allows transport planners to estimate the effects of supplementing infrastructure to alleviate the problem of congestion on this line by enabling the development of new operation plans for alternate infrastructural environments and the simulation of traffic and congestion at each station for each alternative. The simulations allow authorities to then analyze and compare solutions to keep traffic flowing and minimize travel time for users.

Using the smart card data to build models has been key in Seoul because it has given city authorities the ability to reliably predict the use of public transport for years to come and, as a result, create long-term plans for mobility policy (Box 4.1). In general, it enabled the city government to work in a way that is proactive instead of reactionary.

KRRI Principal Researcher Jaehong Min explains why the need for dynamic predictive data tools like TRIPS will be in greater demand in the coming years. "As telecommuting increases after the COVID-19 pandemic, there will be an increased need for new mobility models in the future. We are currently seeing an increase in the desire to use a passenger car, which causes various social problems such as congestion, accidents, and the greenhouse effect. So we need to increase the use of public transportation, but public transportation cannot keep up with passenger cars in terms of flexibility. For this reason, we will need to develop efficient public transportation operation technologies that will satisfy diverse needs for transportation while making it safer and easier to use public transportation. Self-driving shuttle buses have already become commercialized in Europe, and research in Korea is underway. Also, with the emergence of unstructured semipublic transportation services such as PM (personal mobility such as electric scooters), big data-based 'optimal operation and linkage system' technology will be developed as an operational technology that links all public transportation in real time. TRIPS will be developed to lead this trend."

6.6 Other cases: Integrate with other big data

TRIPS has helped Seoul and other cities in South Korea develop mature and dynamic data-driven policies based on real data collected by smart cards. To further the usefulness of the tool, especially for cities where fares are not based on distance and the type of data available is different because users do not tag out when exiting a mode of transport, TRIPS is working with telecom operators to bring the same kind of data-driven solutions used in Seoul. TRIPS has developed an alighting location estimation algorithm which has shown more than 90% accuracy within two stops.

Also, TRIPS has a forecasting function that uses AI technology integrated with land use data. It can estimate the expected number of users by origin-destination for new bus stops. This function can be used in areas of new development to help public transportation operators create more efficient operations plans.

Although not created through the TRIPS tool but using similar methodology, an example of how Seoul is combining data sources to create policy to

Box 4.1 Interview with CIO/Executive Vice-Mayor of Seoul (2011–13).

We had the great pleasure and honor to meet the CIO/Executive Vice-Mayor of Seoul (2011–13), Dr. Jong Sung Hwang (Fig. 4.14). Dr. Hwang is currently the Master Planner for the Busan Eco Delta National Pilot Smart City and a member of South Korea's National Smart City Committee. In the following text, we share the main points raised during this interview.

Question: The public transport system is Seoul is often cited as one of the best in the world. What was the vision for creating the 2004 reforms that transformed the city's transport system?

Answer: The key vision was sustainable urban transport, in line with the concept of ESSD, environmentally sound and sustainable development, proposed by the UN. One of the methods was to change transport policy to a walking and public transportation-focused one, nudging citizens not to use cars and to use public transportation and walking instead.

Question: A Unified Fare Smart Card was quite advanced for 2004, so it is easy to imagine that the creators of this plan got a lot of pushback on this idea. What were the main obstacles that had to be overcome to implement these reforms and how did the government overcome them?

Answer: In fact, Korea as a whole had a high level of innovative culture at that time, as a result of successes in digital transformation initiatives including broadband Internet and e-government. Resistance to innovation like the smart card was not so strong and tangible. The city government, however, had to provide strong incentives to bus companies to restructure bus lines across the city and innovate fare systems. As a result, a semipublic bus system was introduced.

Question: Was obtaining transport user data an objective when the city government was designing the 2004 transport reforms? If not, when did they realize the value of the data from the Unified Fare System (the smart card)?

FIG. 4.14 Dr. Jong Sung Hwang, former CIO/Executive Vice-Mayor of Seoul.

Continued

Box 4.1 Interview with CIO/Executive Vice-Mayor of Seoul (2011–13)—cont'd

Answer: When we started the new transport system, data analysis was not one of our main goals. The concept of and technologies for big data did not exist. It was after 2010 that the city government tried to use smart card data for transport policy and other purposes. It could be said that analysis of smart card data became a sort of routine and important policy tool when the city government developed a transport data analytics system, called TRIPS in short, Travel Record-based Integrated Public transport operating planning System in 2014.

Question: When you were CIO/Executive Vice-Mayor of Seoul, governments were just starting to realize how they could use data for optimizing city services and making the city more socially and environmentally sustainable. What were the key phases in the development of Seoul as a data-driven city?

Answer: Personally, I wanted to make an evolution in digital strategy from an information-based one to a data-based one long before I became the CIO of the Seoul Metropolitan Government in 2011. When we designed a long-term national digital strategy in the mid-1990s, we had in mind that information flow is not the end, and it is just a building block for a digital society, in which data-driven decisions became a new normal. When I started my job as the CIO, the city government had a well-developed city-wide database and data-use infrastructures. On top of that, we developed a public data-sharing system in 2012, allowing anyone to access and use public data created and managed by the city government.

Question: In general terms how has the use of data-driven policies changed the lives of citizens in Seoul?

Answer: One of the biggest benefits from data-driven policies was the increase of trust in government. It has dispelled citizen's doubts about fairness of public policy to a certain degree by providing objective basis of policies and decision-making. Another benefit could include the strengthening of government capabilities. For instance, city government became able to recognize and solve problems with data analytics before citizens complained about them.

Question: And how has the Smart Card and data it produces changed the way the city government manages the transportation system?

Answer: The city government can monitor transportation services quickly and accurately and design solutions based on simulation and other data analytics techniques. Smart card data provides almost real data, not sample data. All subway passengers and "almost" all bus users use a smart card, so that smart card data helps the city government monitor and analyze situation quite accurately.

Question: How have you resolved the problems of data privacy/security/confidentiality, especially when you collect personal data?

Answer: It mostly depends on national laws and regulations on privacy and security. Korea is one of those countries that protect privacy very strongly. The reason for this is because the Korean people experienced problems during the 1960s through the 1980s due to the authoritarian regimes that breached privacy often and easily. In terms of data management, personal data collected by the smart card company is under close control of the city government.

> **Box 4.1 Interview with CIO/Executive Vice-Mayor of Seoul (2011–13)—cont'd**
>
> The company needs approval from the city government every time it uses personal data for any purpose other than the original intended use.
>
> **Question**: What are the main stakeholders (private or public or hybrid companies, citizens?) involved in your main projects/strategy?
>
> **Answer**: It depends on types of projects. Usually private sectors and citizens are the biggest stakeholders.
>
> **Question**: How do you manage this business ecosystem of companies and their interrelated actions for a common goal? What are the main issues you had to face?
>
> **Answer**: Institution or investment. The best way to make private players to act for a common goal is to provide effective incentives for that goal with institutions including law, regulation, and culture. But it takes time to develop good institutions. For a short and midterm effect, the city government can use financial investment as a tool to induce private players toward a common goal.
>
> **Question**: What will be your recommendations/good practices based on your experience for future city managers that would like to transform their city and make it data-driven city?
>
> **Answer**: It usually takes a long time to make a data-driven city. There is no way to do it quickly. So it is necessary to have a long-term view and strategy and take a step-by-step approach. One of the must-have items for that approach is an overall architecture. Any city should have their own data and decision-making architecture that works best in their city. In addition, more focus should be placed on common infrastructure than on the individual use case. In many cases, city government tries to develop successful use cases. But without common infrastructure, such efforts cost a lot or cannot sustain itself.

improve the lives of citizens is the Owl Bus, a late-night city bus operating in Seoul since 2013. It is not part of the regular Seoul transport network but has routes between principle areas of the city from midnight to 5 a.m. The routes were determined through analysis of taxi data and mobile phone data during these late-night hours to cover transport demand during the hours when the Seoul metro is closed. Responding to a clear need in the city, the data-driven service was awarded both the "Best Policy" award by citizens and the Presidential Award after its first year of service.

A Appendix I: Questionnaire

This questionnaire helps to identify at what stage of the smart city lifecycle a particular city is in, according to the model defined in Section 2.2. This model defines four stages: inception (I), launching (L), growing (G), and maturity (M).

148   Implementing data-driven strategies in smart cities

We have also considered that the city has not initiated (N) the lifecycle in specific aspects. The questionnaire considers the following aspects:

The internal *organization* of the city hall, as the focal organization of the smart city ecosystem.
The *technology* adopted in data-driven city projects.
The *management of data* obtained in different data-driven smart city projects.
The degree of involvement of the *stakeholders* in the smart city project.

A.1 Organization

Data-driven city strategy:

Concepts like a smart city or data-driven city are absent from the organizational strategy debate (N).
There is growing awareness in local government about the smart city and data-driven city concepts (I).
A strategy plan for achieving the status of data-driven city has been approved and implemented (L).
The city has a strategy to develop data-driven projects and capabilities, including key performing indicators (G).

Data-driven city structure:

City hall is considering developing data-driven or smart city projects (I).
Smart city projects are developed in different city hall departments, with the help of external partners (L).
The city hall has developed an organizational unit to undertake data-driven projects (G).
The city hall has a data-driven decision center reporting directly to the mayor, and each city hall department has a chief data officer (CDO).

A.2 Technology

The city is currently implementing data-driven city projects using the following technologies (choose those that apply):

Web content (I).
Social media (I).
Mobile apps (L).
Data analytics (L).
Artificial intelligence (e.g., chat bots) (G).
Internet of things (e.g., sensors) (G).
Virtual reality/augmented reality (G).
Twin city in the cloud (M).
None of the above (N).

A.3 Data management

Data maturity:

> The city council has no plans to collect and store data from the city (N).
> Some projects are being carried out to collect data from the city, but the amount of data collected so far is limited (I).
> Several projects of data collection have been implemented so far, and a considerable amount of data has been collected from them (L).
> There is an ongoing plan to collect data from the city systematically and to store it in an integrated repository (G).
> The city implements cutting-edge technologies of data collection to build a twin city in the cloud (M).

Data quality covers topics related with:

> Data integration, meaning that data coming from data-driven is stored in a format compatible with data coming from other projects.
> Quality assurance (e.g., data cleansing, treatment of outliers and missing data, etc.).
> Quality control, consisting of defining standards to allow integration of data in existing applications.

The situation of the city regarding data quality can be described as:

> No data is gathered from the city, so data quality is not a concern (N).
> There are plans to develop smart city projects in the near future, but data quality is not a concern (I).
> Data is gathered in specific projects, but there is no data quality plan (L).
> Data across projects are integrated (G).
> Data gathered in the city is integrated, and there are data assurance and control processes implemented (M).

Data exploitation:

> There are concerns about gathering data from the city, but no data is exploited at the moment (I).
> Data coming from a data-driven project is used only for that project (L).
> All data from data-driven projects is stored at a repository accessible at the organizational level, to be reused in future projects (G).
> All data from data-driven projects is stored at a repository accessible to the digital business ecosystem (M).

A.4 Involvement of stakeholders in the data-driven city (quadruple helix)

Drawing on the quadruple helix model of innovation, we can distinguish four key stakeholders in the process of building a data-driven city:

> Local government.

Industry.
Universities.
The public (civil society and media).

The participation of **industry** in data-driven projects can be described as:

No involvement (N/I).
Involvement in specific projects (L).
Systematic involvement (G).
Institutionalized involvement (e.g., city-industry agreements, joint institutions) (M).

The participation of **universities** in data-driven projects can be described as:

No involvement (N/I).
Involvement in specific projects (L).
Systematic involvement (G).
Institutionalized involvement (e.g., city-industry agreements, joint institutions) (M).

The awareness of the **civil society and media** on the data-driven city can be described as:

No awareness (N/I).
Interests for specific projects (L).
Citizens are educated as users of the data-driven city (G).
Being a data-driven city is a central element of city's identity (M).

References

Adner, R., & Kapoor, R. (2016). Innovation ecosystems and the pace of substitution: Re-examining technology S-curves. *Strategic Management Journal*, *37*, 625–648. https://doi.org/10.1002/smj.2363.

Albino, V., Berardi, U., & Dangelico, R. M. (2015). Smart cities: Definitions, dimensions, performance, and initiatives. *Journal of Urban Technology*, *22*(1), 3–21. https://doi.org/10.1080/10630732.2014.942092.

Bunnell, T. G., & Coe, N. M. (2001). Spaces and scales of innovation. *Progress in Human Geography*, *25*(4), 569–589. https://doi.org/10.1191/030913201682688940.

Burke, W., Beskow, L., & Trinidad, S. (2018). Infomed consent in translational genomics: Insufficient without trustworthy governance. *The Journal of Law, Medicine & Ethics*, *46*, 79–86.

Derqui, B., & Grimaldi, D. (2020). Data on the sustainability profile and food waste management in primary and secondary schools: The case of the Catalonia region in Spain. *Data in Brief*, *28*. https://doi.org/10.1016/j.dib.2019.104825. In press.

Grimaldi, D. (2019). Can we analyse political discourse using Twitter? Evidence from Spanish 2019 presidential election. *Social Network Analysis and Mining*, *49*. https://doi.org/10.1007/s13278-019-0594-6. In press.

Grimaldi, D., Diaz, J., Arboleda, H., & Fernandez, V. (2019). Data maturity analysis and business performance. A Colombian case study. *Heliyon*, *8*(1). https://doi.org/10.1016/j.heliyon.2019.e02195. In press.

Grimaldi, D., & Fernandez, V. (2017). The road to school. The Barcelona case. *Cities*, *65*, 24–31. https://doi.org/10.1016/j.cities.2017.01.013. In press.

Grimaldi, D., & Fernandez, V. (2019). Performance of an internet of things project in the public sector: The case of Nice smart city. *The Journal of High Technology Management Research*, *30*(1), 27–39. https://doi.org/10.1016/j.hitech.2018.12.003. In press.

Grimaldi, D., Fernandez, V., & Carrasco, C. (2018). Heuristic for the localization of new shops based on business and social criteria. *Technological Forecasting and Social Change*, *142*, 249–257. https://doi.org/10.1016/j.techfore.2018.07.034. In press.

Grimaldi, D., Fernandez, V., & Carrasco, C. (2019). Exploring data conditions to improve business performance. *Journal of the Operational Research Society*, *4*(12), 1–11. https://doi.org/10.1080/01605682.2019.1590136. In press.

Gymrek, M., McGuire, A. L., Golan, D., Halperin, E., & Erlich, Y. (2013). Identifying personal genomes by surname inference. *Science*, *339*(6117), 321–324. https://doi.org/10.1126/science.1229566.

Harrison, C., Eckman, B., Hamilton, R., Hartswick, P., Kalagnanam, J., Paraszczak, J., & Williams, P. (2010). Foundations for smarter cities. *IBM Journal of Research and Development*, *54*(4), 1–16.

Janssen, M., & Kuk, G. (2016). The challenges and limits of big data algorithms in technocratic governance. *Government Information Quarterly*, *33*(3), 371–377. https://doi.org/10.1016/j.giq.2016.08.011.

Kashin, K., King, G., & Soneji, S. (2015). Systematic bias and nontransparency in US Social Security Administration Forecasts. *Journal of Economic Perspectives*, *292*, 239–258. https://doi.org/10.1257/jep.29.2.239.

Komninos, N., Pallot, M., & Schaffers, H. (2013). Special issue on smart cities and the future internet in Europe. *Journal of the Knowledge Economy*, *4*, 119–134.

Kummitha, R. K. R. (2019). Smart cities and entrepreneurship: An agenda for future research. *Technological Forecasting and Social Change*, *149*, 119763. https://doi.org/10.1016/j.techfore.2019.119763.

Madlener, R., & Sunak, Y. (2011). Impacts of urbanization on urban structures and energy demand: What can we learn for urban energy planning and urbanization management? *Sustainable Cities and Society*, *1*, 45–53.

Reisman, D., Schultz, J., Crawford, K., & Whittaker, M. (2018). Algorithmic impact assessments: A practical framework for public agency accountability. *AI Now Institute*. https://ainowinstitute.org/aiareport2018.pdf.

Tran Thi Hoang, G., Dupont, L., & Camargo, M. (2019). Application of decision-making methods in smart city projects: A systematic literature review. *Smart Cities*, *2*(3), 433–452. https://doi.org/10.3390/smartcities2030027.

United Nations, Department of Economic and Social Affairs. (2018). *Population division (2019)*. New York: United Nations. https://www.un.org/development/desa/dspd/wp-content/uploads/sites/22/2018/07/1-1.pdf.

Zygiaris, S. (2013). Smart city reference model: Assisting planners to conceptualize the building of smart city innovation ecosystems. *The Journal of the Knowledge Economy*, *4*, 217–231. https://doi.org/10.1007/s13132-012-0089-4.

Chapter 5

Enabling technologies for data-driven cities

Carlos Carrasco-Farré[a], Ramon Martín de Pozuelo[b], and Didier Grimaldi[c]

[a]*Ramon Llull University—ESADE Business School, Barcelona, Spain,* [b]*Research Group on Internet Technologies & Storage, Department of Engineering—La Salle University, Manila, Philippines,* [c]*Ramon Llull University, La Salle Faculty, Barcelona, Spain*

This chapter focuses on the technologies that enable one to translate real-world scenarios in the city into a collection of data. Data-driven cities are only possible if they rely on technologies that allow one to monitor what it is happening in the urban space. We need a city ICT infrastructure able to digitalize and transform city problems into streams of digital raw data that can be processed to react and plan consequently.

The chapter table of contents is structured as follows:

- "Data-driven Cities and Smart Cities: Technology is the tool, not the goal"
- "Which technologies are needed in a data-driven city? From IoT to Big Data"
  - Data collection
  - Data transportation
  - Data storage
  - Data preparation
  - Data analysis
  - Data visualization

1 Data-driven cities and smart cities: Technology is the tool, not the goal

Data-driven cities and smart cities concepts define, without a doubt, very complex ecosystems in which numerous technologies and multiple agents are involved that implement, operate, and use them. These technologies also face challenges such as scalability, capacity, mobility and information security, and privacy management. Therefore, to fully understand the value chain of the services proposed within the framework of the smart city, it is also necessary to understand what technology can offer.

Creating a data-driven city is much more than providing certain novel IT-enabled services. Deploying a data-driven city is associated with the creation of a series of infrastructures as well as having information management mechanisms and different platforms. And all this is integrated from a global perspective.

However, technologies should never be considered the goal, neither the data itself. Technologies mean nothing without a specific purpose that benefits the city management or the citizens. The usage of the technology is normally focused on obtaining data that helps one to have better knowledge of the city system's behavior and be more efficient in its management. Even for the technologies used in that direction and provide data that could be relevant for the city managers, data means nothing without the correct interpretation. When addressing the implementation of an initiative to move toward a smart city, we must think, first of all, about citizens and how to increase their happiness, making their lives easier and more comfortable.

Technologies should be considered as enablers of the management of the cities' data lifecycle. In this way, thanks to the data collected from sensors distributed across the smart city, transported to a storage system, and correspondingly analyzed and visualized, the municipal authorities and other data owners can:

- Attend to emergencies as soon as possible, emitting an alarm when an incidence occurs based on sensor signals.
- Check the state of progress of the different KPIs, matching them with the objectives defined in the data-driven city plan and reviewing their level of compliance.
- Analyze the historic recorded data to draw conclusions and establish recurring behavioral patterns to predict future trends and plan accordingly.

The rest of this chapter will focus on listing and detailing those technologies that are relevant for the efficient deployment of the data-driven cities, but it is important to highlight that the focus of the city should always remain on the citizens, and the deployment of efficient smart cities and data-driven cities must go beyond a technological perspective to adopt a humanistic perspective. And for this, technologies are enabling a means to reach an end focused on improving people's lives. To achieve this vision, any data-driven initiative has to be conceived as a long-term project, defining objectives and priorities, which may be different for each city (although all major cities share basic problems) and in which a public-private collaboration is substantiated. A project led by the local administration must include, as a relevant chapter, a change in management that helps citizens to know and understand the transformation of their habitat.

2 Which technologies are needed in a data-driven city? From IoT to big data

There is not a single standard approach to categorize the different technologies that enable the deployment of data-driven cities, providing the technological infrastructure to collect the data from the physical real world and converting it into meaningful information that can be helpful for assisting the urban services management.

Considering the different phases in the data lifecycle, we propose to divide it in the following categories:

- *Data collection*: In the first place is the stage of data collection of the city. This task is performed using sensors, actuators, and different devices, which must include people's own mobile phones, different devices in the home environment, vehicles, as well as measuring devices located in fixed infrastructures, such as in street furniture, in buildings, in piping systems and pipes, in weather stations, and so on.
- *Data transportation*: Second, the data collected from the city are transmitted through communication networks. This is done through a combination of wireless, mobile, and fixed infrastructure depending on the mobility, bandwidth, and latency needs of the particular application. In some cases, wireless and mobile networks will be the only ones available. The architecture of this network will be very varied. As a general rule, the sensors will transmit the information through lightweight protocols to coordinators or gateways, which in turn will route the data through mobile or fixed lines and will make it reach the databases and platforms that facilitate the provision of services.
- *Data storage*: The following phase comprises the storage of the data. It generally is a question of storing the data collected in a central platform in the environment of the city at the same time as it facilitates the back processing by means of different analytical systems. To do this, the information repository must not be volatile, also allowing for subsequent use of data by applications and services.
- *Data preparation*: Before going into the analysis of the data, normally raw data must be adapted to be processed by the data analytical tools. Furthermore, it should be also considered that data preparation processes could be also done before the data storage or even data transportation phases if it helps to reduce the amount of data to be stored or transmitted. In fact, this is done in most of the cases to be as efficient as possible in the usage of ICT resources.
- *Data analysis*: Fifth, the data is processed to extract meaningful information that can be used to monitor the behavior of the system (i.e., transportation, energy, parks irrigation, citizens' behavior, and services' demands, etc.) better planning its management in the future. Sometimes, the analysis

is done in real-time to extract anomalous patterns and trigger alarms. That should activate certain procedures by the city administration to revise them and actuate when necessary (i.e., increase police support in a certain area, alert the fire station, etc.).
– *Data visualization*: Finally, when necessary, data is integrated in a platform or tool that allows a fast visual analysis for the provision of services. This platform can also facilitate the provision of services in the field of the data-driven city and made up of modules that allow it to deploy specific services with third parties and the citizens. Hence, in those cases, the objective of the platform is also to incorporate interfaces that will be used to implement the services that will be delivered to end customers.

Finally there are smart city services, which may be developed by the same agents involved in the rest of the technology value chain or by other agents, in many cases, the agents already involved in the provision of each service in concrete areas of the city belonging to the different sectors and economic areas (i.e., power energy suppliers, public transportation, or waste management subsidiaries). The provision of services within the smart city framework will necessarily involve the participation of numerous agents of different nature and character who will play diverse roles. There is no single ecosystem model. There are multiple possibilities and multiple models, and even in different city implementations, the same agents can play different roles.

Combining technologies for a Smarter City: The case smart lampposts

Under the umbrella of the European project GrowSmarter, the cities of Barcelona, Cologne, and Stockholm implemented a series of augmented lampposts. More in particular, the measure was about the integration of lighting, environmental sensors, and communication devices (in the case of Barcelona); sensors were used to collect and analyze data about vehicle flow and emissions (in Stockholm) and electric charging (in Cologne) into a single respective lighting pole. In general, the idea was to prove that lampposts can not only provide lighting, but also they can be transformed into multifunctional smart towers.

Each city showcased a use case for a new generation of lamppost. For example, in the case of Stockholm, real-time data collected by sensors gave an understanding of how people travel to events taking place in the area where the lampposts were deployed, making possible the development of applications for lowering transport-based emissions. Similarly, in the case of the Barcelona's "SmartTower" solution, the city transformed the traditional lamppost into new telecommunication micro-sites that integrate wireless communication devices and sensors. In addition, Barcelona's SmartTowers are connected to the Fiber Optic Backbone Network. By doing so, these new lampposts offer a solution for hyperconnected areas that serve a growing demand for wireless and mobile connectivity. Furthermore, in the case of Cologne, the city combined electrical charging with street lighting poles. The aim was to make walkable urban areas ubiquitously connected and to enable a shared sensing infrastructure in the open street spaces. In general, all three

Enabling technologies for data-driven cities Chapter | 5 157

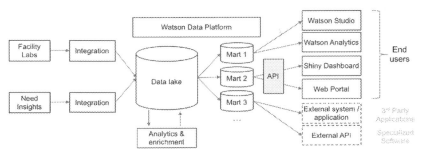

FIG. 5.1 IBM's platform architecture for Stockholm in GrowSmarter Project. *(Source: IBM.)*

deployments were based on the concepts of connectivity, positioning, and electricity with the aim to not just offering traditional services (like lighting) or more new ones (like mobile connectivity) but also to offer the opportunity to develop new services for citizens.

This is important because the growing demand of broadband mobile communications requires a dense network of small urban sites deployed around the city to support all the wireless connectivity needs (Fig. 5.1). However, the need for a denser network comes at a cost: the deployment of new infrastructure. With the aim to rationalize the deployment of dense networks based on small cells and microsites, the implementations in Barcelona, Cologne, and Stockholm took advantage of existing urban furniture, like street lighting poles, through their transformation into smart infrastructures. One of the examples of new usages of the deployed lampposts is that vehicle sensors combined with air pollution sensors can be used in cities and areas where the air pollution from traffic exceeds the levels set by the EU. In addition, this information can be communicated to drivers through digital screens that personalize the information based on the type of vehicle passing by.

However, despite the positive results of these measures, there are also challenges, being the multiplicity of administrators involved one of the main issues. In the cited cities, the stakeholders in charge of the infrastructure deployment had to interact with different administrations or administrative departments, whether it was for getting permits and licenses or for getting access to data. In that sense, having some procedures to overcome interdepartmental relationships and siloed routines in administration can facilitate the successful and timely deployment of this type of technology. For example, city administrators could facilitate the implementation by shifting away the procurement process from the classic model based on price toward other models in which the expected and desired value to be delivered plays a central role.

Moreover, before going into depth on the most relevant technologies that are used on the previously mentioned phases, it should be noted that, sometimes, the sensing systems included in the data collection and data transportation phases are already provided with some intelligence. In those cases, they can act autonomously to provide certain services or parts of the service without the need to connect to the central server. This fact blurs the categorization of those technologies because they offer functionalities of almost all the phases. An example in this sense could be that of irrigation systems, which could be activated with a schedule that also takes into account the humidity of the environment, so that some part of the service, with its logic or intelligence, could work autonomously without the need to connect to a central server. In addition, the system could be activated remotely or report data to the central system to later be used to analyze how to optimize the maintenance of gardens, learn from the usage, etc. All in all, we will include the technologies considering the category in which its functionalities fit most and are essential for that phase.

Next, we present and categorize some of the main technologies of those phases that will be the protagonists of these changes in the cities of the 21st century.

2.1 Data collection

2.1.1 Sensors and internet of things (IoT) devices

Sensors are integrated into all the physical devices that make up the Internet of Things ecosystem. From our smart watches to vehicles, smart homes, or traffic lights. These sensors collect information from the environment and transmit that data to the cloud. In this way, all the elements can function as a network.

Some of the changes for the smart cities of the future include smart traffic lights, which efficiently analyze and direct traffic flow, streetlights that illuminate according to the passage of pedestrians, monitoring air quality, or even buildings that control their own sanitation network.

Everything that is part of a smart city must be connected so that it can communicate with each other as part of a whole.

IoT is moving into an IoE (Internet of Everything) trend, so in addition to connected objects (containers, bins, streetlights, traffic lights, buses, pickup trucks, sprinklers, etc.), we will have connected and sensorized living beings: trees, pets, even people. We will be sensorized, and we will transmit our position, in addition to certain parameters that will improve the management of the city itself.

2.1.2 Mobile phones and wearables

As mentioned, those sensors are not just included on specialized objects that are located at specific points in the urban infrastructure. Citizens are increasingly part of the data collection process. Thanks to our mobile phones and wearables, and through municipal and third-party apps, we are already offering valuable information to administrations that, with anonymized data, are detecting the habits, preferences, and behaviors of citizens and are crossing them with other

Open Data variables, such as meteorological data or the calendar of events to be able to predict future behaviors. This information with data mining techniques and data analytics can also be used afterward to improve public services.

2.1.3 Geolocation technology

Another trend in these new cities has to do with geolocation. The right way to build urban planning for smart cities requires precision and the analysis and use of detailed data. This is exactly the role that geospatial or geolocation technologies play. They provide the underlying basis on which each smart city solution can be built. Geospatial technology provides the location and framework needed to collect and analyze data, transforming that data to facilitate software-based solutions around smart city infrastructure.

2.1.4 Robotics

If we talk about the infrastructure that is interacting with the real world, we should not only consider sensors but also actuators. The integration of robots into urban spaces is rapidly transforming some of the most technologically advanced cities. Experts in the field of robotics are positive about the benefits that robots can bring to society in various fields. Collaboration between humans and robots must take into account two things: how robots work and how humans decide to use them. Robots are part of the previously mentioned technologies that blur the city data phases, as they can be self-dependent, integrating functionalities from all the phases, sensing, storing the data, analyzing it, and reacting to the stimulus emulating human behaviors. Examples of its usage are already demonstrated in Tokyo (autonomous taxis), Singapore (delivery services), or Dubai (public services, transportation, policing, and surveillance).[a]

2.2 Data transportation

2.2.1 5G

The 5G standard has been designed to support an extremely wide range of situations like those that can occur in a big city. From the concentrations of high demanding mobile traffic in urban centers up to much denser and data-consuming IoT deployments than the current ones, going through critical applications that require low latency and high availability. 5G provides universal, unrestricted connectivity via sensor networks (IoT) or mobile devices of citizens.

Without a powerful network, nothing would be possible in a smart city. 5G technology enhances the next level of connectivity for industries and society. Without 5G, none of the other smart city technologies mentioned would be

---

a. https://www.smartcity.press/robotic-system-integration/#:~:text=After%20having%20understood%20the%20rolecities%20as%20the%20emerging%20prototypes.

possible. The idea is that this high-speed connection allows improvements in communication between IoT devices, sensors, or promotes the implementation of autonomous vehicles.

This extended network will become ubiquitous and it will move a massive amount of data that will no longer come only from mobiles but a large number of devices such as sensors, actuators, cameras, and vehicle infrastructure. 5G offers the kind of quality and service guarantee that, until now, was associated only with the deployment of physical networks such as cable or fiber. It will be taken for granted that people and things will be able to connect to the network without having to consider the deployment step of physical networks through civil works. This step was hitherto inevitable in many deployments, long and costly, and caused inconvenience to citizens.

The 5G network can become an invisible network that supports all technologies needed to meet the challenges of cities. The 5G network consists of a series of layers ranging from mobile devices and sensors to the virtual network that supports data applications. Between the physical world and the cloud, 5G deploys a redesigned and potentially much denser radio network than current ones, a virtualized network core and, when necessary, a local process network (MEC or multiaccess edge computing).

2.2.2 Low power wide area networks (LPWAN)

There are two types of wireless communication technologies for the IoT: short-range networks such as Wifi, Bluetooth, ZigBee (and other IEEE 802.15.4 variants (Baronti et al., 2007)), or radiofrequency identification (RFID), with a range from a few centimeters to a few hundred meters, and long-range networks, effective up to several thousand kilometers thanks to antenna networks. Among those long-range networks, we find the traditional cellular networks (GSM, GPRS, etc.) already used for machine-to-machine (M2M) communications. However, for a use that requires the implementation of numerous sensors capable of transmitting a very small amount of data at low speed, the solution of traditional cellular networks would be oversized. This is where LPWAN networks come into play, created to anticipate the planned obsolescence of GPRS networks. 2G modules have been efficient in their day and still are, but more refined technologies were needed.

Wireless mobile communications are optimal for connecting devices in a massive and ubiquitous way, but it is necessary that connected objects can extend the life of their batteries for years instead of months, that the range of communications is sufficient to deploy IoT networks over large areas without having to extend communications infrastructures, and the price of modules is low enough to offer a realistic ROI to companies interested in deploying IoT solutions. However, there are several technologies approaching these LPWANs that have arisen in the last few years.

Before the appearance of standards, companies were form dedicated to offering specific connectivity services for IoT, such as Sigfox (Zuniga & Ponsard, 2016) or groups of companies around a technology such as Lora (Bor, Vidler, & Roedig, 2016), with very appreciated characteristics such as low power consumption or low cost of modules and data, as well as the long range of communications. Weightless, for example, is one of the most used in IoT, within the Weightless SIG group (Raza, Kulkarni, & Sooriyabandara, 2017). It is an open LPWAN technology, highly optimized for IoT in terms of cost and battery life. There are three variants of the technology: Weightless N, Weightless P, and Weightless W, the latter being the fastest in terms of transmission bitrate.

However, on the other hand, 3GPP (Wang et al., 2017), the body that defines standards for mobile communications, took note of the shortcomings that 3G and 4G had for IoT communications and prepared an LTE standard as appropriate technologies for their usage. That resulted in the NB-IoT (Narrowband IoT) standard (Ratasuk, Vejlgaard, Mangalvedhe, & Ghosh, 2016), which focuses specifically on indoor coverage, low cost, long battery life, and high connection density. NB-IoT uses a subset of the LTE standard, deployed over the existing infrastructure for 4G, but it is also capable of taking advantage of 5G in the future.

2.3 Data storage

2.3.1 Hybrid cloud

The IoT is going global, and the most common predictions raise the number of connected devices above 25,000 billion in 2021 (Gartner, 2018). The huge amount of data originated by these IoT devices need to be stored somewhere, and the ability of public administration and private organizations to store and extract useful information will be the key to long-term success. We need scalable storage systems that allow sustaining and efficiently managing all that generated Big Data. Here is where cloud computing/storage will play a big role.

A characteristic of the IoT is that we can expand the number of devices very easily and, therefore, the cloud has to respond to this change in scale with agility. Fortunately, the ability to scale is one of the main advantages of the cloud.

Among the different approaches to deploy cloud infrastructure (Jamsa, 2012), the most trending option nowadays is the hybrid cloud, which tries to bring the best advantages from both options.

Hybrid clouds combine local infrastructure (or private clouds) with public clouds. In a hybrid cloud, data and applications can move between private and public clouds for more flexibility and deployment options. For example, you can use the public cloud to meet high-volume needs with less security, such as web email, and the private cloud (or other on-premises infrastructure) for sensitive privacy-critical or business-critical operations, such as sensors that are collecting sensitive personal data from citizens. It provides much more flexibility, and an application or resource can run in the private cloud until there is a spike in demand (for example, when adding a new set of sensors that are placed only for the control of a sporadic public event). At this point, the organization can "scale" to the public cloud to leverage more computing resources.

2.3.2 Edge/fog computing and distributed storage

Edge/Fog computing is a distributed computing paradigm that brings computation and data storage closer to the location where it is needed, to improve response times and save bandwidth. It is a solution that simplifies the relationship between the IoT and the cloud because it brings the processing of part of the data closer to the place where it was generated.

In this way, by processing part of the data almost in situ, sending the rest of the data to the cloud:

- We gain in response speed, reducing latency for critical calculations.
- We enable real-time applications, like many of the autonomous car operations, for example.
- We reduce both the expense and the need for bandwidth.

2.3.3 NoSQL databases

In the early years of databases, each application stored data in its own unique structure. When developers wanted to build applications to use that data, they had to know a lot about the particular data structure to find the data they needed. These data structures were inefficient, difficult to maintain, and difficult to optimize for good application performance. The relational database model was designed to solve the problem of several arbitrary data structures. That was very important at that time, but the technological evolution of society and the massive participation of users and IoT smart objects that produce and host content every second required a more flexible way of storing, ordering, and capturing more data. That is what has helped to fix the NoSQL databases. A NoSQL (originally referring to "non-SQL" or "nonrelational") database provides a mechanism for storage and retrieval of data that is modeled in means other than the tabular relations used in relational databases. The main characteristic of NoSQL databases is that they do not use the SQL (Stonebraker, 2010) query language, and they are also especially designed to allow for storage and management of large data banks. As their main characteristic, the NoSQL Databases solve the main problems that we were currently face:

- Horizontal scaling: We no longer need to depend on a hardware vendor to power our solutions.
- Data availability: We can distribute as much equipment and economic capacity as we have if we need them to be robust.

- Solution to network failures or outages: We have an interconnected ecosystem that, to a great extent, will always have data availability.

2.3.4 Cybersecurity, Blockchain, and distributed ledger technologies (DLTs)

Connected cameras, intelligent road systems, and public safety monitoring systems can provide an extra layer of protection and emergency support to help citizens when needed. But what about protecting smart cities themselves from vulnerabilities? How can we defend ourselves against hackers, cyberattacks, and data theft? In cities where multiple participants share information, how do we trust participants to be who they claim to be? And how do we know that the data they report is true and accurate? The answer lies in physical data vaults and robust authentication and ID management solutions. Smart cities can only work if we can trust them. All ecosystem partners (governments, businesses, software vendors, device manufacturers, power providers, and network service providers) must do their part and integrate solutions that meet four basic security objectives:

- *Availability*: Without actionable, real-time, reliable data access, the smart city cannot thrive. How data is collected, distilled, and shared is critical, and security solutions must avoid the negative effects on availability.
- *Integrity*: Smart cities depend on reliable and accurate data. Steps must be taken to ensure that the data is accurate and free of manipulation. Smart cities depend on reliable and accurate data
- *Confidentiality*: Some of the data collected, stored, and analyzed will include sensitive information about consumers. Steps must be taken to prevent the unauthorized disclosure of confidential information.
- *Responsibility*: Users of a system must be responsible for their actions. Your interactions with sensitive systems must be recorded and associated with a specific user. These records should be difficult to falsify and have strong integrity protection.

DLTs will play a key role in this process to ensure the incorruptible and unchanging value of the data with which other technologies work. A DLT (also called a shared ledger or distributed ledger technology) is a consensus of replicated, shared, and synchronized digital data geographically spread across multiple sites, countries, or institutions. A peer-to-peer network is required as well as consensus algorithms to ensure replication across nodes is undertaken, and unlike with a distributed database, there is no central administrator. Blockchain system is the most well-known form of DLT, although not the only one.

The value provided by 5G, IoT, robotics, geoposition, AI, or machine learning depend on the verification of the data managed and its veracity. DLTs/Blockchain's main goal is to ensure that information gets from its source to its management in databases. Hence it is known as the Internet of Trust. It is precisely this feature that allows the immutability of information, which has been used to solve the problem of double-spending (mathematical foundation) for the development of sectors such as Fintech. But DLT goes much further, as its applications in the field of smart cities will be crucial in the development of new business models that will significantly affect its sustainability. Models of circular, collaborative economy or even new models of labor contracts, focused on the management of the intellectual rights of our work, will be possible.

2.4 Data preparation

In Big Data, the words "data preparation" include all activities related to the collection, combination, and organization of messy, inconsistent, and nonstandardized data from diverse sources. In practically every Big Data project, we will find ourselves faced with the need to validate, clean, and transform the data we have collected. Once we have completed all these "data preparation" tasks, we will have managed to structure them and we will be able to analyze them with business intelligence tools. Data preparation has traditionally been a very manual task and consumed the bulk of most data project's time. Profiling data, standardizing it, and transforming it has traditionally been very manual and error prone. Fortunately, the latest generation of tools, typically powered by NoSQL technologies, takes a lot of this pain away. They enable users with reasonable technical skills to rapidly explore, understand, and analyze datasets ranging from small data to data that is petabytes in scale. Some of the most prominent commercial solutions in this regard are Microsoft Power BI, Tableau Prep, Trifacta, DataWatch, Paxata, Alteryx, Lavastorm, SAP Lumira, Platfora, Teradata Loom, and Datameer.

The list is large, and new solutions are appearing every year, but, at the end, the goal of all of those solutions is to facilitate the process of preparation, blending, and refining of data, providing a much better and smoother data analysis experience. This helps the administration and businesses gain practical insights to improve their functions. Moreover, most data preparation software also provides governance, control, and management of metadata and machine learning functionality to speed up the data analysis process.

2.5 Data analysis

2.5.1 Artificial intelligence

The large amount of data generated by a smart city would be useless without using Artificial Intelligence (AI) to process it to generate valuable information. The data obtained from the Machine to Machine (M2M) interaction is processed and analyzed. There are countless applications in smart cities, where AI can play a key role. From traffic improvement, to intelligent parking management and the safe integration of autonomous vehicles, AI can help in the planning of autonomous public transport routes, the management of the electricity network, the intelligent management of traffic, the piloting of drones, autonomous postal services, or units of sanitary facilities, among others. There are several technologies that help on data analysis, such as code languages (e.g., R, Python), open source libraries such as MLFlow and DVC, or specific commercial solutions (e.g., Alteryx, Databricks, Dataiku, SAS, DataRobot, ModelOp, BigML, etc.) that are making data model management and operations easier for data science teams.

Big tech providers are also providing their technologies integrated with their cloud solutions, such as Microsoft's Azure Machine Learning or Google's BigTable.

2.6 Data visualization

2.6.1 Smart cities control panels

One of the fields in which the visual expression of data for its analysis has gained the most is that of smart cities or smart cities. By using control panels, the urban environment can be managed more efficiently, basing decisions on reliable and up-to-date information.

This data can be collected in various ways, from sensors strategically located throughout the city's geography, to information generated by citizens' mobile phones, cameras, the consumption of their credit cards, mobile applications, or open data portals.

Through this information, we can draw conclusions in a wide range of facets that shape the government of a city. For example, we can record noise levels in certain areas, with the importance of this to improve the quality of life and health of neighbors.

Big Data platforms

Theoretically, consolidating, aggregating, and using existing and new sensor data from infrastructure, traffic, and users will generate a new base for innovation to support a new generation of management, control, and policies (Fig. 5.1). That is precisely what the cities of Barcelona, Cologne, and Stockholm also tested under the GrowSmarter project umbrella (although each city had their own corresponding needs and adaptation to the local situation). For example, in the case of Stockholm, their Big Data platform collected information from a specific geographical area of the city with a large variety in flows due to several amenities located there (see previous Box to know more about the collection technology). The idea was to use all this information to better understand the flows and help the planning, decision, and policy-making within the city.

Regarding the technical platform, the city of Stockholm used the IBM Cloud platform that offered the services and application programming interfaces (APIs) to inform city managers and citizens. In particular, the platform had information about vehicle passage data, Wifi ping data, weather data, event information, and information from different sensors. The overall architecture of the platform is shown in Fig. 5.1:

Based on the platform, the city also created the MetroLIVE application with the aim to help visitors in the area plan their movements with real-time information. One of the main services of the app is to provide heatmaps of the number of visitors and to provide alternative walking routes to avoid the crowd.

Similarly, the city of Cologne also deployed their own Big Data platform. Cologne's platform also relied on real-time data to store and process urban information and to enable vertical and horizontal integration of services. However, Cologne had something else in mind. The access to the platform should not be only for the city but also for other stakeholders. While all departments of the city council had access and contributed with data, there were also several external stakeholders that were doing so. In some cases, these stakeholders were public (like the municipal utility groups Rheinenergie AG or KVB), while others were private (like Cambio, a car-sharing company, or Ampido, a sharing economy company for parking spaces).

On the other hand, Barcelona opted for a platform that allowed exploring, querying, and visualizing data.

A data-driven approach of the mobility ecosystem

The introduction of digital technologies to the transport sector has been catalyzed by the design and deployment of Intelligent Transport Systems (ITS), which focuses on providing intelligence placed at the roadside or in vehicles to improve traffic safety, minimize traffic problems, and make the usage of transportation infrastructure more efficient. At its basis, the technology model of ITS rests on the sensorization and digitization of the transport infrastructure, with the introduction of traffic sensors, weather stations, and communication systems (including wireless and fiber-optics), among other technologies. The collection, warehousing, and real-time processing of data en masse is also a characteristic of ITS systems, where data is used to power digital analytical solutions, capable of understanding the status of traffic at different segments, detecting events as they occur, and predicting risks and situations to agilize and optimize the servicing and maintenance operations. In this context, Advanced Traffic Management Centers (A-TMC) have proven themselves as the vital component of ITS architectures, by centralizing the collection and analysis of sensor-collected data in real time for empowering operations and traffic management. A-TMCs have also gained intelligence and became capable of managing several aspects of traffic autonomously (e.g., red-light settings, lane closures, deployment of servicing vehicles, etc.).

Arguably, the last mile of ITS systems is user engagement, or the communication between systems and commuters or drivers. The purpose of establishing such communication is to provide information, guidance, trip planning, and mobility services to drivers and commuters to improve traffic control and management capacities, and facilitate mobility especially in urban settings. In addition, this communication also allows ITS systems to collect data on the mobility of people and vehicles to complement the existing sensing mechanisms.

Under ITS systems, the ecosystem of transportation, which consists of infrastructure elements, vehicles of different types, commuters, and services and service providers, becomes connected and centralized in A-TMCs and monitoring and communication systems. For such ITS systems to scale, there is an inherent need for decentralization. This implies that authority and decision-making in terms of traffic management is partially delegated from central A-TMCs to local actors in the transportation ecosystem (e.g., drivers and vehicles). In this context, a new paradigm for transportation systems is designed to adopt and exploit this decentralization trend by introducing the notion of collaboration in the system's management model.

Whereas ITS focuses on intelligence and data-driven management, C-ITS (which stands for Collaborative Intelligent Transport Systems) extends its focus to the communication, interaction, and coordination between vehicles and the road infrastructure. This collaboration is expected to significantly improve road safety and the efficiency of traffic management by supporting powerful and complex traffic management strategies that can be deployed and executed automatically based on the real-time microscopic evaluation of the traffic status at different segments of the infrastructure. These strategies are executed by combining systems and people, including variable message signs, instructions to automated vehicles, directions to drivers, and other traffic control components. The benefits of C-ITS also include reduced congestion, increased highway throughput, and improved customer satisfaction.

C-ITS systems are heavily reliant on communication technologies to function effectively. Therefore, several approaches have been implemented, sometimes complementarity, to provide connectivity between vehicles, infrastructure, and services. A main component of these communication technologies are cellular networks, and more recently 5G networks that are capable of supporting ultra-fast real-time communication and data exchange between a larger set of actors. The effective networking of vehicles and infrastructure is a key element of C-ITS systems as an enabler of a more advanced, autonomous, and orchestrated model of transportation.

In concord, the increased sensorization of vehicles is improving their environmental awareness, which in turn can empower their collective intelligence. When nearby vehicles share information about conditions and incidents, the scope of their vision is effectively enlarged, and their actions can be coordinated to avoid risks and improve safety, and also to navigate and cruise more effectively. In essence, this is the fundamental module of collaborative transport systems, which also includes centralized nodes or services that help to improve the overall system capabilities and performance.

On the macro level, and by collecting data from vehicles in real time, a very detailed view of traffic can be generated. Data-driven macro- and microsimulations have studied how dynamic traffic control policies can be applied to effectively manage traffic and improve the throughput of transport infrastructure (Aramrattana et al., 2019; Codecá & Härri, 2017). The application of such dynamic control policies can lead to a reduction in traffic jams and in the overall travel time invested to transport goods and people, with a consequential noticeable reduction in emissions association with transport. Dynamic control represents the intelligent layer of C-ITS and is empowered by advanced digital technologies, such as Artificial Intelligence, Machine Learning, Cloud and Edge processing, Internet-of-Things, among others.

Besides the technological infrastructure required (including advanced communication systems), C-ITS also rely on services that allow vehicles and infrastructure to share and use information for coordinating their actions collaboratively. These C-ITS services are also referred to as Cooperative, Connected, and Automated Mobility (CCAM) services. They constitute an innovative array of applications, enabled by digital connectivity among and between vehicles and transport infrastructure. These services are expected to significantly improve highway management on several fronts, such as safety, traffic efficiency, driving comfort, highway capacity and congestion, fuel consumption, and CO_2 emissions, among other effects. From a customer perspective, they create new communication channels, improve customer experience and retention, and help to accommodate new usages for highway travel.

In the context of designing and developing a European C-ITS Platform (Europa, 2016), a list of CCAM "Day 1 services" was defined to represent applications that can be made available in the short term, given their technical requirements, the maturity of their related or required technologies, and the state of market-driven deployment of C-ITS infrastructure. Also, a list of other highly desired CCAM "Day 1.5 services" was defined to encapsulate the services for which specifications or standards may not be completely ready yet. These are envisioned as part of a second phase deployment after Day 1 services have been successfully put into function. With the rise of 5G communication technologies, and in the context of planning and facilitating 5G deployment, a list of CCAM "Day 2 services" was defined to support the initial phases of automation (Car-2-Car, 2019). Similarly, initial plans for Day 3 use cases where cooperation is supported have been drafted, as well as Day 4 use cases to describe future mobility scenarios that are not expected to materialize before 2040. This is illustrated in Fig. 5.2.

A large number of CCAM services, in particular security-related services, can be supported by establishing V2I communications using RSUs and ITS-G5 communication. However, to transition to a more evolved phase of C-ITS deployment (mobility services, infotainment, etc.), the integration of cellular networks as an integral part of the mobility communication model becomes essential. In this respect, the effectiveness of C-ITS can be improved

Enabling technologies for data-driven cities Chapter | 5 169

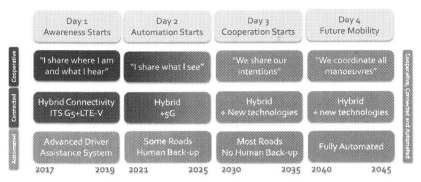

FIG. 5.2 CCAM services by expected maturity phase. *(Source: Cooperative, connected and automated mobility: Challenges for the automotive industry. In:* Presentation by Joost Vantomme, Smart Mobility Director. PZPM conference, Warsaw *2018.)*

and optimized by combining both the ITS-G5 and the standard cellular networks as part of a hybrid communication approach represented in Fig. 5.3. This communication model integrates existing cellular networks (3G/4G), which will later be supported by 5G, and will enable V2V collaboration scenarios, the real-time or near-real-time usage of cloud-based services, and third-party mobility applications. This technology-neutral approach to C-ITS architecture will support the two "Cs" in Cooperative, Connected, and Automated Mobility (CCAM).

Under this hybrid communication model, CCAM services are also set to create new innovative business models in transportation, such as Mobility as a

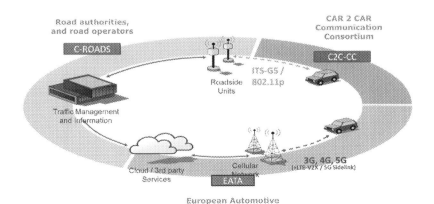

FIG. 5.3 Envisioned hybrid communication model for C-ITS. *(Source: Radio frequencies designated for enhanced road safety in Europe—C-Roads position on the usage of the 5.9 GHz band.)*

Service, and manage transportation services (or Logistics as a Service). So far, it has been clearly noted that since C-ITS and CCAM services hinge on data (which could be owned or governed by a number of different stakeholders), the control or partial-control over this data is an important leverage that allows stakeholders active in the mobility sector to consolidate and expand their role in CCAM-driven business models (e.g., as data brokers and/or as service providers), and consequently benefit financially from CCAM services.

Cooperative, connected, and automated mobility business models

In total, by 2020, over 24+ different elemental CCAM use cases have so far been defined under Day 1 and Day 2 classes (Car-2-Car, 2019), which are shown in Fig. 5.4. The majority of these services are being implemented and evaluated in different publicly-funded research and innovation projects in the United States and European Union, including Nordic Ways, C-ROADS, UK-CITE, DigiTrans, Brainport, Virginia Smart Roads, Arctic Intelligent Transport Ecosystem, Catalonia Living Lab, C-ITS Corridors, ALP.Lab, K-City, SCOOP@F, Midlands Future Mobility, Horiba-MIRA, TIC-IT, AV Living Lab, iMove Australia, and other small-scale pilots.

As the technology and services layers of future transportation systems mature, new opportunities start to crystallize in the business layer. In particular, the digital transformation of infrastructure monitoring and management creates new opportunities for companies to expand or pivot to the transportation sector to provide enabling services and technologies, such as video analytics, intelligent monitoring systems, predictive modeling of surface conditions, operational intelligence solutions for road maintenance, infrastructure monitoring, traffic monitoring, floating-car data, fleet management, automated mobility, and digital twining, among others.

However, the technological development of ITS/C-ITS does not necessarily translate into customer value and successful business to companies active in the transport and Mobility sector (Aapaoja, Kostiainen, & Leviäkangas, 2017). Public-private partnerships can accelerate the development of business ecosystems for and over ITS/C-ITS infrastructure, beyond enabling technologies and services. These partnerships have created the first autonomous transport services, clear-air-zones, and smart mobility hubs, among other solutions. The sprouting Mobility-as-a-Service businesses and local mobility ecosystems are expected to contribute to the sustained development of the transport sector.

To facilitate an economy of scale for mobility services, cross-platform and cross-border integrations are being conducted according to newly developed standards for data exchange and collaboration. These cross-border integrations allow one to maintain CCAM services seamlessly on the larger transport network, thereby increasing the economic viability of operations for services providers.

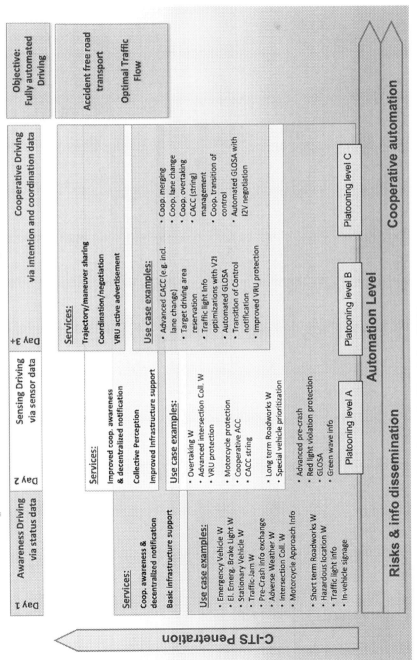

FIG. 5.4 Use case definitions of CCAM services. (*Source: Car2Car platform 2019.*)

References

Aapaoja, A., Kostiainen, J., & Leviäkangas, P. (2017). ITS service platform: In search of working business models and ecosystem. *Transportation Research Procedia, 25*, 1781–1795.

Aramrattana, M., et al. (2019). A simulation framework for cooperative intelligent transport systems testing and evaluation. *Transportation Research Part F: Traffic Psychology and Behaviour, 61*, 268–280.

Baronti, P., Pillai, P., Chook, V. W., Chessa, S., Gotta, A., & Hu, Y. F. (2007). Wireless sensor networks: A survey on the state of the art and the 802.15.4 and ZigBee standards. *Computer Communications, 30*(7), 1655–1695. https://www.sciencedirect.com/science/article/pii/S0140366406004749.

Bor, M., Vidler, J. E., & Roedig, U. (2016). *LoRa for the internet of things.* https://eprints.lancs.ac.uk/id/eprint/77615/.

Car-2-Car. (2019). *Guidance for day 2 and beyond roadmap.* CAR 2 CAR Communication Consortium https://www.car-2-car.org/fileadmin/documents/General_Documents/C2CCC_WP_2072_RoadmapDay2AndBeyond.pdf.

Codecá, L., & Härri, J. (2017). Towards multimodal mobility simulation of C-ITS: The Monaco SUMO traffic scenario. In *2017 IEEE vehicular networking conference (VNC), Torino* (pp. 97–100). https://doi.org/10.1109/VNC.2017.8275627.

Europa. (2016). *C-ITS platform final report.* https://ec.europa.eu/transport/sites/transport/files/themes/its/doc/c-its-platform-final-report-january-2016.pdf.

Gartner. (2018). https://www.gartner.com/en/newsroom/press-releases/2018-11-07-gartner-identifies-top-10-strategic-iot-technologies-and-trends.

Jamsa, K. (2012). *Cloud computing: SaaS, PaaS, IaaS, virtualization, business models, mobile, security and more.* Jones & Bartlett Publishers. https://books.google.com/books?hl=en&lr=&id=msFk8DPZ7noC&oi=fnd&pg=PR1&dq=cloud+computing+saas+paas+iaas&ots=oZ1FQj9FFo&sig=LC2vE4KAUIwN3p-z8NcF-C3ixpA.

Ratasuk, R., Vejlgaard, B., Mangalvedhe, N., & Ghosh, A. (2016, April). NB-IoT system for M2M communication. In *2016 IEEE wireless communications and networking conference (pp. 1–5).* IEEE. https://ieeexplore.ieee.org/abstract/document/7564708/.

Raza, U., Kulkarni, P., & Sooriyabandara, M. (2017). Low power wide area networks: An overview. *IEEE Communications Surveys and Tutorials, 19*(2), 855–873. https://ieeexplore.ieee.org/abstract/document/7815384/.

Stonebraker, M. (2010). SQL databases v. NoSQL databases. *Communications of the ACM, 53*(4), 10–11. https://dl.acm.org/doi/abs/10.1145/1721654.1721659?casa_token=QoY_h48zuZ0AAAAA:YjLALaagzX0t7s007FhMWfSNzuc_UuMK-qA085BHQq_4z_SgnBDv3nsguTSB39i9sliP3quiV6an8g.

Wang, Y. P. E., Lin, X., Adhikary, A., Grovlen, A., Sui, Y., Blankenship, Y., et al. (2017). A primer on 3GPP narrowband internet of things. *IEEE Communications Magazine, 55*(3), 117–123. https://ieeexplore.ieee.org/abstract/document/7876968/.

Zuniga, J. C., & Ponsard, B. (2016). Sigfox system description. In *LPWAN@ IETF97, Nov. 14th, 25.* https://datatracker.ietf.org/meeting/97/materials/slides-97-lpwan-25-sigfox-system-description-00.pdf.

Chapter 6

Data analysis, modeling, and visualization in smart cities

Carlos Carrasco-Farré[a], Ignasi Alcalde[b], and Didier Grimaldi[b]
[a]*Ramon Llull University—ESADE Business School, Barcelona, Spain*, [b]*Ramon Llull University, La Salle Faculty, Barcelona, Spain*

1 Introduction

The rise of data is a fact, and its volume is estimated to double every 1.2 years. After data is collected, processed, and modeled, the relationships need to be visualized so a conclusion can be made. Organizations have two things in abundance: data and unanswered questions (Derqui & Grimaldi, 2020; Grimaldi, Diaz, Arboleda, & Fernandez, 2019; Grimaldi, Fernandez, & Carrasco, 2019).

The challenge is not generating and capturing more data but rather discovering new ways to condense, interpret, and make decisions regarding this data. And for that the key lies in data visualization, which is one of the best-known methods to reduce and illustrate data in a simplified and visual way.

But there is a preconceived idea that good data visualization is easy to achieve with today's visualization tools. There are multiple data visualization tools with more or less complexity, such as Tableau, Power BI, Qlik, R, D3.js, etc. that allow you to visualize data more or less quickly in just a few clicks, but this is just the last step of multiple iterative stages. Getting to the final visualization involves a series of prior decision-making at each stage of the data visualization process (Grimaldi, 2019; Grimaldi, Diaz, & Arboleda, 2020; Grimaldi, Fernandez, & Carrasco, 2019).

Technical steps like acquiring, analyzing, and refining the data are part of the process. In addition, a data visualization professional must ensure that data is not inadvertently hidden, distorted, or skewed on their graphs. In every decision process, correctly viewing not only the data but its correct meaning will change our experience as users, clients, or consultants. Reading a static graph from an infographic is not the same as interacting with information from a dashboard.

But to create useful data visualizations is not an easy task. As humans, we are not "designed" to process complex numbers and associate those numbers with abstract concepts. But we have an innate capacity to recognize visual patterns at a glance, but representing complex numbers as visual patterns allows us to take advantage of our natural analytical skills. Let's start from the beginning.

This chapter is divided into five major blocks: what is data visualization, methodology, graphs and principles of design, dashboards, and principles.

2 What is data visualization?

We can define data visualization as a process that consumes data as input and transforms it into insights, so we have data as a raw material and insight as a refined product. It is exploring some data to answer questions or ask new ones and analyzing patterns, relationships, and atypical values between data to tell a story with data.

It is also the representation of data or information in a graph, chart, or other visual format to communicate insights from data through visual representation. It is often used interchangeably with terms such as information graphics, statistical graphics, and information visualization.

But also as Andy Kirk states in his book *Data Visualization: A Handbook for Data Driven Design*, we can also define it as "the representation and presentation of data, using proven design techniques to bring alive the patterns, stories, and key insights that are locked away." As we know, the main goal is to distill large datasets into visual graphics to allow for easy understanding of complex relationships within the data. In other words, to facilitate understanding and help to make decisions.

Data visualizations are usually created in the digital media, and we have two major data visualization types: exploratory and explanatory. When we talk about exploratory data visualization, you interact, interrogate, and explore the data, which can help you answer the recuse questions you have about it, so that means you need to the context of the data. Thus data visualization not only solves doubts, it also invites you to create new questions that were not even imagined.

One clear example is this one, where we can explore in several ways how the world has changed in the last 40 years. We can explore by GPD per capita, life expectancy, birth per woman, world areas, etc. (Fig. 6.1).

A subgroup of explorative data visualization are dashboards.

A dashboard is a tool that allows you to monitor the status of a system. It visually tracks, analyzes, and displays key performance indicators (KPI), metrics, and key data points to monitor, for example, the income and expenses organization by different departments and segments of products and customers. Dashboards usually have data in real time or at least frequently renewed.

Dashboards are created by users who are experts in the subject of the dashboards, or at least they know the data and the context of the data very well, so they have goals to pursue with it. Summarizing, they are doing visual analytics with the dashboard.

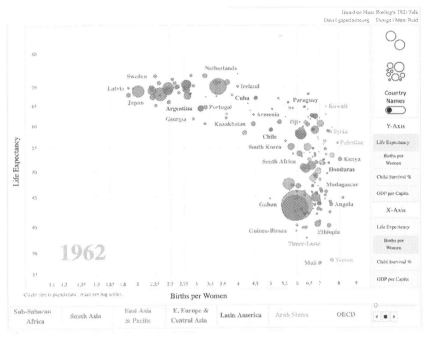

FIG. 6.1 How has the world changed since 1962? *(Source: Marc Reid, datavis.blog https://datavis.blog/2020/01/21/tableau-animated-transitions/.)*

On other hand, explanatory data visualization visuals are meant only to show us the important things, and there should be little to no intended analytical value. This type is also called data storytelling and is usually created in a static way, so we can print the final result. Infographics are a perfect product type of explanatory data visualization.

Here, we have a clear example to explain with data how we get to zero greenhouse gas emissions (Fig. 6.2).

A well-known group of explanatory data visualizations are infographics. An infographic is a representation of information and data in a graphic format designed to make the data easily understandable at a glance.

Infographics are used to quickly communicate a message, to simplify the presentation of large amounts of data in a visual and impactful way. There is data storytelling in an infographic, so that means that narrative and data work together.

3 Data essentials

Data is the "raw material" that is all around us, which is created in our current daily activity. But what exactly is it? We can define data as a record of

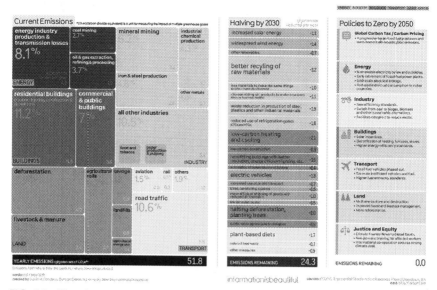

FIG. 6.2 How do we get to zero greenhouse gas emissions? *(Source: Information is beautiful https://information.isbeautiful.net/visualizations/how-to-reduce-the-worlds-carbon-footprint-by-2050/.)*

observations; in other words, we observe reality and then we "measure" and register it. We can define it as a value assigned to a thing. Every object has a lot of data attached to it, like color, category, condition, diameter, price, etc. Even a human being has a lot of data attached, like your first name, family name, date of birth, weight, height, nationality, etc. All of these things are data.

We can also say that data is the minimal information unit. For example, we can say the temperature is 4°C as a data point. But if we don't define the data with some context, the raw data means nothing. However, if we say the temperature is 4°C in Barcelona, Spain, on July 22 at 5:00 p.m., then we have context and, at the same time, we have information.

If we add some extra information, it helps the audience make decisions, for example, the average temperature in Barcelona at that time during the last 10 years (22°C), and then we visualize this with a line chart of the temperature evolution day-by-day in July. With this visualization, we not only understand that temperature that day was not normal, we can "make a decision" and get out to the street with warmer clothes to protect ourselves from this unusually cold temperature.

4 Data types

There are two major data categories: **qualitative** and **quantitative data.**

Qualitative data is everything that refers to the quality of something: a description of colors, texture, and feel of an object or interview quotes.

Qualitative data has subgroups called Categorical and Ordinal. Categorical data, also called Nominal, refers to data that can be sorted according to a group or category, for example, types of products sold, gender, hair color, etc.

Ordinal is a type of categorical data where there is a clear ordering of the variables, in other words, they are listed in an ordered manner. For example, the Olympic medals are bronze, silver, and gold, or satisfaction criteria can be either Very satisfied, Satisfied, Indifferent, Dissatisfied, or Very dissatisfied.

Quantitative data can be counted or measured; all values are numerical and usually refer to a number. For example, the number of windows on a house, its size and price, or a score on a test, etc. Quantitative data has two main groups: Discrete data and Continuous data.

Discrete data is numerical data that has a finite number of possible values, for example, the number of employees in the office, shoe sizes, etc.

Continuous data is numerical data that is measured and has a value within a range. In continuous data, all values are possible with no gaps in between, for example, height, weight, length, the rainfall in a year, etc. Some continuous data will change over time, like the temperature in a room throughout the day.

5 Methodology

The process to create data visualization has three different stages: planning and tactics, data, and design.

In the first stage, planning and tactics, we define the goals of the data visualization by thinking about the main subject and audience. We also focus on targets and indicators, and we research and analyze data from different angles and ensure that the right data is available for a good visual analysis.

In the second stage, data, the aim is to transform data into information. It is often said that if we want to have information, we have to clean and format data, by organizing, structuring, and contextualizing it. Afterward, it may be necessary to also process data analysis in a deeper way, running very complex algorithms, to get some insights and give more value to the data. When analyzing data, search for patterns or interesting insights such trends, correlations, and outliers.

The third stage, design, refers to the drawing and charting process that allows us to achieve the goal defined during planning and tactics in a visual and functional way. The design process is an iterative design methodology focused on the user that involves sketching and prototyping with the result of a final product.

6 Charts and data relations

When analyzing data, the analysis usually consists of a comparison, transition, relationship, or examination of the composition of data. For example, a comparison illustrates the highs and lows of the dataset, and then we represent it with a chart. A chart is a graphical representation of data. There are several different types used for quite different things. The most common are probably line graphs, bar graphs, histograms, and pie charts.

But there is a large number of charts. You can explore the website https://datavizcatalogue.com/index.html to get an idea of the different possible ways to represent data in a graphical way.

The data itself has no value and only begins to have value when we relate it. When choosing a graph, we must think about what type of relationships we want to graph. The most common can be divided into seven categories: Comparison, Time series, Part to whole, Distribution, Correlation, Ranking, and Maps.

- **Comparison**: Shows size comparisons of quantitative values of subcategories. These can be relative (counted number) or absolute (calculated rate or percent). For example: the number of tourists from various countries.
- **Time series**: Tracks changes in values of a quantitative metric over time. Focuses on changing trends. For example: monthly stock price variation.
- **Part to whole**: Shows a subset of data compared with the larger whole. It helps to understand the contribution from different categories to a total. For example, percentage of population in different continents.
- **Distribution**: To understand the shape and properties of a variable. Shows values in a dataset and how often they occur around a central value. It's a way to visualize the uniformity or equality in the data. For example: the age of players on a football team.
- **Correlation:** To understand the relationship between two or more variables that may demonstrate a positive or negative correlation to each other. For example: criminality according to unemployment rate.
- **Ranking**: Shows how two or more values compare to each other in relative magnitude. It's used when an item's position in an ordered list is more important than its absolute or relative value. For example: urban population growth, ranked from the most populated to least.
- **Maps**: Displays categorical data, using intensity of color or bubbles to represent values of specific geographic regions. Maps are used when precise locations or geographical patterns in data are more important to the reader than anything else. For example: comparing world population in every country.

We can find a list of the most common charts for every category in a visual vocabulary online resource created Inspired by the Graphic Continuum by Jon Schwabish and Severino Ribecca at https://ft-interactive.github.io/visual-vocabulary/.

7 Data design principles

After choosing the right charts, it important to think of the best way to represent them. Edward R. Tufte, an American statistician and one of the most reputed pioneers in the field of data visualization, says:

> *Visual displays rich with data are not only an appropriate and proper complement to human capabilities, but also such designs are frequently optimal.*

That is why we should have in mind some design principles that will allow us to understand why we make certain visual representational decisions.

A basic principle is visual thinking, which is the process of thinking through visual processing to activate our innate visual memory. In data visualization, the key memory is the iconic memory. Iconic memory deals with information received by the brain from visual receptors. It is processed quickly and without us being aware of it: we call it "preattentive" processing. It is not intended to be an exhaustive analysis of everything we see but rather to extract a subset of relevance such as color or shape.

There is also a long-term memory, which refers to the storage of information over an extended period. It has a limited capacity: different studies say that it can store between five and nine items (depending on the person and the type of task you are performing). To make good data visualizations, we should choose the appropriate visual attributes to take advantage of the attentive processing capability of the iconic memory (color and shape) and also be consistent with the use of the layout and format of the elements to empower long-term memory.

Another basic principle is called preattentive attributes, which are visual properties that we.

notice without using conscious effort to do so. They are a very powerful tool in data visualization to determine what your audience notices first when they look at your dashboard.

Colin Ware, states in his book, *Information Visualization: Perception for Design:*

> *...the human visual system is a pattern seeker of enormous power and subtlety. The eye and the visual cortex of the brain form a massively parallel processor that provides the highest-bandwidth channel into human cognitive centers.*

He has defined the preattentive visual properties in four major categories: color, form, movement, and spatial positioning.

7.1 Color

Color can be defined as visual perception that enables one to differentiate otherwise identical objects and can be expressed in many different ways: RGB (Red, Green, Blue), CMYK (Cyan, Magenta, Yellow, and Key), or HSL (Hue, Saturation, and Lightness). Intensity and hue can be used to separate visual elements from their surroundings and focus the attention quickly.

7.2 Form

We can define form as the visible shape or configuration of a visual object. Colin Ware explains that there is set of attributes (listed in Fig. 6.3), and form

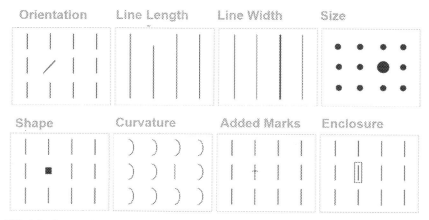

FIG. 6.3 Preattentive visual attributes. *(Source: Ware, C. (2019).* Information visualization: Perception for design. *Morgan Kaufmann.)*

can be adjusted to call or reduce attention to a member of the dataset. For example, using a size (bigger or smaller) to indicate its importance or not in a dataset by making it larger or smaller.

7.3 Movement

Movement can be defined as a motion or action, or as a shift in position. This data visualization field has two subattributes, flicker and motion.

7.4 Spatial positioning

This can be defined as the ability to discern the position of two or more objects in space relative to each other. The main preattentive attribute for spatial positioning is 2D positioning, which Is considered the most accurate attribute representing quantitative data to be processed visually.

8 Dashboard basics

Dashboards are organized as concise visual representations of various KPIs (Grimaldi & Fernandez, 2017; Ramirez, Palominos, Camargo, & Grimaldi, 2021).

KPIs are measures that help organizations confirm that they are on track to meet goals and objectives. They can be oriented to the various roles of the organization (senior management, functional departments, and operational divisions), but ultimately they all converge on the overall goals and objectives of the organization. Some KPIs are product- and industry-specific.

When we choose a KPI, it should respond to a previously established objective. This objective must be relevant, measurable over time, and relevant to your objective and strategy, since otherwise you will be obtaining data that will not provide you any value. "Measurable over time" means that the KPI has to vary over time. In this way, you can make comparisons over time to see how it has evolved and establish results.

Dashboards will vary depending on the different end users for which they are designed. It is a "fixed" photo of the main indicators of our business, not a place to study a certain topic, such as cross-variables, etc.

It is used to make decisions that optimize the company's strategy, but it is not used to define a specific corrective action or to study a certain area in detail.

A dashboard should help and guide us to identify the origin of positive or negative data that we have detected, which allows us to make a decision about it; a detailed analysis of the "whys" should be done in a specific report or in another tool designed for it.

To create a dashboard, we should keep in mind the following premises:

- Identify measurable, appropriate, and actionable KPIs.
- Agree on uniform data definitions and metrics.
- Avoid too much or too little information.
- Evaluate the value and timeliness of the data.
- Establish baselines and objectives.

The most common indicators in a dashboard are proportion, percentage, currency, and all kinds of units we can count: activities, product, people, time, transactions, leads, etc. Dashboards usually have segmentation filters like a range of time (day, week, month, quarter, real time, year) and some sociodemographic indicators.

8.1 How to lie with maps

The goal of data visualization is to convey meaningful insights arising from data patterns in a quick and easy way. However, there is often a trade-off between aesthetics and capturing the true results of data analysis. This trade-off is evident in the case of maps, where one could rearrange the visualization to present contradicting results. For example, think about the geographical distribution of Airbnb apartments in a given city.

Barcelona is one of the most prominent tourist destinations in Europe, proven by the number of hotels in the city: 655 as of December 2019. Despite its social and economic importance for the city, tourism also generates some tension with local citizens. For example, in a 2016 municipal survey, almost 50% of citizens thought that the city has reached its capacity limit for tourism. The interesting thing is that residents in touristic areas showed a much higher percentage, while residents in nontouristic areas thought that more tourism could benefit them. In other words, the decentralization of tourism could benefit the city, and here is where digital platforms come into play.

One of the main promises of Airbnb is that it helps neighborhoods that traditionally do not benefit from tourism. In other words, the accommodation platform helps cities by spreading tourism far from touristic areas. To illustrate our example on how to lie with maps, we downloaded data from Airbnb in the city of Barcelona.

In December 2020, there were 19,641 Airbnb listings in the capital of Catalonia. If we visualize each listing as a point, the map looks like this (Fig. 6.4).

Looking at the previous map, we could conclude that, effectively, Airbnb is helping the city to spread tourism in nontouristic areas. If we compare it with the location of traditional accommodation services (like hotels), the result is this (Fig. 6.5).

Here, we depict the number of hotels per neighborhood in Barcelona. As can be seen, the majority of neighborhoods have zero hotels, while three neighborhoods have more than 66 hotels (main touristic area of the city). If we compared both maps, we could wrongly conclude that Airbnb is delivering its promise of spreading tourism out of congested areas. The reason is because we are playing with an optical illusion that shows how we can lie with maps (Fig. 6.6).

For example, what if we change the size of points in the Airbnb listings maps?

Just by dividing the size of points by two, the story starts to seem different. While we still see Airbnb listings outside the touristic area, we can start to see a concentration in the same neighborhoods where the majority of hotels are

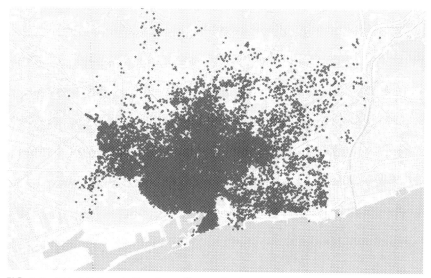

FIG. 6.4 Airbnb listings in Barcelona. *(Source: Book authors.)*

Data analysis, modeling in smart cities Chapter | 6   183

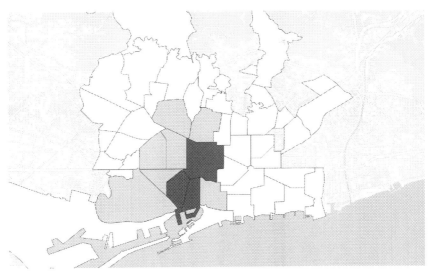

FIG. 6.5 Airbnb listings in Barcelona per neighborhood. *(Source: Book authors.)*

FIG. 6.6 Airbnb listings in Barcelona (smaller size). *(Source: Book authors.)*

located. However, if instead of visualizing each point we rely on heatmaps, the story is radically different.

Using a Kernel Density Estimator (a nonparametric way to estimate the probability density function of a variable), we can visualize a heatmap of the Airbnb listings concentration in Barcelona. In our case, we selected a bandwidth

184 Implementing data-driven strategies in smart cities

of 300 m, which is a plausible value for perceiving "tourism intensity" within walking distance of someone's home area (Fig. 6.7).

Now we see a completely different story that leads us to a radically different conclusion. While looking at the first map of Airbnb listings geolocation, it may seem that the platform offers accommodation in nontouristic areas; the reality is that a majority of them are concentrated in touristic areas. This is important not just from the internal point of view of the city council (avoiding wrong conclusions) but also from the external point of view when facing evidence of other stakeholders trying to mislead public opinion.

9 A data-driven approach to predict the COVID-19 effect on urban retail

EIXOS Economic Observatory, about whom we already talked in Chapter 3, used their data to predict the effect of COVID-19 on urban retail. They did so by using different forecasting methods and models that drew upon a database of almost 1,000,000 geolocated retail activities. The aim was to answer questions like how public interventions to stop the virus (like lockdowns) would affect retailers of different cities. However, how do they do that?

9.1 Measuring the effect of COVID-19

Because at this moment we are still under the effects of the COVID pandemic, we do not have data about how the future looks. To avoid this situation, EIXOS Economic Observatory compared different potential scenarios. In particular,

FIG. 6.7 Airbnb listing density in Barcelona. *(Source: Book authors.)*

they compared four scenarios: the retail situation preconfinement, the retail situation during the lockdown, and two future scenarios.

These scenarios were based on a comprehensive review of existing scientific literature, which include some newly published academic articles regarding the influence of COVID on retail. Through this review, they identified retail categories that, because of their characteristics, will face a tough situation after the lockdown. Of course, all retailers will face a challenging future due to financial stress and a potential decline in consumption, but some of them will need to overcome different problematics.

Of course, the model has some simplifications of reality. Since it is impossible to have information about the financial status of each one of the retailers in a city, they decided to make all their calculations using the retail category. Furthermore, they used these calculations to predict the future of retail areas. Among all the key indicators, they focused on the Retail Occupancy Index (ROI), which is defined as the percentage of active retailers over the total available storefronts in a given area. For that indicator, the threshold to define an area as having a healthy retail sector is a limit of 80% occupation. Below that number, the area faces a potential retail desertification problem, with those below 70% being in severe risk of desertification. Therefore, they had a indicator and baselines against they wanted to compare the results of the predictive models (Fig. 6.8).

FIG. 6.8 Retail activity in NYC. *White dots*: Stores open during the lockdown. *Red dots* (*black* in print version): All stores open normally before lockdown. *(Source: EIXOS Economic Observatory.)*

9.2 How EIXOS identified the retail categories most affected by the COVID-19 lockdown?

To quantify the potential effects of the lockdown, EIXOS relied on several indicators that they weighted differently for each retail category. First of all, they considered whether a retail activity is likely to have perishable goods (for example, food) or stock that is highly dependent on seasonality (for example, fashion). In addition, they considered the amount of people working, on average, for each retail category. This is important because having more employees, even during a lockdown, is likely to create financial stress on the retailer. Furthermore, they used data from a paper published by MIT researchers to estimate the risk of infection by retail category (using the geolocation of mobile phone data). Finally, through surveys they collected information about the importance that citizens gave to each of the available categories as a measure of how likely they were to consume there when the lockdown ended (Fig. 6.9).

9.2.1 Prelockdown scenario

Before assessing the effect of the COVID pandemic on retail, it is important to know the context before the pandemic. To do so, we use the EIXOS Economic Observatory retail dataset of 2019 that geolocates each retail store in Manhattan. Based on this database, we know that the average retail occupancy in Manhattan was 90% in 2019.

9.2.2 COVID-19 scenario

In this scenario, we analyze what happened during the lockdowns implemented to slow down the spread of the pandemic. In this scenario, only essential activities (mainly food and pharmacies) were opened. Therefore, the occupancy rate went down from 90% to 26%.

9.2.3 Medium effect scenario (postlockdown)

Once we have the pictures before and during the lockdowns, we can move on to analyze future scenarios for Manhattan's retail. In this scenario, we apply the medium effect weights for the variables included in the predictive model described before. The results of this model show that, in a moderate scenario, Manhattan's retail activity will be around 80% of occupancy rates. However, to manage the situation, the city council also needed to account for worst scenarios.

9.2.4 Doomsday scenario (postlockdown)

In this scenario, the predictive model assumes that all activities come back to normal except apparel stores and only 50% of bars and restaurants are able to open again. The occupancy rates for this scenario are slightly below 70%, which means that, on average, Manhattan would be at the edge of severe

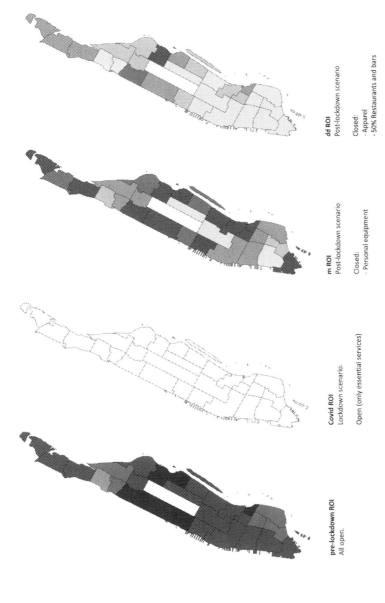

FIG. 6.9 COVID-19 effect scenarios. *(Source: EIXOS Economic Observatory.)*

188 Implementing data-driven strategies in smart cities

desertification, well below the minimum threshold of 80% occupancy to be considered a healthy retail area.

ntacode	Neighborhood	ROI	ROI m	ROI dd	ROI covid	Minimum leap
MN25	Battery Park City-Lower Manhattan	94.65	86.50	65.31	41.44	8.16
MN03	Central Harlem North-Polo Grounds	80.30	76.46	70.10	17.78	3.84
MN11	Central Harlem South	89.90	79.80	70.83	21.04	10.10
MN27	Chinatown	80.96	74.26	63.81	21.37	6.70
MN15	Clinton	92.16	90.26	69.43	40.76	1.89
MN34	East Harlem North	86.52	81.68	72.75	25.65	4.85
MN33	East Harlem South	97.65	93.07	86.77	16.48	4.57
MN22	East Village	83.29	75.85	58.68	30.95	7.44
MN21	Gramercy	93.70	88.05	70.76	36.83	5.65
MN04	Hamilton Heights	79.90	74.79	67.55	19.60	5.11
MN13	Hudson Yards-Chelsea-Flatiron-Union Square	86.24	75.77	63.41	26.10	10.47
MM31	Lenox Hill-Roosevelt Island	92.01	84.96	72.52	26.83	7.06
MN14	Lincoln Square	97.00	84.36	72.43	24.80	12.64
MN28	Lower East Side	81.53	78.41	69.25	21.33	3.12
MN06	Manhattanville	80.67	76.89	69.96	18.91	3.78
MN01	Marble Hill-Inwood	91.38	85.14	75.87	26.24	6.24
MN17	Midtown-Midtown South	90.07	69.56	53.34	28.93	20.51
MN09	Morringside Heights	95.74	93.04	84.14	18.38	2.71
MN20	Murray Hill-Kips Bay	94.12	89.18	71.76	36.00	4.94
MN24	SoHo-TriBeCa-Civic Center-Little Italy	92.15	68.14	58.59	21.32	24.01
MN50	Stuyvesant Town-Cooper Village	100.00	93.10	77.59	37.93	6.90
MN19	Turtle Bay-East Midtown	92.44	86.55	69.08	34.54	5.88
MN40	Upper East Side-Carnegie Hill	93.05	65.05	57.19	16.60	28.00
MN12	Upper West Side	96.30	87.20	75.25	25.13	9.10
MN35	Washington Heights North	91.49	81.59	75.82	20.63	9.91
MN36	Washington Heights South	91.79	85.63	78.93	25.09	6.16
MN23	West Village	89.33	75.60	59.73	31.41	13.74
MN32	Yorkville	98.47	92.52	76.79	32.65	5.95
	Average	90.46	81.91	69.91	26.60	8.55

Of course, the pandemic effects are not homogeneously spread throughout the city. Depending on the preexisting retail composition, some neighborhoods are more at risk than others in terms of retail closures and, eventually, potential desertification.

While we see neighborhoods with moderate damage, there are others that can be severely affected by the COVID pandemic. The later will face persistent closures derived from high presence in the apparel sector, as well as restaurants and hotels. Understanding the potential effect of the pandemic at the aggregate level and at the neighborhood level allows for micro-targeted policies to avoid a catastrophic scenario. In that sense, focusing on the more at-risk areas will move the effect from a doomsday scenario to a moderate scenario. Indeed, this can only be accomplished through the transformative power of public-private collaboration.

Public administrations at various levels (from local to federal) are key to ensure that the financing mechanism reach those who need them the most, not just at the retail store level, but also at the neighborhood level. Because we need to remember that one closure increases the probability of another closure next to it through what is known as the "empty store effect." This effect is similar to the "broken-window effect." This effect explains that a broken window may be signaling that a building or area is not well-maintained or patrolled, and that nobody cares about the area, which will bring more crime and, eventually, more broken windows. Something similar happens with retail. When a store closes in a specific retail street, there will be fewer visitors to that street. If another store closes due to the reduced traffic, the people passing by will be even fewer, creating a domino effect or, in other words, the "empty store effect."

This is highly unlikely—in general terms—in Manhattan because its retail structure resembles a Mediterranean city, which is a highly resilience model, with retail stores spread throughout the entire built environment and not just concentrated in specific retail streets or main streets. However, it is perfectly possible that the effects are severe in specific micro-areas, leading to "islands of desertification."

In addition, all the scenarios carry out another challenge: the loss of distinctiveness. Independent businesses were, until now, fundamental to meet the needs of our cities. However, replacing independent businesses with chain stores and big retailers can lead to clonification problems, which is basically that all streets in all cities will, potentially, look the same.

In summary, it is important to take decisive actions led by public administrations in conjoint efforts with the private sector to make sure that the effect of the pandemic is reduced to the minimum. Especially because the effect will not only be felt during or right after the pandemic, but it can also lead to radical changes in our cities.

How not to lie with maps

Maps are powerful tools to analyze how social needs and opportunities are distributed through a territory and can be used to see where a certain service can be more useful or have a better outreach. Therefore, maps are an essential tool for urban planning and policy-making. However, as we have seen with the Airbnb example, maps can be easily misleading, and if it is true that they have a big explanatory power, it is not less true that they easily hide information that the observer, unless they are an expert, cannot grasp.

190 Implementing data-driven strategies in smart cities

An interesting paradox is to see how the appearance of the map changes when changing the spatial level of aggregation of the unit of analysis when the underlying data is the same. This is especially true when maps choose to represent a variable that is categorical, such as which candidate gained the most votes in the last national election. The next map shows the 2020 US election results aggregated at the state level (left) and at the county level (right) (Fig. 6.10).

To make it even more interesting, if we are not experts in US geography, these maps don't show us which candidate obtained most votes, and they also don't communicate very efficiently if and how urban density correlates with voting for democrats or republicans. For doing so, the same data can be plotted showing the size of each electoral county, and the map looks even more different than the previous examples. So, maps are great tools to tell one story, but for doing so, they ignore other stories that are also true (Fig. 6.11).

However, not only is the level of aggregation important, but also how boundaries are also set is key. Political scientist have coined the concept of "gerrymandering" to refer to the practice of manipulating district boundaries to establish an unfair political advantage for a particular party or group. The next figure shows how different boundaries can led to three different outcomes

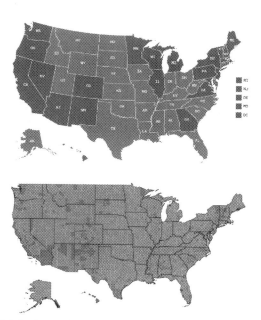

FIG. 6.10 2020 US election results. *(Source: https://www.nbcnews.com/politics/2020-elections/president-results; http://www.econ.cam.ac.uk/news/pesaran-us-elections-2020-forcast.)*

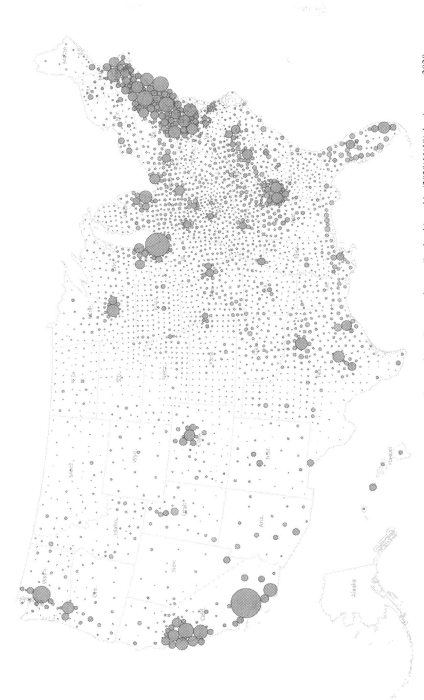

FIG. 6.11 Number of votes separating the candidates in each county. (*Source: https://eu.usatoday.com/in-depth/graphics/2020/11/10/election-maps-2020-america-county-results-more-voters/6226197002/.*)

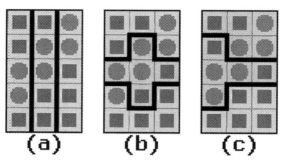

FIG. 6.12 Visual representation of gerrymandering. *(Source: https://en.wikipedia.org/wiki/Gerrymandering.)*

having the same underlying data. This practice of intentionally manipulating the boundaries to obtain advantageous results can be also practiced by data analysts, who can perform a trial-and-error process until they get a map that better fits the story that is to be explained. So, when interpreting a visualization, it is important to understand the underlying data behind the visualization and be aware of how small changes can lead to different outcomes (Fig. 6.12).

The use of isochrones to represent distances in time units

Another issue regarding the interpretation of maps occurs when comparing physical distances and distances measured in time units. The former is accurately represented by maps and the latter is not, although it might be unconsciously inferred by the observer. Most of the time, we are interested in distances measured in time, since time distance is what really shapes citizens' experience and accessibility to urban services. To overcome this challenge and visually show how long does it takes to move from different places, we can turn to the idea of isochrone maps, which gives us an idea of real services and opportunities available from a specific location.

Isochrone maps show the area accessible from a certain point within a certain time threshold. The next figure shows which areas of Melbourne were accessible in 1910 within different thresholds of time by train (Fig. 6.13).

The availability of big data and the computational power of modern engines, such as Google StreetView, makes isochronic maps easily available to urban planners and policy-makers who want to know which urban areas are most in need of certain services. The next figure shows the case of the city of Barcelona and Primary Care facilities available to its citizens: each of the 5290 building blocks of the city are classified according to the walking distance needed to reach the closest public primary care facility; the green areas are the ones that are closer to primary care facilities (within 15 min), and the red

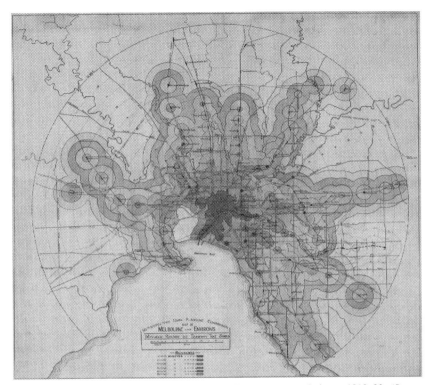

FIG. 6.13 Early isochrone map of Melbourne rail transport travel times, 1910–22. *(Source: Wikipedia.)*

areas are the ones where more time is needed to access a music school (more than 30 min). In between, we find a continuum of travel time distances. As a result, the observer can see that most of the areas of the city are really close to the service of interest (Fig. 6.14).

When repeating the same visualization for other services, some patterns are found, such as the neighborhoods nearer the mountain are the ones that have less accessibility to different services. These maps are more informative to policymakers and urban planners than just showing the physical location of each service of interest; it is difficult to infer which areas are better off and which could be geographically excluded of a service. However, again, there is information that the map does not show: how many people live in each distance area? Are these areas more densely populated than the city average? How wealthy or poor are the people living in those areas? This information has to be explored in other visualizations.

194 Implementing data-driven strategies in smart cities

FIG. 6.14 Walking distance in minutes in Barcelona. *(Source: https://ciutat15minuts.shinyapps.io/Ciutat15minuts/.)*

Graph analytics to improve data for city resilience

An emerging trend to complement data science in the field of resilient cities is the graph (Wikipedia, 2021) analytics techniques used to analyze relationships between the different systems and subsystems in a city. By using graph algorithms, analyzing interdependencies and potential cascading effect complement data science when facing effects.

Graph analytics and Machine Learning (ML) can help organizations discover patterns of transaction (Loshin, 2013). In cities, a graph can help to build taxonomies, understand the flow of data, and how the different urban services will be disrupted.

Graph theory simplifies complex systems into nodes and edges to identify network structure; this can help cities to better understand how it works as a system of systems. Different stakeholders that are interrelated when an effect strikes (critical urban service operators, first responders, urban and emergency planners, etc.) can better understand their dependencies if their have worked together modeling a graph of how they will respond.

An emerging market for cloud-based graph analytics solutions is expected to grow (Marketsandmarkets, 2021) and can boost the capacity of cities and its platforms to create graph algorithms to improve resilience of mobility, emergency services, or operations management.

References

Derqui, B., & Grimaldi, D. (2020). Data on the sustainability profile and food waste management in primary and secondary schools: The case of the Catalonia region in Spain. *Data in Brief, 28*. https://doi.org/10.1016/j.dib.2019.104825, 104825.

Grimaldi, D. (2019). Can we analyse political discourse using Twitter? Evidence from Spanish 2019 presidential election. *Social Network Analysis and Mining, 12*, 9–49. https://doi.org/10.1007/s13278-019-0594-6.

Grimaldi, D., Diaz, J., & Arboleda, H. (2020). Inferring the votes in a new political landscape: The case of the 2019 Spanish Presidential elections. *Journal of Big Data, 1*, 1–19. In press.

Grimaldi, D., Diaz, J., Arboleda, H., & Fernandez, V. (2019). Data maturity analysis and business performance. A Colombian case study. *Heliyon, 5*, 8. https://doi.org/10.1016/j.heliyon.2019.e02195. e02195.

Grimaldi, D., & Fernandez, V. (2017). The road to school. The Barcelona case. *Cities, 65*, 24–31. https://doi.org/10.1016/j.cities.2017.01.013.

Grimaldi, D., Fernandez, V., & Carrasco, C. (2019). Exploring data conditions to improve business performance. *Journal of the Operational Research Society*, 1087–1098. In press.

Grimaldi, D., Fernandez, V., & Carrasco, C. (2019). Heuristic for the localization of new shops based on business and social criteria. *Technological Forecasting and Social Change, 142*(1), 249–257. https://doi.org/10.1016/j.techfore.2018.07.034.

Loshin, D. (2013). Using graph analytics for big data. *Big data analytics: From strategic planning to enterprise integration with tools, techniques, NoSQL, and graph*. Elsevier (Chapter 10).

Marketsandmarkets. (2021). https://www.marketsandmarkets.com/Market-Reports/graph-analytics-market-10738263.html.

Ramirez, F., Palominos, P., Camargo, M., & Grimaldi, D. (2021). A new methodology to support smartness at the district level of metropolitan areas in emerging economies: The case of Santiago de Chile. *Sustainable Cities and Society, 67*. https://doi.org/10.1016/j.scs.2021.102713, 102713.

Wikipedia. (2021). https://en.wikipedia.org/wiki/Graph_theory.

Chapter 7

Data-driven policy evaluation

Marçal Farré[a], Federico Todeschini[a], Didier Grimaldi[b], and Carlos Carrasco-Farré[c]

[a]Catalan Institute of Public Policy Evaluation (Ivalua), Barcelona, Spain, [b]Ramon Llull University, La Salle Faculty, Barcelona, Spain, [c]Ramon Llull University—ESADE Business School, Barcelona, Spain

1 Introduction

Public policies should be designed and implemented, whenever possible, using evidence as rigorous as possible. Urban interventions then should be no exception. In recent times, we have witnessed increasing efforts to transform information into knowledge, and thus help policymakers make better decisions. In this chapter, we will explore how public policy evaluation helps municipal governments tackle social problems and how big data can improve the design and implementation of more effective, efficient, and transparent policies.

The structure of this chapter is as follows: First, we describe what public policy evaluation is, what knowledge it produces, and how it can be used for designing and implementing better polices. Second, we describe the role of data in public policy and what new opportunities and challenges arise from big data in the context of urban interventions. Third, examples of evaluations that use big data to generate valuable insights for urban policies are shown. Finally, the chapter concludes by summarizing the main learnings and takeaways to leverage the power of big data to inform and support decision-making.

2 Types of policy evaluations and evaluation questions

Policy evaluation or public policy evaluation entails many different concepts. All of them, however, coincide with the idea that evaluation is an activity aimed at developing an understanding of the merit, worth, or utility of a policy by closely examining its different elements or components. However, the nature of the question that can be answered differs significantly depending on what elements the evaluation focuses on.

A general framework to guide policy evaluation is the one that conceptualizes public interventions as a relation between social problems or needs that are to be addressed and a continuum of resources, activities, and products that constitute the core of the public policy, followed by the effects or outcomes that are expected to occur as a consequence of the policy. This framework is usually called change theory or logic framework (McLaughlin & Jordan, 2015), and it exposes the main hypothesis that constitutes a public intervention and the different activities and resources necessary to attain the objectives of the intervention. As we can see in Fig. 7.1, the role of evaluation is to identify and test the underlying hypotheses and produce evidence that can be used in the decision-making process.

It is quite infrequent to evaluate all the components of the change theory of an intervention at once. Most often, the evaluation focuses on those components that are considered more relevant to policymakers. As such, policy evaluation will usually produce different sets of knowledge depending on the type of questions that need to be answered. And as we shall see, that will require different types of methodologies and data.

2.1 The role of evaluation in the decision-making process

Different models have been developed to represent how public policy works. The traditional model for policy analysis, known as the heuristic model (Fig. 7.2), describes policy as a process involving different steps. Although the model has been criticized by many authors for being too simplistic and describing the policy exclusively from a top-down perspective (Sabatier, 2019), it is very useful to analyze what kind of information and evidence fit in different moments of the process. The first stage of the model, agenda setting, is the phase when problems are identified and defined as such, deciding which of them deserve government's attention. In the subsequent stage, alternative

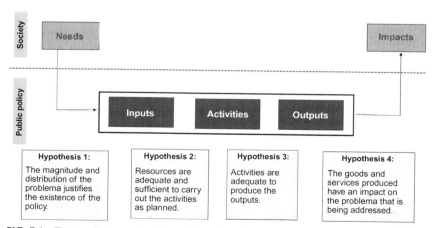

FIG. 7.1 Theory of change of public policies and underlying hypothesis. *(Source: Own elaboration, based on Blasco, J. (2009). Com iniciar una avaluació: oportunitat, viabilitat i preguntes d'avaluació. Catalan Institute of Public Policy Evaluation (Ivalua).)*

FIG. 7.2 Cycle of policy formation. *(Source: Own elaboration, based on the heuristic model described by Sabatier, P. A. (2007). The theories of the policy process (2nd Edition). Boulder, Colorado: Westview Press.)*

courses of action are formulated. Ideally, this is done by setting clear objectives and developing a sound theory on how policy will solve or mitigate the problem as previously defined. From the different alternatives, the chosen policy is then adopted. This phase typically involves seeking support among different stakeholders and legislative or executive approval. Finally, organizational resources are mobilized to make sure that the policy is implemented.

As we previously mentioned, evaluation usually produces different types of knowledge and evidence depending on the type of questions that are set to answer. The type of knowledge needed to answer a particular question, that is, contrast a hypothesis, will usually determine on what part of the policy process the evaluation is most needed. In this chapter, three different types of policy evaluation are described: needs assessment, implementation evaluation, and impact evaluation. While needs assessment can be useful during the agenda setting, the construction of policy alternatives and policy design, implementation, and impact evaluation can be carried out during the implementation to inform policy redesign, replication, scale-up, or discontinuity.

2.2 Needs assessment

Needs assessment involves questions regarding problem definition, resource allocation, and population targeting. It usually includes the description of an unsatisfactory situation that has led to the intervention, its quantification and spatial distribution, as well as the enumeration of the relevant factors and circumstances surrounding it, as well as the quantification of the resources needed to address the problem (Royse, Staton-Tindall, Badger, & Webster, 2009).

Let's suppose a policymaker is commissioned to present an urban strategy to improve educational outcomes in the most disadvantaged areas in his town. The first steps would be to clearly define and quantify the problem that needs to be addressed and understand its causes and consequences to design the right strategy for the problem. Once this has been done, it is important to quantify its prevalence and spatial distribution. At this point, the policymaker can start considering different potential solutions to address the problem (e.g., social mentoring programs, extracurricular training, leisure activities, etc.) and estimate the level of service provision that should be in place to attend the target population and the amount of resources needed.

In next section, we analyze an example of needs assessment using mobile and satellite data to estimate the magnitude and spatial distribution of a social problem.

2.3 Implementation or process evaluation

Some policies are more straightforward to implement once designed, such as property tax collection or traffic light control and coordination, as its implementation is highly determined by its original design. However, some policies deviate from its original design or purpose, and parameters such as quality of delivery, degree of execution, citizen response, or reach on the target population can vary a lot from what was initially envisaged, sometimes even causing a shift in its original goals. These problems show that well-designed policies are not enough to tackle the problem: how it is implemented is key. A common example of this is the low take-up rate of mean tested welfare benefits programs (Atkinson, 1996). The concept on nontake-up (NTU) refers to people who are eligible to receive a benefit but do not apply; it is an implementation problem that erodes policy capacity to tackle poverty and social exclusion and that have been well documented in different contexts.

In Germany, the benefits of the Income Support for Job Seekers scheme are targeted to unemployed people, job seekers, and low-income households whose resources are not sufficient to cover their basic needs. Harnisch (2019) shows that nontake-up rate has been quite high and stable between 2005 and 2014. On average, during that period, the share of households that do not claim benefits despite eligibility amounts to 55.7% of all eligible households. Nontake-up are also present at the municipal policy level. Eurofound (2015) shows the case of nontake up in the cities of Milano and Torino, where city councils initially didn't plan to make a public announcement about a benefit targeting low-income families with at least one minor (*Nuova carta acquisti sperimentale*, NSC) but rather focused on collecting applications only among households already assisted by social services. Different evaluations have shown that individual, institutional, and policy design factors have a key role explaining NTU rates (Laís, 2020).

Another perspective regarding implementation evaluation is to place the focus on the processes through which services are organized and delivered rather than on the outputs of the program or the target population. Although challenges present during policy implementation are specific to different circumstances, some general categories and factors arise in different contexts, such as financial and material resources, staff, organizational structure, norms, organizational culture, or IT. Some researchers have theorized and documented the role of street-level bureaucrats in these processes.

Lipsky (1980) characterizes street-level bureaucrats as *"public service workers who interact directly with citizens in the course of their jobs, and who have substantial discretion in the execution of their work"*. Accordingly, this sort of frontline practitioner, through the use of autonomy and discretion, became policymakers rather than policytakers; their decisions therefore have important consequences on how policies are implemented and, as a consequence, on people's lives. According to Lipsky's theory, street-level bureaucrats use coping mechanisms to deal with their clients' demands and limited resources available. The relevance of this perspective is to use knowledge about street-level bureaucracies to improve the conditions and incentives under which public servants operate.

2.4 Impact evaluation

Interventions are designed and implemented to attain certain objectives. However, it is not necessarily the case that an intervention will be successful in doing so. Impact evaluation tries to measure to what extend an intervention contributed to attain those objectives.

According to Gertler (2011), impact evaluation "seeks to answer cause-and-effect questions" and should be structured to answer questions such as what the effect of an intervention on a certain outcome is. In that sense, impact evaluations are interested in separating those changes that are a (direct) consequence of the intervention. Therefore, the key to an impact evaluation is the focus on causality and causal attribution: we would like to know the difference between what we observe with the intervention and what we would have observed without it.

While we often formulate causal questions, answering them can be quite challenging. Going back to the previous example on an urban intervention to improve educational outcomes, policymakers would probably be interested in knowing whether 1 year after implementing the different activities if they have generated a significant improvement in educational achievement among those participating in the intervention.

Formally, we want to know the effect of an intervention P over the outcome Y for a certain individual i. To do that, we should calculate the following Eq. (7.1):

$$\beta_{Pi} = (Y_{1i} \mid P_i = 1) - (Y_{1i} \mid P_i = 0) \qquad (7.1)$$

According to Eq. (7.1), the causal effect of an intervention P over outcome Y for a particular individual i is the difference between the value of the outcome when the individual receives the intervention $(Y_{1i} \mid P_i = 1)$ and the value of the outcome had the person who received the intervention had instead not received it $(Y_{1i} \mid P_i = 0)$.

In our example, β_{Pi}, the effect of the education intervention on the standardized test on mathematics for person i is the difference between her score doing the program and her score had she not done the program.

Thus, if we want to know the (causal) effect of the education intervention on person i's math test score, we would need to do the intervention, take the math test, defy the laws of physics, travel back in time, and test her now without doing the intervention and then calculate the difference between the two. Since the only thing that changed for person i is the education intervention, any difference in the math test score will be due to the intervention.

Unlike the two previous types of evaluation, impact evaluation requires going a step further. Answering to what extent an intervention changed a certain situation implies knowing how the situation would have been in the absence of the intervention. This is known as the counterfactual situation. An intervention's impact is therefore the outcome in the factual scenario versus the outcome in the counterfactual scenario. Unfortunately, since time travel is not feasible, we cannot observe what would have happened in the absence of the intervention. This is called the "fundamental problem" of impact evaluation. It does not matter how large our dataset is; at most, it will have half of the data.

Even so, not everything is lost. Under certain assumptions, however, we might be able to obtain an unbiased estimation of it. To estimate it, we need information on people who did not receive the intervention. Using nonparticipants as a proxy for the "absence of intervention" scenario comes at a cost though. For example, in the case of the education intervention, it could be that those who voluntarily enrolled in the program are more motivated to successfully finish high school than those who did not enroll. Should that be the case, then the comparison between the two groups will be biased. In particular, we would be confusing the causes that led to the problem of high school failure (motivation) with the consequences of the program.

Therefore, it is quite important that that those units whose information will be used to estimate the counterfactual are indeed similar to those that received the intervention. First, in absence of the intervention, both groups should be similar on average. Second, both groups should be expected to react in the same way to the intervention. Finally, they should not be exposed to different interventions. If such would be the case, then these nonparticipants would be like clones of our participants in the eye of the intervention and the only (relevant) difference between the two would be the intervention.

2.5 How to (correctly) identify the counterfactual situation?

As commented previously, the counterfactual is not directly observable. Its correct identification will therefore depend on the validity of the assumptions that we make regarding the group of people without the intervention. Some assumptions, therefore, will be less valid and some more. Let's take a look at two strategies that are usually flawed. Let's say we compare the math abilities of those participating in the education intervention 1 year after the start of the intervention with what they had previous to participation.

The identifying assumption here is that the only thing that has changed for participants is the intervention. However, many other contemporaneous things could also have affected education outcomes among the participants at the same time the intervention was planned. For example, if the education intervention was conceived in the midst of an economic depression that reduced income drastically among vulnerable households, this before and after comparison will not be able to separate the effect from the education intervention and the economic depression. That is, a simple before/after comparison is valid only when nothing else that affects the outcome has changed contemporaneously to the intervention.

Another alternative frequently used is the comparison between the recipients of intervention and nonrecipients. For example, 1 year after the intervention starts, we compare the test score in math abilities between those receiving the education intervention and a group of students that did not participate in the program. The identifying assumption in this case is that ex-ante both groups have a similar probability of participating in the program but, unrelated to the outcome (math ability), some decided to participate, and some decided not to. We will probably have arguments to contest that hypothesis. It could be that those not participating considered that they did not need the intervention. Or it could be that they had less motivation. In either case, there is some unobservable variable that is correlated both with receiving the intervention and with the outcome. Since we have reasonable doubts whether the two groups are not equivalent before the intervention, the validity of the identification strategy is under suspicion.

To be a valid comparison, those in the control group should be like those in the treatment group on everything that affects both the probability of receiving the intervention and the outcome, observable or unobservable. The presumption of the authorities is that the control group had better characteristics. Therefore, both groups were different when the program began, and thus we won't know which part of the difference in the probability of developing mental diseases is due to the intervention and which to the initial differences. In the evaluation literature, this bias is known as selection bias since those that do not participate in the program usually have different characteristics, and we should adjust for the preintervention differences (observable and unobservable) to eliminate the selection bias. In case we do not have enough information to adjust for those differences, then the estimator would be biased.

In Fig. 7.3, we can see a summarized idea of the selection bias problem. Let's say P is the intervention, Y is the outcome variable, and M is another

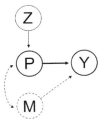

FIG. 7.3 Directed acyclical graph of a very simple intervention. *(Source: Own elaboration.)*

variable. The arrows shows the direction of the relationship. In this case, if we estimate the effect of P over Y without taking into consideration M, P will capture not only the effect of P on Y but also the effect of M on Y. So, unless we block the backdoor path from M to Y, we will not be able to capture the causal effect of P on Y.

3 Experimental and quasiexperimental methodologies

Methods to evaluate the impact of an intervention are usually classified in two groups. The first one is experimental methods, where the allocation of the intervention is random, which guarantees that participation in the intervention does not correlate with any observable or unobservable characteristics, therefore shutting down any backdoor path. This type of method is similar to randomized clinical trials used in medical sciences to decide whether a certain drug is effective (among "data scientists", they are usually referred to as A/B tests).

The second group are quasiexperimental methods. Unlike the previous one, participation here is not decided by a random mechanism controlled by the researcher. For this reason, the assumptions that are necessary to identify the counterfactual situation are usually stronger. Among this second group of methods, we have instrumental variables, difference in differences, regression discontinuity, interrupted time series, and matching methods (Angrist & Pischke, 2014; Imbens & Rubin, 2015).

Let us suppose that we would like to know whether a certain activation policy has benefited its participants. If participation in the program is not exogenous, we might not have the ability to block the backdoor path using observable information. For example, if a desire to learn new skills is driving the willingness to participate in the program, we might not have data to measure this variable. To deal with this problem, we can use instrumental variables. To be valid, an instrumental variable must have a very significant impact on access to the activation program and only affects the outcome variable through program participation. If these two requirements are met, we can use this method to uncover the effect of program participation on participants.

Now, let's imagine that too many people wanted to participate in the program, but only those that meet certain characteristics can be chosen. If access depends on some exogenous threshold set by the authorities, such as age or number of months worked, we could compare those that are just above the threshold to those just below it. This second method is known as regression discontinuity analysis, and the underlying assumption is that, for people who otherwise have the same characteristics in terms of employment skills, level of education, etc., those just below and above the threshold are similar and only sheer chance distinguishes them.

Another possibility to assess the effect of the intervention is to use time variation. Suppose we observe the outcome variable before and after the intervention for those doing the program and those not doing the program. If we have reasons to suspect that in the absence of the intervention, the path followed by the outcome in the treatment group would have been the same that in the control group (that is, the difference between the two would have been constant), then the difference after the program and before the program between those doing the intervention and those not doing it will give a valid estimation of the effect of the intervention. This method is known as double differences or difference in differences and exploits both the cross-sectional and longitudinal dimension of the data.

Another method to assess the effect of a particular policy is interrupted time series, which as was the case of the double differences, also exploits the longitudinal dimension. In this case, a time series of a particular outcome of interest is used to establish an underlying trend, which is affected by an intervention at a known point in time. In its simplest case, the counterfactual situation assumes that the trend would have gone unmodified in the absence of the intervention. For interrupted time series to be a valid research method, we need to know at which specific point in time the intervention was introduced, and we should expect a rapid response from the treated units. Therefore, it is key to have high frequent data. If we suspect time-varying confounders for which we do not have data to control, we should also incorporate a control group whose trend we suspect would have been the same as the treated group in the absence of the intervention.

Last, matching methods try to neutralize the differences due to the distribution of observable characteristics. The assumptions here are that observable characteristics capture the probability of assignment and not the anticipated outcome and, conditional on the observable variables, all the possible candidates have a positive probability of participation. If these two assumptions are valid, the method compares the outcome for beneficiaries and nonbeneficiaries that are close in terms of participation probability. Similar to interrupted time series, matching can be complemented with double differences.

All of the previous methods make certain assumptions to identify the counterfactual situation and estimate the impact of the intervention. These assumptions are nontestable, and therefore their validity should be assessed on the basis of theory and experience. As we shall discuss in the next section, big data can contribute to impact evaluation in at least two dimensions. First, in situations with a natural large number of observations, big data generated is very well suited to deal with randomized control trials in some contexts. Many Internet companies and political campaigns are actually exploiting this feature to improve their systems (Angrist & Pischke, 2014). Second, the ability of big data to capture several dimensions of the determinants of participation can help with the second group of methods (Varian, 2014). That is, information that otherwise would be very difficult to capture can control and block paths and therefore eliminate all the bias from the estimator of the effect of the intervention on the outcome.

4 The role of data in urban policy evaluation

The availability and quality of data is critical to generate valid evaluations (Grimaldi, 2020; Grimaldi, Diaz, Arboleda, & Fernandez, 2019; Grimaldi, Fernandez, & Carrasco, 2019). Probably the reader is familiar with stories of companies that have succeeded using data to improve their performance and to offer a better experience to their customers and expand their market. McAfee and Brynjolfsson (2012) describe how Sears Holdings, by turning to technologies and practices of big data, went from requiring about 8 weeks to generate personalized promotions for their customers to speeding it up to 1 week, at the same time that the quality of the targeting improved.

In this chapter, we show that the same skill sets can be used to address social problems such as poverty or urban inequality. However, first it might be worth highlighting some differences between the most common use of data and the particular use in policy evaluation.

Much of the effort when using big data is placed in prediction without a need to understand the causal underlying mechanism (Grimaldi, 2019; Grimaldi, Diaz, & Arboleda, 2020). For example, certain online recommendations rely on predictive models of what movie you would probably enjoy or what dishwasher you might buy. These algorithms, as shown in previous chapters of the book, can be useful for predicting phenomenon and prescribing preventive action. As shown later in this chapter, prediction can be useful to answer policy questions such as some of the ones posed in Section 1 regarding needs assessment. However, much of the effort in the evaluation literature and practice is placed not in prediction but in causation, in understanding the true causes of social phenomena (Grimaldi & Carrasco, 2019). To differentiate them, while prediction tells us how an outcome varies with a large number of potential predictors, it does not tell us the effect of a single variable on the outcome. Finding what predicts if someone will find a job without knowing why may be useful for certain purposes, but it is insufficient to inform policy decisions regarding an employment program.

Closely related to the previous paragraph, unprecedented quantities of data available and the increase in computing capacity analysis can be undertaken at a higher speed making it easier to find patterns and associations in the data. Some people argue that this possibility makes the role of theory less important, and some even have claimed that data analytics means "the end of theory" (Anderson, 2008). On the other hand, policy analysts and social scientists in general argue that with larger amounts of data, theory plays an even more critical role to answer relevant questions, which take into account what is already known from previous experience and research.

4.1 Typologies of data in public policy evaluation

Chapter 2 of this book explains how a citizen-centered big data approach could be implemented by integrating data from different sources in a unique real-time platform that facilitates and even automates analysis and response. The central idea is that data is collected in the course of citizens' activities and immediately processed for action. In this section, we distinguish different sources of data that city councils currently use in the policy-making process and assess their advantages and limitations due to their attributes in terms of costs of production and processing, frequency, readiness, quality, representativity, and granularity (Table 7.1).

Data for public policy evaluation can come from various sources and in many formats; for simplicity, we classify most common data in three categories: survey data, administrative data, and big data.

4.1.1 Survey data

Survey data collection is a standard tool for empirical research in the social sciences. At the urban level, survey data can unravel relevant information, such as standards of living of the population or citizens' lifestyle, from which specific social needs can be inferred. The survey as instrument and its sampling procedure are designed intentionally for research purposes, which makes it a quality source of information, capable of measuring relevant features in a reliable and valid way. However, survey data typically relies on revealed rather than factual information (e.g., when citizens are asked if they use a service), which sometimes can encompass different sorts of bias. Regarding representativity, although the data it is not always totally free from bias, sampling is done to ensure statistical inference to wider population, which represent a big advantage. However, survey data typically comes at a high cost of production and therefore with a low frequency and low granularity due to sample size limitations, which makes data representative only at a certain level of aggregation (for example, a survey may provide estimates that are representative at a city level but not at a neighborhood level).

TABLE 7.1 Definitions of attributes.

Cost of production: Amount of resources devoted to producing the data to be used. Cost of processing: Amount of resources devoted to preparing the data and analyzing it. Frequency: Number of times the data is updated in a given period. Readiness: Lag of time between the moment when data is captured and when it is ready to be analyzed. Quality: Degree at which data correctly represents the real-world construct to which it refers. Representativity: Degrees in which the data represent a wider population of interest. Granularity: Level of detail within the data that is captured and analyzed.

Source: Own elaboration.

4.1.2 Administrative data

Administrative data, unlike survey data, is collected for administrative purposes by governments or other public administration entities in the course of their regular activities (Crato, 2017), and it typically covers the same individuals or entities over time, creating a panel structure. Data quality is high (Card, Ibarrarán, Regalia, Rosas-Shady, & Soares, 2011) and coverage is universal, ruling out representativity and granularity limitations. Administrative data often allow for cross-section comparative studies between neighborhoods or areas of a city. The cost of producing administrative data is low, since it is already there and it is not produced specifically for evaluation or analytical purposes; however, the cost of processing and analyzing will depend on the degree of data maturity of the city council and other public administrations that produce and manage it. This is one of the reasons why the use of administrative data for policy evaluation may be low. Moreover, the frequency in which the data is available, as well as the variables covered sometimes is insufficient. As an example, in some context poverty rates can be estimated through census data, but this data might be collected every 10 years and often released with a delay of one or more years. However, as we will explore, administrative datasets can be linked to other data sources (Einav & Levin, 2014), allowing us to leverage its advantages and compensate for these limitations.

4.1.3 Big data

Finally, there is big data, which has been defined in previous chapters and offers large volume of data, novel variables, and often with real-time availability and less structure than the previous types of data. Under this category we identify unstructured data coming from sources such as mobile phones, credit cards transactions, or social media. While survey and administrative data have been carefully designed for research or administrative purposes, this type of data are generated through measurements or other automatic procedures that have no relation to these goals. Because of this, although big data are typically produced at a fraction of the cost of surveys, it sometimes can be more difficult to analyze and interpret. On the other hand, big data can have greater reliability, since it often captures aspects that a survey or administrative register cannot directly capture. For example, measuring poverty based on consumption through surveys might be challenging since consumption data can be very noisy due to recall error, but with big data it can be known what some people are buying through their credit cards. However, a new challenge appears: How do we avoid selection bias to preserve representativity of the sample? For example, if a lower proportion of poor people have credit cards than that of the general population, by using credit card data we might be underestimate the number of poor people. In the next section, this challenge is analyzed. Moreover, the number and variety of variables available can be used to find patterns and predict other variables, such as emotions, which would be difficult to elicit through smaller datasets.

Table 7.2 summarizes the attributes described for the typologies of data used for policy evaluation:

The classification presented is used to depict the three main types of data available to policymakers, which are also typically used in public policy research and evaluation. As we showed, each typology tends to have strengths and weaknesses in comparison to the others. These types of data are not mutually exclusive and can be combined in a way that overcomes their weaknesses and leverages their strengths.

One interesting example on how the combination of these data types can help in the design and evaluation of an intervention is the BMincome pilot project of Barcelona City Council (Spain) that was evaluated recently by the Catalan Institute for Public Policy Evaluation (Todeschini & Kirchner, 2019). The program in question was a cash transfer combined with activation policies for low-income families in one of the poorest areas of Barcelona. The combination of different data sources proved to be key to answer questions regarding its design and implementation, as well as the impact of the intervention. First, administrative data helped in identifying the eligible population and inviting them to participate in the program. Also, once they signed up for the pilot project, following them was easier since their ID could be used to extract that from many administrative sources and also to reduce the number of questions that could only be answered using a survey. For example, whether the person was working or not could be answered with social security data, so it was not necessary to include it in the survey. However, administrative data cannot

TABLE 7.2 Typologies of data for policy evaluation.

Attributes	Survey data	Administrative data	Big data
Cost of production	High	Low	Low
Cost of processing	Low	Middle/High	Middle/High
Quality	High	High	Depends
Frequency	Low	Middle/Low	High
Readiness	Middle	Low	High
Representativity	High	High	Depends
Granularity	Low	High	High

Source: Self elaboration.

answer if the person was looking for a job. So, this was included in the survey. Here, big data from their mobile phone can be used to know how they looked for a job and how far they were willing to go to find a suitable job. So, if the design of the experiment is correct, administrative data can tell us whether participants are working more or less than nonparticipants. A survey can tell us whether a job search is different while big data can inform us about the patterns of job search. That way, we would be able to answer whether the cash transfer with activation policies is effective in terms of labor participation, whether households collecting a cash transfer are more willing to search for a job, and whether they are using the appropriate channels. All this information can be later used by policymakers to reformulate the intervention, if necessary, and extend it to other parts of the city.

5 Challenges and opportunities of big data

Big data has several advantages over the other two sources of data we discussed. However, it also poses some challenges that should be considered when carrying out the type of analyses we described earlier. This section explores some of the pros and cons of using big data and how can they be corrected.

One of the most important advantages of big data is readiness. Unlike survey or administrative data, big data can be available almost in real time and therefore track problems right away. At the beginning of 2020, Opportunity Insights developed a model to track the economic impact of the 2020 COVID-19 pandemic using data such as job postings, business revenue, and open small businesses. Oliver et al. (2020) used the information from mobile phones to detect hospital visits and predict the contagion rate at a high level of granularity. This allows policymakers to adapt urban policies with instant feedback from the ground.

Another interesting feature for policy analysis is precision. In certain circumstances, they can help measure social phenomena with more accuracy than traditional data sources. For example, Ajzenman, Cavalcanti, and Da Mata (2020) estimated the impact of the Brazilian president's public declaration on social distance, using georeferenced information from mobile phones to measure human distance. This kind of analysis would be completely impossible using more traditional data sources.

But using big data for policy analysis can lead to wrong conclusions in certain situations if some precautions are not taken. The most obvious one is that big data were not necessarily generated to carry out statistical analyses. That means that the data collection processes can have some imperfections that could lead to biased conclusions.

The first issue is sampling. Big data can easily underrepresent certain groups. Mobile users are a self-selected sample of the population. So using data from mobile users can mean that we won't have data from the poorest part of the population. The Street Bump example here is quite relevant. Street Bump is a mobile app designed by the Boston city council that a uses mobile phone's accelerometer and GPS data to detect potholes and report them automatically. After the app the was released, city officials realized that they were fixing potholes only where rich people lived; poor neighborhoods equally or more likely to have potholes but were neglected because they were less likely to have smartphones suitable to install the application or even less likely to download it and install it in the first case. Even though this methodological problem was eventually corrected, it shows some of the perils from considering big data a substitute and not a complement of traditional data.

Biases are not new in social sciences. However, expanding the generation of data might amplify it by reproducing the social differences in the use of these devices to the samples at use. For example, if the use of smartphones varies across age or socioeconomic segments of the population, the data from smartphones will reproduce those differences and, taken at face value, those estimations will not be useful to make an inference about the population of interest. Depending on the data source, one could assign a disproportionate weight to certain social groups. Another source of bias that limits the representativity is data only available from one company or service provider. If we want to assess mobility patterns during the COVID-19 lockdown using mobile data, we should be aware that Android and Apple smartphones are different populations.

Fig. 7.4 shows the location of Twitter users who use Android (green dots, gray in print version) and iPhone (red dots, dark gray in print version) in the city of New York and its surroundings. As we can see, the proportion of iPhone is comparatively more concentrated around wealthy areas, such as Manhattan, while Android users are relatively more present in areas such as Newark.

The combination of big data with other sources can be used to assess and improve the representativeness of the data. Hill et al. (2019) describe different examples presented to the "Big Data Meets Survey Science" conference held in

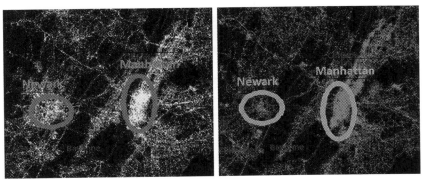

FIG. 7.4 Location of Twitter users who use Android and iPhones in New York and its surroundings. *(Source: From https://labs.mapbox.com/bites/00245/brands/#.)*

October 2018 that shows how machine learning and web-scraping applications can be used to create or augment official statistics estimation. Pedraza, Visintin, Tijdens, and Kismihók (2019) compared the number of vacancies in the economy inferred by survey methods by the Netherlands Statistical Office (NSO) obtained from web posts. Although the numbers show that the NSO data produced a higher value of vacancies over the entire period, indicating greater coverage of the phenomenon, the authors show that the web and NSO time series vacancy data were generated by the same underlying phenomenon: the real number of new vacancies appearing in the Dutch labor market, supporting the idea that web-sourced data are able to capture aggregate economic activities.

Big data quality, that is, the degree at which data correctly represents real-world constructs, can show significant variation. According to Pulse (2012), the United Nations initiative to promote big data and artificial intelligence for sustainable development, big data is similar to *"the shadows of objects passing in front of the fire"*, drawing a parallel with Plato's cave myth. The question then is how well these shadows represent relevant aspects of the intervention and how can we use them to answer relevant questions. Some authors have expressed their concerns, warning that sometimes online data might be false or fabricated by individuals who try to interfere. This is especially challenging in social media, where some accounts are used by multiple people, there are bots that produce automated content, and the notion of an active account is problematic (Boyd & Crawford, 2012). Moreover, large datasets from Internet sources are often unreliable, prone to outages and losses, and these errors and gaps are magnified when multiple datasets are used together (Boyd & Crawford, 2012). Pedraza et al. (2019) reviewed literature that evaluated data quality of online sources such as Twitter, Wikipedia, Google searches, voluntary web surveys, and Open Data Government portals, concluding that quality and representativeness depend on the context, target population, and research goal. This stresses the importance that, working with big data, as when working with any other type of data, requires an understanding of where the data comes from and how the data has been produced.

Representative surveys are not necessarily immune to concerns such as selective responses and heterogeneous response quality (Einav & Levin, 2014). However, in the case of big data, this is particularly relevant because often the generation of data is mediated by technological devices, consumer patterns, or cultural norms that have a correlation with the socioeconomic conditions.

Another potential challenge for big data is the interpretation of the data. While survey data is constructed following certain methodological rules, this is not the case with big data (and frequently neither the case of administrative data). Let's take the example of text sentiment analysis for example. Natural language has certain unwritten rules that change and evolve through time and context. What is acceptable in Twitter is certainly not in an economic journal, and thus our interpretation of the text should adapt to the source. In the evaluation of Erasmus+, an European Commission program to promote education, training, and sport, the team of evaluators sought to assess the relevance and visibility of the program by collecting social media posts from Twitter, Facebook, and Instagram. Sentiment analysis was used to classify each post connected to Erasmus+ as negative, positive, or neutral. According to the consulting firm who performed the evaluation, sometimes the algorithm misjudged sentiments, especially when complex sentences, jokes, or sarcasm were used. Very negative sentiments were inferred from messages coming from the United Kingdom. However, a deeper analysis showed that those comments were in fact not directed to the program but were concerns about its continuation after the Brexit referendum. This kind of risk might be present when trying to infer some information that is not self-evident in the data, such as sentiments. However, recent advances in this field look remarkably promising (Lachaux, Roziere, Chanussot, & Lample, 2020).

Another concern when using big data comes from biases that are not present in the data but are embedded in how the human brain works. An example of this is confirmation bias, which is defined as the tendency to select, interpret, and recall information in a way that confirms or strengthens one's preexisting beliefs. Confirmation bias can be present when working with any kind of data, but it is particularly prone to appear when dealing with big quantities of data and when the computational capacity allows for checking for all kinds of correlations and patterns in the data, some of which might be the product of spurious relations or randomness.

As Nassim Taleb states in his book "*Fooled by randomness: The Hidden Role of Chance in Life and in the Markets*" (Taleb, 2005), when one throws the computer at data looking for just about any relationship, it is certain that a spurious connection will emerge. Some authors argue that massive quantities of data encourage the practice of apophenia: seeing patterns where none exist (Boyd & Crawford, 2012) or even that there is a danger that, as machine learning techniques automates and accelerates the analysis, processes will facilitate the industrial-scale production of spurious results through multiple hypothesis testing (Ashworth, Berry, & Mesquita, 2014).

If evaluation should generate knowledge to support decision-making, these aspects should be taken into account when using big data for policy analysis.

6 Examples of policy evaluation

In this section, we analyzed big data's contribution to policy evaluation by exposing examples of evaluations performed with different data sources, including mobile data, satellite data, credit cards, and administrative registers.

6.1 Big data contribution to impact evaluation

Section 1 of this chapter described quasiexperimental methods that are frequently used in impact evaluation, including instrumental variables, difference in differences, regression discontinuity, interrupted time series and matching methods. All these methods make certain assumptions to identify what would have happened in the absence of the policy being evaluated, that is, the counterfactual situation, and estimate the impact of the policy by comparing it to what really happened, the factual situation. As stated in Section 2, the measurement of variables that determine the participation or exposition to a certain policy, together with frequent updates, brings new opportunities to build comparable groups.

In this section, three different examples of quasiexperimental studies are presented, each of them using different combinations of the three data sources described in Section 2: administrative data, surveys, and big data. The first example shows the potential of (unstructured and potentially big) administrative records for impact evaluations, especially in those contexts where the public administration has developed and perfected systems of recording information in a systematic way. However, as shown in the second and third example, big data can provide information that otherwise would be too hard and/or expensive to collect, which therefore widens research opportunities and speeds up the production of valuable evidences.

7 Case study: Fudging the nudge: Information disclosure and restaurant grading in New York (Meltzer et al., 2015)

Municipalities are typically responsible for different services, such as public schools, street cleanliness, or public transport (Grimaldi & Fernandez, 2017). To keep track of its performance and quality service, it is common to use grading systems. Grades, as a policy, try to influence or "nudge" the citizens or organizations instead of directly imposing a behavior and can be used as a warning when some service is not working well, or as a tool to identify good practices that might be replicable or scalable, allowing for greater improvements.

The New York City Department of Health and Mental Hygiene (DOHMH) is responsible for inspecting the city's restaurants to guarantee food safety. To do so, the DOHMH randomly assign inspectors to restaurants, scheduling the timing of inspections within a window of 2 months. In July 2010, the DOHMH started assigning each restaurant a grade to reflect the restaurants' food safety compliance, and the grade was required to be posted in the entrance near eye-level, so that passers-by could easily discern it. The theory of the grading policy is based on the hypothesis that the grades will provide information to citizens, and they will use this information to reduce their consumption in places more likely to bear foodborne illnesses. This fact, in turn, is expected to have an impact on restaurants' attention and behavior about sanitation.

Previously, Ho (2012) analyzed publicly available restaurant grading data for New York City from an implementation perspective. The author explored the extent to which inspection scores are consistent, observing that prior scores had very low prediction power of future ones, attributing this to inconsistencies in the inspection process. Later, Wong et al. (2015) provided evidence on improved consistency since the beginning of the public grading policy, showing increases in the probability of a restaurant scoring in the A-range during unannounced initial inspections. Finally, Meltzer et al. (2015) answered questions related to the policy impact: Does such a policy improve food safety? Does it help or harm the economic viability of the restaurants? What are the costs and benefits for the municipality from such a grading scheme?

According to Meltzer et al. (2015), New York City's grading policy has impacted restaurant sanitary conditions and fines. Final inspection scores decline (i.e., sanitation improves) by about 4 points (about 17% of the pregrading mean) upon policy implementation and then continue to decline at about ¼ point per quarter. On the other hand, impacts on sales and revenues are less clear. The results indicate that the policy influenced restaurants, which improved food safety compliance but did not influence their revenue.

Meltzer et al. (2015) implemented a systematic analysis using large datasets that include data from the DOHMH and Department of Finance (the agency that houses the business sales revenue data), including food safety compliance and sales activity for the universe of graded restaurants over multiple years both before and after the grading policy's implementation. As we have seen in Section 2, administrative data has several advantages: the data already exists besides research purposes, it has a certain quality, and typically it's representative and granular since it includes all the population of interest. As shown in this example, when administrative data is well connected and frequently updated, and when combined with regression analysis, it can be used to capture causal effects. However, in some cases, the fragmentation of administrative data and low frequency at which it is updated might be an obstacle to conduct such analysis. In the next examples, it is shown how big data can contribute to overcome these caveats.

8 Case study: Consumer response to the COVID-19 crisis (Andersen, Hansen, Johannesen, & Sheridan, 2020)

One question that arises from the COVID-19 crisis is how consumer spending has been reshaped in the short term and whether we can see any distinguishable patterns that can inform urban policymakers, particularly if such crises can become more frequent. Andersen et al. (2020) investigated three questions. First, how average consumer spending, the main component of private demand, reacted to the Danish lockdown of March 11, 2020. Second, whether there is evidence of heterogeneity across expenditure changes that can evidence spillovers across sectors through demand. Finally, whether spending response is different for different types of consumers.

On March 11, the Danish government introduced a national lockdown where all nonessential business were shut down and workers were urged to work from home. Also, borders were effectively closed as well. On March 18, the government introduced further restrictions such as prohibiting concentrations of more than 10 individuals. At the same time, it introduced some policies to cope with the resulting economic damage and liquidity problems. For example, it paid 75% of those workers who were temporarily sent home and partially compensated firms for the fixed cost. It is very hard to distinguish the part of the effect due to COVID from the part due to the measures from the government. However, we could estimate the effect of the whole.

The identification equation for that analysis is relatively simple, and it mimics the difference in difference methodology we commented on previously. The authors compared excess demand in the postlockdown period with excess demand in the prelockdown period. In this context, excess demand is considered the ratio of spending in a given day of 2020 and spending 364 days before. This eliminates the cyclical component as they are comparing the same day of the week, almost the same moment in the month, and the same moment in the annual spending cycle. The identification assumption, therefore, is that the year-to-year growth in consumer spending would have remained similar in the event that no lockdown (nor COVID-19) would have been introduced.

The distinguishable part of the analysis is the data the authors use: transaction-level customer data. The authors are able to exploit every purchase made with payment cards, including date, amount, branch code, and location of the shop of the more than 760 individuals with an account. The data source is the Dankse Bank, the largest bank in Denmark, and it covers the period that spans from January 1, 2018 to May 5, 2020. Besides the transaction, the authors have access to some basic demographic characteristics that allows construction of a consumer's profile. Importantly, there are no significant differences between the sample and the population.

According to the results from the research, the drop in aggregate purchases from the COVID crisis is a massive 25%, taking into consideration that job losses are estimated to have an impact of 10% reduction (Ganong & Noel, 2019). Now, this reduction is different for certain types of individuals. The two groups with the largest difference are health risk and type of consumption. For example, those aged 65 years or more reduce consumption more than younger people. Looking at the proportion of their consumption prelockdown in those sectors affected by the lockdown, there is a significant difference in the consumption reduction between those in the highest quantile and those in the first quartile. Similar people who differ on their stock exposure in their wealth reduced spending more than those without such a position. Everything else equal, those in the private sector reduced consumption by more.

Another decomposition is between sectors that were affected by the government intervention and those that were not. While the sectors affected by the government represent approximately 50% of the economy, they registered an increase of 10% due to the lockdown. On the other hand, those closed by the government, which accounts 25% of the economy, registered a 70% decrease due to the lockdown. Those constrained, which account for 25%, suffered a reduction of around 40%. However, there is evidence of a certain negative spillover from the demand side, although it seems to be modest.

Carvalho et al. (2020) ran a similar analysis with similar data for Spain, but they also exploited the geographical feature of the data. Consistent with the nature of the Spanish lockdown (relative to the same period in the previous year), expenditures in commodities related to basic needs more than doubled during the lockdown period. On the other hand, expenditures in goods with higher elasticity almost vanished.

Another interesting conclusion from the analysis is about the geographical distribution of the effect of the lockdown. First, there is no evidence that a differential exposure to the pandemic across regions affected regional expenditure. However, at a more granular level (zip code level), there is evidence of heterogeneous effects. That is, zip codes with a higher incidence of COVID cases witnessed larger decrease in expenditure.

It should be clear that without access to transaction-level customer data, it would have been impossible to test the underlaying hypothesis answer and answer the questions. These data are available at big quantities and with high granularity, which allows exploitation of all kinds of features present in the sample, such as differences between economic sectors, people's profile, or geographic areas. Granular data can provide opportunities to identify counterfactuals, such as the comparison of neighborhoods affected by a certain regulation to others not affected by it or seeing the changes in a relative short period of time that yearly or monthly aggregation would miss. Finally, even though processing and exploring big data is complex, its rapid availability since the moment it is captured allowed the authors to complete the study in a very short period of time.

9 Case study: The impact of public health interventions during the COVID pandemic

Use of masks are another example of how a combination of administrative data and big data can help uncover the effects of public interventions in almost real time. Using an experimental design (which we described in Section 2) Mitze, Kosfeld, Rode, and Wälde (2020) exploited the fact that, in Germany, the region of Jena introduced an obligation to wear masks much earlier than other regions. From the other municipalities of Germany without a mask obligation, the authors constructed a synthetic control counterfactual that mimics the COVID-19 trend of Jena before the mandatory masks.

According to the results, the introduction of mandatory masks reduced the accumulated number of COVID-19 by 23% (equivalent to a reduction of 1.3% in daily growth rate or a relative decrease of 60.1% in the daily growth rate). Taking into consideration what we know from the previous papers regarding the effect of lockdown on the economy, a mask mandate is a potential substitute for lockdowns and thus can save up to 5% of the GDP.

The final example regarding the effect of COVID prevention policies is the effect of a large-scale experiment in India (Banerjee et al., 2020). The treatment group consisted of 25 million individuals who were sent an SMS containing a 2.5-minute video clip that encouraged reporting symptoms to local public health workers and emphasized social distance and hand washing. The control group consisted of 3 million individuals who received messages pointing them to government information. Messages were randomized at a postal index number level. Five to fifteen days after the SMS was sent, the authors surveyed 677 health workers and 1883 individuals by phone.

According to Banerjee et al. (2020), the campaign doubled the reporting to health authorities of fever and/or respiratory symptoms, decreased mobility outside's their own village by 20% from a 37% baseline, and increased hand washing when returning home by 7% from a 65.7% baseline. Also, it increased the use of mask-wearing and social distancing.

10 Case study: Effect of smart technology on consumer's behavior

Unlike electricity production costs, retail prices usually do not change from hour to hour and are usually fixed during the month, which leads to a mismatch between wholesale and retail prices that creates a situation of inefficient allocation of resources. In the current global warming context, many economists have advocated for the use of time-of-use pricing to reflect marginal costs better and therefore reduce consumption during on-peak periods.

The question is, however, under which conditions consumers have the ability to react to that type of pricing, and whether sociodemographic characteristics and usage level can predict differences in the ability. Harding and Lamarche (2016) tried to assess how responsiveness are households to time-of-use pricing.

The paper investigates the effect of smart meters under time-of-use pricing in the southern United States. Upon signing up for the intervention, households were randomized to one of the following three groups: smart meters with time-of-use pricing, information provision regarding tariffs and consumption, and the standard tariff (status quo). The experiment gathered 1100 households. To capture household responsiveness over the course of the day, the registered electricity consumption was over a 15-minute interval (11 million observations).

According to the results, smart meters are particularly effective at enabling households to respond to such pricing schemes because they provide real-time information on consumption and pricing as well as allow households to program device use for different times of the day, and thus anticipate and respond to price changes in advance. Information provision alone, however, does not achieve such a significant impact.

Furthermore, it is relevant to understand how the responsiveness to time-of-use pricing combined with enabling technologies varies with demographic characteristics. According to the results, younger and high-income households are more responsive to time-of-use pricing relative to poorer or older households. However, there is not a significant difference between high-usage costumers relative to low-usage costumers, even though the former are in a position to benefit in terms of cost reductions from the enabling technologies. A back-of-the-envelope estimation suggests that the reduction of CO_2 emissions is marginal and under 4 pounds for the mean consumer.

The urban policy implication is that the combination of time-of-use pricing with enabling technologies are an effective alternative to reduce energy consumption. However, the heterogeneous response to time-of-use pricing can raise distributional considerations. However, in terms of energy conservation, it is less well suited and does not achieve large reductions in CO_2 emissions.

These examples shows that big data can complement more traditional sources of data in urban policy evaluation and can be adapted to both experimental and quasiexperimental methods. In the first two cases, big data provide granularity and timeliness that can be used to track the reaction of the society and evaluate the impact of government interventions almost in real time. Exploiting these data usually requires a collaboration with the public sector to combine it with administrative and census data that can allow adjusting the data for sociodemographic characteristics and therefore mitigate selection bias.

And as we can see from the SMS example from India, big data can be used to design and implement interventions while survey and administrative data can be the source of information for the outcome variable.

11 Big data contribution to needs assessment

As shown in previous examples, big data can be used to exploit exogenous changes to estimate the policy effects on a particular variable, such as service quality or economic activity. When the question that has to be answered is not causal in nature but descriptive, big data can also be of big help. This is the case for needs assessment, a type of evaluation in which the focus is placed in understanding and dimensioning a specific problem and quantifying the resources needed to address it. For this kind of policy evaluation, predictive and classification methods are of great value to estimate who suffers the particular problem of interest and what are the factors surrounding this problem. The next example shows how the combination of administrative data and big data can be used to learn what variables are good predictors of a certain condition of interest (poverty in this example) and not only realize frequent updates but also gaining deeper understanding of its dimension, spatial distribution, and surrounding factors.

12 Case study: Mapping poverty using mobile phone and satellite data

According to the World Bank, latest poverty estimates from 2016 to 17 in Bangladesh show remarkable gains in poverty reduction since 2000. Upper poverty rates have halved to 24.3% while extreme poverty rates have reduced by two-thirds to 12.9%. Per capita consumption is used to assess household's poverty status, and poverty lines are set at the cost of consuming certain levels of Cal per person and per day and an allowance for non-food expenditure.

However, these estimates are produced by using household expenditure data collected in the nationally representative quinquennial Household Income Expenditure Survey (HIES), being the latest round collected in 2016–17. Steele et al. (2017) proposed a complementary approach using big data to provide novel insight into the spatial distribution of poverty, gaining a deeper understanding of how poverty is distributed in the rural and urban areas. They combine sensing and geographic information system data (hereafter called RS data) and mobile operator call detail records (CDRs) to map poverty in urban and rural areas of Bangladesh. RS provides data of physical properties, such as rainfall, temperature, and vegetation capture information related to agricultural productivity, while distance to roads and cities reflects access to markets and information. CDR features a range of metrics such as basic phone usage, top-up patterns, and social network to metrics of user mobility and handset usage.

To estimate poverty rates, Voronoi polygons were built, which size allowed to maintain the fine spatial detail in mobile phone data within urban areas. Each polygon was assigned RS and CDR values, and survey data measuring poverty was matched. Nonspatial generalized linear models were constructed to identify and select a set of poverty predictors and were then used in a hierarchical Bayesian geostatistical approach (BGMs) to produce predictions of each poverty metric for each polygon. Model performance was based on out-of-sample validation statistics. As a result, highly granular maps of predicted poverty rates were constructed for commonly used indicators of living standards.

Fig. 7.5 shows the predicted percentage of people living below $2.50 per day.

According to the authors, models employing a combination of CDR and RS provide better predictive power and lowest error rates than models based on either data source alone. The method performed better at predicting poverty indicators measured through wealth than consumption and income.

The findings indicate the possibility of exploiting correlations between different data sources to estimate and understand the distribution of human living conditions. This information can be very useful to dimension resources and policies aimed at solving specific problems and to improve the targeting strategies to reach the population. Furthermore, this example shows how big data and prediction methods can be used to complement administrative and survey data and provide more granular and regular updates.

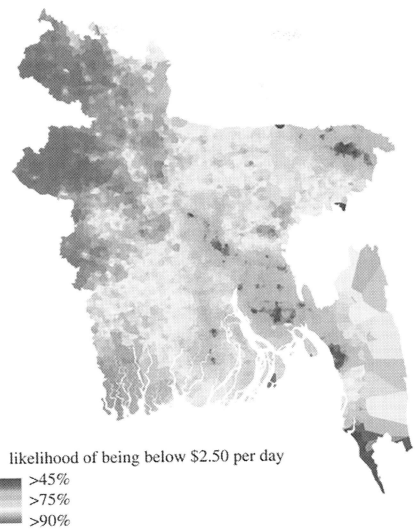

FIG. 7.5 Likelihood of households of being below $2.50/day. *(Source: From Steele, J. E., et al. (2017). Mapping poverty using mobile phone and satellite data.* Journal of the Royal Society Interface, *14, 20160690. https://doi.org/10.1098/rsif.2016.0690.)*

13 Conclusions

Data are essential for policy evaluation. We have witnessed a trend in the last two decades toward more rigorous public policy evaluation using empirical data. From this perspective, the advent of big data offers an opportunity to take advantage of the availability of large volume, fast velocity, variety, and the ability to link many datasets. This should allow better prediction of social and economic phenomena, improve causal inference, and the possibility to answer relevant questions such as:

- What is the magnitude and geographic distribution of a certain social problem?
- How are policies that try to address this problem being implemented?
- What is the impact of such interventions on the urban problem?
- For whom and under which circumstances do these policies work?

However, the materialization of these opportunities is far from generalized. The examples presented in this chapter are standalone efforts rather than pieces of a systematic inquiry. On the one hand, the availability and access to data may involve partnering with private firms that limit researcher freedom, and thus the capacity to analyze and draw conclusions from it. The ideas and recommendations presented in previous chapters of this book are key so that the evaluation practices become commonplace, especially the contributions of Chapter 2, regarding the importance of developing a citizen-centered big data urban governance, and Chapter 4, where the process of implementing a data-driven transformation is described along its different phases: inception, launching, growing, and maturity. These are preconditions for a greater use of policy evaluation.

On the other hand, big data may suffer from selection bias depending on how and by whom data are being generated, and thus the conclusions we can draw from them should be taken with a grain of salt. In this chapter, it has been described what policy evaluation can bring to urban policies and how big data can contribute to it, exploring its strengths, limitations, and complementarities with other sources of information. As stressed in Section 2, it is important that the analysts are aware of how the data has been produced and what its limitations are. Despite some data sources lacking a structure that facilitates its analysis, recent advances show the potential of machine learning and web-scraping techniques to generate precise estimates that can complement, add depth, or even expand the perimeter of what is being measured through other methods.

At the same time, the possibility to connect different data sources will contribute to obtain higher precision of estimates and identify new opportunities for policy analysis and evaluation purposes. Although more data is neither a substitute for better data nor for methodological soundness, high frequency of data and granularity can generate new methodological opportunities, such as exploiting discontinuities and exogenous variation in the intervention to construct comparison groups that are similar enough to those receiving the intervention, and thus infer what would have happened in the absence of the policy.

Finally, due to the increased automation of data treatment and analysis, policy evaluation may no longer be considered as a separate function from other activities aimed at knowledge generation, such as reporting or monitoring, and it may be treated as one of the outputs of the integrated information systems that will be adopted by local governments. How this opportunity is undertaken will depend on political and organizational priorities.

References

Gertler. (2011). *Impact evaluation in practice*. World Bank.

Angrist, J. D., & Pischke, J. S. (2014). *Mastering' metrics: The path from cause to effect*. Princeton University Press.

Ajzenman, N., Cavalcanti, T., & Da Mata, D. (2020). More than words: Leaders' speech and risky behavior during a pandemic. *SSRN Electronic Journal*.

Andersen, A. L., Hansen, E. T., Johannesen, N., & Sheridan, A. (2020). Consumer responses to the COVID-19 crisis: Evidence from bank account transaction data. *SSRN Electronic Journal*.

Anderson, C. (2008). *The end of theory: The data deluge makes the scientific method obsolete*. Wired Magazine.

Ashworth, S., Berry, C. R., & Mesquita, E. B. D. (2014). All else equal in theory and data (big or small). *PS—Political Science and Politics, 48*(1), 89–94. Cambridge University Press https://doi.org/10.1017/S1049096514001802.

Atkinson, A. B. (1996). The case for a participation income. *The Political Quarterly, 67*(1), 67–70. https://doi.org/10.1111/j.1467-923x.1996.tb01568.x.

Banerjee, A., Alsan, M., Breza, E., Chandrasekhar, A., Chowdhury, A., Duflo, E., et al. (2020). *Messages on COVID-19 prevention in India increased symptoms reporting and adherence to preventive behaviors among 25 million recipients with similar effects on non-recipient members of their communities*.

Boyd, D., & Crawford, K. (2012). Six provocations for big data. *SSRN Electronic Journal*. https://doi.org/10.2139/ssrn.1926431.

Card, D., Ibarrarán, P., Regalia, F., Rosas-Shady, D., & Soares, Y. (2011). The labor market impacts of youth training in the Dominican Republic. *Journal of Labor Economics, 29*(2), 267–300.

Carvalho, V. M., Garcia, J. R., Hansen, S., Ortiz, Á., Rodrigo, T., Mora, J. V. R., et al. (2020). *Tracking the COVID-19 crisis with high-resolution transaction data*.

Crato, N. P. (2017). *A call to action for better data and better policy evaluation*. https://doi.org/10.2760/738045.

Einav, L., & Levin, J. (2014). The data revolution and economic analysis. *Innovation Policy and the Economy, 14*(1), 1–24.

Eurofound. (2015). *Access to social benefits: Reducing non-take-up*. Luxembourg: Publications Office of the European Union. https://www.eurofound.europa.eu/publications/report/2015/social-policies/access-to-social-benefits-reducing-non-take-up.

Ganong, P., & Noel, P. (2019). Consumer spending during unemployment: Positive and normative implications. *American Economic Review*. https://doi.org/10.3386/w25417.

Grimaldi, D. (2019). Can we analyse political discourse using Twitter? Evidence from Spanish 2019 presidential election. *Social Network Analysis and Mining, 9*(49). https://doi.org/10.1007/s13278-019-0594-6.

Grimaldi, D. (2020). Factors affecting big data analytics based innovation processes. A Spanish evidence. *International Journal of Innovation and Technology Management, 8*. https://doi.org/10.1142/S0219877020500364. In press.

Grimaldi, D., & Carrasco, C. (2019). Heuristic for the localization of new shops based on business and social criteria. *Technological Forecasting and Social Change, 51*(1). https://doi.org/10.1016/j.techfore.2018.07.034.

Grimaldi, D., Diaz, J., & Arboleda, H. (2020). Inferring the votes in a new political landscape: The case of the 2019 Spanish Presidential elections. *Journal of Big Data, 7*(58). https://doi.org/10.1186/s40537-020-00334-5. In press.

Grimaldi, D., Diaz, J., Arboleda, H., & Fernandez, V. (2019). Data maturity analysis and business performance. A Colombian case study. *Heliyon*, *8*(1). https://doi.org/10.1016/j.heliyon.2019.e02195Get.

Grimaldi, D., & Fernandez, V. (2017). The road to school. The Barcelona case. *Cities*, *65*, 24–31. https://doi.org/10.1016/j.cities.2017.01.013.

Grimaldi, D., Fernandez, V., & Carrasco, C. (2019). Exploring data conditions to improve business performance. *Journal of the Operational Research Society*, *4*(12). https://doi.org/10.1080/01605682.2019.1590136.

Harding, M., & Lamarche, C. (2016). Empowering consumers through data and smart technology: Experimental evidence on the consequences of time-of-use electricity pricing policies. *Journal of Policy Analysis and Management*, *35*(4), 906–931.

Harnisch, M. (2019). *Non-take-up of means-tested social benefits in Germany*. https://www.diw.de/documents/publikationen/73/diw_01.c.616586.de/dp1793.pdf.

Hill, C. A., Biemer, P., Buskirk, T., Callegaro, M., Lucía, A., Cazar, C., et al. (2019). Exploring new statistical frontiers at the intersection of survey science and big data: Convergence at "Big-Surv18". *Survey Research Methods*, *13*(1), 123–135. https://doi.org/10.18148/srm/2019.v13i1.7467.

Ho, D. E. (2012). Fudging the nudge: Information disclosure and restaurant grading. *The Yale Law Journal*, *122*. https://digitalcommons.law.yale.edu/ylj/vol122/iss3/2.

Imbens, G. W., & Rubin, D. B. (2015). *Causal inference: For statistics, social, and biomedical sciences an introduction* (pp. 1–625). Cambridge University Press. https://doi.org/10.1017/CBO9781139025751.

Lachaux, M.-A., Roziere, B., Chanussot, L., & Lample, G. (2020). *Unsupervised translation of programming languages*. https://docs.python.org/2/library/2to3.html.

Laís, B. (2020). *"Qui no plora, no mama"? o perquè hi ha gent que no sol·licita prestacions econòmiques*. http://lleiengel.cat/gent-no-sollicita-prestacions/.

Lipsky, M. (1980). *Street level bureaucracy. Dilemmas of the individual in public services* (p. 272). Russell Sage Foundation. https://doi.org/10.7758/9781610447713.5.

McAfee, A., & Brynjolfsson, E. (2012). Big data: The management revolution. *Harvard Business Review*. https://hbr.org/2012/10/big-data-the-management-revolution.

McLaughlin, J. A., & Jordan, G. B. (2015). Using logic models. In *Handbook of practical program evaluation* (pp. 62–87). John Wiley & Sons, Inc. https://doi.org/10.1002/9781119171386.ch3.

Meltzer, R., Rothbart, M. W., Schwartz, A. E., Calabrese, T., Silver, D., Mijanovich, T., et al. (2015). *Is public grading worth the costs? An evaluation of New York City's restaurant grades policy*. https://www.appam.org/assets/1/7/Impact_paper_9-30-15.pdf.

Mitze, T., Kosfeld, R., Rode, J., & Wälde, K. (2020). *Face masks considerably reduce COVID-19 cases in Germany: A synthetic control method approach*.

Oliver, N., Letouzé, E., Sterly, H., Delataille, S., Nadai, M. D., Lepri, B., et al. (2020). *Mobile phone data and COVID-19: Missing an opportunity?*. http://arxiv.org/abs/2003.12347.

Pedraza, P. D., Visintin, S., Tijdens, K., & Kismihók, G. (2019). Survey vs scraped data: Comparing time series properties of web and survey vacancy data. *IZA Journal of Labor Economics*, *8*(1). https://doi.org/10.2478/izajole-2019-0004.

Pulse, U. N. G. (2012). *Big data for development: Challenges & opportunities*. http://data-arts.appspot.com/globe-search.

Royse, D., Staton-Tindall, M., Badger, K., & Webster, J. M. (2009). *Needs assessment*. https://doi.org/10.1093/acprof:royes/9780195368789.001.0001.

Sabatier, P. (2019). The need for better theories. In *Theories of the policy process* (pp. 3–17). Routledge. https://doi.org/10.4324/9780367274689-1.

Steele, J. E., Sundsøy, P. R., Pezzulo, C., Alegana, V. A., Bird, T. J., Blumenstock, J., et al. (2017). Mapping poverty using mobile phone and satellite data. *Journal of the Royal Society Interface*, *14*(127), 20160690. https://doi.org/10.1098/rsif.2016.0690.

Taleb, N. N. (2005). *Fooled by randomness: The hidden role of chance in life and in the markets*. New York: Random House.

Todeschini, F., & Kirchner, L. (2019). *Informe de resultados preliminares del proyecto piloto BMincome*. Ajuntament de Barcelona.

Varian, H. R. (2014). Big data: New tricks for econometrics. *Journal of Economic Perspectives*, *28*(2), 3–28. https://doi.org/10.1257/jep.28.2.3.

Wong, M. R., McKelvey, W., Ito, K., Schiff, C., Jacobson, J. B., & Kass, D. (2015). Impact of a letter-grade program on restaurant sanitary conditions and diner behavior in New York City. *American Journal of Public Health*, *105*(3), e81–e87. https://doi.org/10.2105/AJPH.2014.302404.

Index

Note: Page numbers followed by *f* indicate figures, *t* indicate tables, and *b* indicate boxes.

A

Advanced Traffic Management Centers (A-TMC), 166–167
Airbnb listings, Barcelona, 182–184, 182–184*f*
Automated Fare Collection system (AFC), 139–140, 140*f*

B

Big data
  assessment, 219
  challenges and opportunities, 210–213, 211*f*
  consumer's behavior, 219
  contribution, policy evaluation, 214
  data-driven cities and smart cities
    Barcelona platform, 166
    Cologne platform, 166
    data preparation, 164
    GrowSmarter project, 165
    internet of things (IoT), 161
    Stockholm platform, 165–166
  selection bias, 222
  urban policy evaluation, 208–210, 209*t*

C

Call detail records (CDRs), 220
City resilience, 4
  data visualization, 194*b*
Collaborative Intelligent Transport Systems (C-ITS), 167–168, 169*f*
Commission on Public Information and Communication (COPIC), 8
Connected Boulevard project, 132, 136–137
Cooperative, Connected, and Automated Mobility (CCAM) services, 168–171, 169*f*, 171*f*
COVID-19
  CO_2 emissions, 2
  data visualization
    EIXOS Economic Observatory, 184–194, 187*f*, 188*t*, 190–194*f*
    Retail Occupancy Index (ROI), 185, 185*f*
  economic downturn, 2–3
  New York City, 10
  Swiss response
    agent-based modeling, 73
    characteristics, 74
    public transportation system, 74
    Swiss COVID app, 73–74
    Swiss National COVID-19 Science Task Force (SN-STF), 73
COVID-19 crisis
  consumer response, 215–217
  public health interventions, 217–218

D

Dashboard
  data visualization
    Airbnb listings, Barcelona, 182–184, 182–184*f*
    creation of, 181
    decentralization of tourism, 181–182
    indicators, 181
    Kernel Density Estimator, 183–184
    key performance indicators (KPI), 180–181
Data design principles, data visualization
  color, 179
  form, 179–180
  long-term memory, 179
  movement, 180
  "preattentive" processing, 179
  spatial positioning, 180
  visual thinking, 179
Data-driven (DD) approach
  big data
    assessment, 219
    challenges and opportunities, 210–213, 211*f*
    contribution, 214
    selection bias, 222
    urban policy evaluation, 208–210, 209*t*
  COVID-19 crisis
    consumer response, 215–217
    public health interventions, 217–218
  experimental and quasiexperimental methodologies, 204–205

227

Data-driven (DD) approach *(Continued)*
  mobile phone and satellite data
    call detail records (CDRs), 220
    Household Income Expenditure Survey (HIES), 220
    likelihood of households, 220, 221*f*
    poverty rate, 220
  New York City
    administrative data, 215
    Department of Health and Mental Hygiene (DOHMH), 214
    grading policy, 215
  policy evaluation
    big data contribution, 214
    change theory/logic framework, 197–198, 198*f*
    counterfactual situation, 202–204, 203*f*
    impact evaluation, 201–202
    implementation/process evaluation, 200–201
    needs assessment, 199–200
    role of, 198–199, 199*f*
  smart city (SC)
    bibliometric methodology, 47
    clusters analysis, 50, 52–53*t*
    complementary search equations, 48, 48*t*
    density distribution, 56, 57*f*
    disaster, search equations, 55–56, 55*t*, 56*f*
    Increase Rate (IR$_y$), 48–49
    Philippine Disaster Resilience Foundation (PDRF), 56–66, 60*f*
    private sector, search equations, 55–56, 55*t*, 56*f*
    resilience, search equations, 55–56, 55*t*, 56*f*
    Scopus database, 48–50
    VOSviewer software, 50–55, 50–51*f*, 54*f*
  smart technology, consumer's behavior
    big data, 219
    energy conservation, 219
    smart meters, 218–219
    time-of-use pricing, 218–219
  urban policy evaluation
    administrative data, 208
    attributes definition, 206–207, 207*t*
    big data, 208–210, 209*t*
    survey data, 207
Data-driven cities and smart cities
  big data
    Barcelona platform, 166
    Cologne platform, 166
    data preparation, 164
    GrowSmarter project, 165
    internet of things (IoT), 161
    Stockholm platform, 165–166
  challenges, 153–154
  data analysis, 155, 164–165
  data collection
    geolocation technology, 159
    mobile phones and wearables, 158–159
    process, 155
    robotics, 159
    sensors and internet of things (IoT) devices, 158
  data preparation, 155, 164
  data storage
    cybersecurity, blockchain, and distributed ledger technologies (DLTs), 163–164
    edge/fog computing and distributed storage, 162
    hybrid cloud, 161–162
    NoSQL databases, 162–163
    process, 155
  data transportation
    5G network, 159–160
    low power wide area networks (LPWAN), 160–161
    process, 155
  data visualization, 156, 165–171
  GrowSmarter project, 157, 157*f*
  Intelligent Transport Systems (ITS)
    Advanced Traffic Management Centers (A-TMC), 166–167
    characteristics, 166
    Collaborative Intelligent Transport Systems (C-ITS), 167–168, 169*f*
    Cooperative, Connected, and Automated Mobility (CCAM) services, 168–171, 169*f*, 171*f*
    dynamic control, 168
  lampposts, 156–157*b*
  technology, 154
Data-driven smart city
  anonymization forms, 129–130
  assets, agents, and activities, 118
  challenges, 119
  compliance approach/binding corporate rules, 130
  consent given, 129
  data exploitation, 149
  data maturity, 149
  data quality, 149
  definition, 111–112
  development roadmap, 118, 118*f*

Index   **229**

economic transformation, 114
encryption technology, 129
global alliance, 120
governance, 114, 114f
governance and management, 119
Health Insurance Portability and Accountability Act (HIPAA) standard, 129
holistic approach, 113
information and communication (ICT), 111–112
information principle, 127–128
Korean Railroad Research Institute (KRRI), 141
legitimation
  big data, 123–125
  European GDPR, 125–127
  U.S. model (HIPAA), 127
lifecycle
  growing, 115
  inception, 115
  launching, 115
  maturity, 116, 116f
Nice (France)
  Connected Boulevard project, 132, 136–137
  infrastructure, 132
  InQBarna, 136–137
  metropolitan area, 132
  Nice City Pass app, 132–137, 133–134f, 134–136t
  stages of, 137, 137t
pact for, 119–120
quadruple helix model, 116–117, 117f, 149–150
Seoul (Korea)
  Automated Fare Collection system (AFC), 139–140, 140f
  data capture, 140–141, 140f
  data cleaning, 141
  data modeling, 143–144
  data strategy, 139–140
  transport systems, 138–139
  TRIPS, 142–147, 142f, 145f
Seoul public transport system, 143–144
smart city approach, 111–112
smart index
  economy, 121–122, 122f
  government dimension, 122–123, 123f
  mobility dimension, 121, 121f
  smart infrastructures, 121, 121f
  society dimension, 122, 123f

  sustainability, 121, 121f
  social transformation, 114
  stakeholders, 149–150
  strategy plan, 148
  structure of, 148
  symposiums and awards, 120
  technology, 148
  transformation to, 112–113
  TRIPS, 141–147, 142f, 145f
  urban transformation, 113
  value model
    business ecosystem, 130
    downstream actors, 131
    Korean Railroad Research Institute (KRRI), 131
    smart city ecosystem, 130, 131f
    triple bottom line, 131
    upstream actors, 130
  vision of, 118–119
Data science
  association problems, 92
  backbone of, 100
  causality problems, 92–93
  classification problems, 91
  clustering problems, 92
  computer skills, 94
  data reduction problems, 92
  Data Scientist, Google searches, 93–94, 93f
  definitions, 89
  DTFT, 101–102
  German Panzers, 90
  German tank problem, 90–91
  indicators, urban retail
    commercial occupation, 109
    EIXOS Economic Observatory, 108
    empty commercial premises, 106–108
    importance of, 103–104
    principle of agglomeration, 104–105
    retail location, 105–106
    Retail Occupancy Index (ROI), 107
    retail streets, 104–105
    selection, 104
  management of
    Big Data analytics canvas, 97, 97f
    data architecture, 99
    data exploration, 99
    data sources, 97
    departments and organizations, 96
    domain experts, 95
    insights generation, 100
    problem statement, 97, 98f
    teams, 94–95, 95f

Data science *(Continued)*
  projects of, 101
  similarity matching problems, 91
  statistics skills, 94
  strategic planning team, 101
  urban resilience, 102–103b
  value estimation problems, 91
Data visualization
  chart, 177–178
  city resilience, 194b
  correlation, 178
  COVID-19
    EIXOS Economic Observatory, 184–194, 187f, 188t, 190–194f
    Retail Occupancy Index (ROI), 185, 185f
  dashboard
    Airbnb listings, Barcelona, 182–184, 182–184f
    creation of, 181
    decentralization of tourism, 181–182
    indicators, 181
    Kernel Density Estimator, 183–184
    key performance indicators (KPI), 180–181
  data design principles
    color, 179
    form, 179–180
    long-term memory, 179
    movement, 180
    "preattentive" processing, 179
    spatial positioning, 180
    visual thinking, 179
  data essentials, 175–176
  definition, 174
  distribution, 178
  explanatory
    data storytelling, 175
    infographics, 175
    zero greenhouse gas emissions, 175, 176f
  exploratory
    changes in world, 174, 175f
    dashboard, 174
  graph analytics, 194b
  maps, 178
  part to whole, 178
  qualitative data, 176–177
  quantitative data, 177
  ranking, 178
  size comparison, 178
  stages
    data, 177
    design, 177
    planning and tactics, 177
    technical steps, 173
    time series, 178
    tools, 173
Department of Health and Mental Hygiene (DOHMH), 214

E

EIXOS Economic Observatory, 184–194, 187f, 188t, 190–194f
  data science, 108
Encryption technology, 129
Entrepreneurship
  social, 6–7
  urban, 7–18
European GDPR, 125–127
Explanatory data visualization
  data storytelling, 175
  infographics, 175
  zero greenhouse gas emissions, 175, 176f
Exploratory data visualization
  changes in world, 174, 175f
  dashboard, 174

G

General Data Protection Regulation (GDPR), 123–124
Geolocation technology, 159
Geospatial technology, 159
Global urban population
  challenges, 1
  economic competitiveness, 2–3
  environment issue, 1–2
  quality of life, 3
  resilience, 4
  sustainability, 3, 4f, 13f
Green entrepreneurs and ventures, 7
GrowSmarter project, 157, 157f, 165

H

Health Insurance Portability and Accountability Act (HIPAA) standard, 129
Heuristic model, 198–199, 199f
Household Income Expenditure Survey (HIES), 220

I

ICT infrastructure, 153
Infographics, 175
Information and communication technologies (ICTs)
  smart city, 4–5

top-down approach, 5
Intelligent Transport Systems (ITS)
    Advanced Traffic Management Centers (A-TMC), 166–167
    characteristics, 166
    Collaborative Intelligent Transport Systems (C-ITS), 167–168, 169f
    Cooperative, Connected, and Automated Mobility (CCAM) services, 168–171, 169f, 171f
    dynamic control, 168
Internet of things (IoT), 158, 161

K
Kernel Density Estimator, 183–184
Key performance indicators (KPI), 180–181
Korean Railroad Research Institute (KRRI), 141

L
Low power wide area networks (LPWAN), 160–161

M
Master Data Model (MDM), 80–81
Mayor's Office of Data Analytics (MODA), 8–10
Mobile phone and satellite data
    call detail records (CDRs), 220
    Household Income Expenditure Survey (HIES), 220
    likelihood of households, 220, 221f
    poverty rate, 220

N
New York City
    administrative data, 215
    Commission on Public Information and Communication (COPIC), 8
    COVID-19, 10
    Department of Health and Mental Hygiene (DOHMH), 214
    ensuring quality of and access, 10
    grading policy, 215
    inclusion and empowering communities, 9
    innovation, 8
    Mayor's Office of Data Analytics (MODA), 8–10
    Open Data Coordinator (ODC), 11
    Open Data Law, 8
    Open Data Week, 9

Nice (France)
    Connected Boulevard project, 132, 136–137
    infrastructure, 132
    InQBarna, 136–137
    metropolitan area, 132
    Nice City Pass app, 132–137, 133–134f, 134–136t
    stages of, 137, 137t
Nonrelational database. *See* NoSQL database
NoSQL databases, 162–163
NYC Recovery Data Partnership, 12b

O
Open Data Coordinator (ODC), 11
Open Data Law, 8
Open Data Week, 9

P
Philippine Disaster Resilience Foundation (PDRF), 56–66, 60f
Public-Private-People Partnerships (4Ps), 7–17

R
Resilience, 4
Retail Occupancy Index (ROI), 185, 185f
    data science, 107

S
Seoul (Korea)
    Automated Fare Collection system (AFC), 139–140, 140f
    data capture, 140–141, 140f
    data cleaning, 141
    data modeling, 143–144
    data strategy, 139–140
    transport systems, 138–139
    TRIPS, 142–147, 142f, 145f
Smart citizen initiative, 6
Smart city (SC)
    COVID-19, 73–75
    data-driven (DD) approach
        bibliometric methodology, 47
        clusters analysis, 50, 52–53t
        complementary search equations, 48, 48t
        density distribution, 56, 57f
        disaster, search equations, 55–56, 55t, 56f
        Increase Rate (IR_y), 48–49
        Philippine Disaster Resilience Foundation (PDRF), 56–66, 60f
        private sector, search equations, 55–56, 55t, 56f

Smart city (SC) *(Continued)*
  resilience, search equations, 55–56, 55*t*, 56*f*
  Scopus database, 48–50
  VOSviewer software, 50–55, 50–51*f*, 54*f*
  New York City
    Commission on Public Information and Communication (COPIC), 8
    COVID-19, 10
    ensuring quality of and access, 10
    inclusion and empowering communities, 9
    innovation, 8
    Mayor's Office of Data Analytics (MODA), 8–10
    Open Data Coordinator (ODC), 11
    Open Data Law, 8
    Open Data Week, 9
    Public Private Partnership (PPP), 10
  people-oriented approach/social smart cities, 5–6
  social entrepreneur, 6–7
  taxonomy of, 4–5
  technology-oriented approach/top-down, 5
  urban entrepreneur, 7–18
  urban governance
    big data citizen centered approach, 69–83, 71*f*, 80*f*
    challenges, 68–69
    policy informatics, 68
    public regulation, 68
    public service delivery, 68
    public supervision, 68
Smart index
  economy, 121–122, 122*f*
  government dimension, 122–123, 123*f*
  mobility dimension, 121, 121*f*
  smart infrastructures, 121, 121*f*
  society dimension, 122, 123*f*
  sustainability, 121, 121*f*
"SmartTower" solution, 156–157
Smart urban governance. *See* Urban governance
Sociable smart cities, 5–6
Social entrepreneurship, 6–7
Swiss National COVID-19 Science Task Force (SN-STF), 73

T

Travel Record-based Integrated Public Transport Operation System (TRIPS), 141–147, 142*f*, 145*f*

U

Urban entrepreneurship, 7–18
Urban governance
  big data citizen centered approach
    data life cycle management, 75–77
    data quality management, 82
    data security and privacy, 82–83
    Master Data Model (MDM), 80–81
    organization model, 70–72, 71*f*
    real-time urban platform, 77–80, 80*f*
    Swiss response, COVID-19, 71*f*, 73–75
  challenges, 68–69
  policy informatics, 68
  public regulation, 68
  public service delivery, 68
  public supervision, 68
Urban resilience, data science for, 102–103*b*
U.S. model (HIPAA), 127

Printed in the United States
by Baker & Taylor Publisher Services